"Dani Fry Jackson's *Math Problem Solving Through Small Group Instruction* is a practical, engaging resource for teachers. Filled with thoughtful lessons, activities, and anchor charts, it provides clear guidance on what's important and why. Jackson truly understands the art of teaching, offering tasks that are both effective and realistic."

Jennifer Lempp, *Author of* Math Workshop *and Educational Consultant*

"So much valuable guidance on meeting the needs of all students is provided in *Math Problem Solving Through Small Group Instruction*! The implementable actions are clear and concise and will help students learn. This is a great addition to your bookshelf!"

Kevin Dykema, *Co-Author of* Productive Math Struggle *and Former NCTM President*

Math Problem Solving Through Small Group Instruction

Problem solving in math is complex. When students struggle, it can be difficult to diagnose where the breakdown is happening. This book defines how reading comprehension, math computation, and self-efficacy impact students' problem solving abilities and how you can support them in each area, with a particular focus on the use of small group instruction.

Chapters break down the process of problem solving into an easy-to-follow progression, with lessons provided throughout. There is a step-by-step guide to help you analyze students' work, with tips on managing flexible small groups. Learning targets help show when students have mastered each step of a problem or flag difficulties you can assist with along the way. The author includes tasks for each grade level with an example response plan as a guide, alongside meaningful research informing small moves that can make big gains.

Great for math educators of grades K–5, administrators, and math curriculum coordinators, this book will leave you feeling confident in identifying student behavior related to mathematical problem solving and addressing it with detailed ways to respond with exactly what your students need.

Dani Fry Jackson is an elementary math curriculum coordinator in Frisco, TX. Dani's writing about math instruction has been featured on Edutopia and highlighted within the Marshall Memo, Education Slice, and K–12 Dive.

Also Available from Routledge
Eye On Education
(www.routledge.com/eyeoneducation)

Teaching 6–12 Math Intervention:
A Practical Framework To Engage Students Who Struggle
Juliana Tapper

There Is No One Way to Teach Math:
Actionable Ideas for Grades 6–12
Henri Picciotto and Robin Pemantle

Mathematics Teaching On Target:
A Guide to Teaching for Robust Understanding at All Grade Levels
Alan Schoenfeld, Heather Fink, Alyssa Sayavedra,
Anna Weltman and Sandra Zuñiga-Ruiz

Exploring Math with Technology:
Practices for Secondary Math Teachers
Allison W. McCulloch and Jennifer N. Lovett

Introducing Nonroutine Math Problems to Secondary Learners:
60+ Engaging Examples and Strategies to
Improve Higher-Order Problem-Solving Skills
Robert London

Reaching and Teaching Neurodivergent Learners in STEM:
Strategies for Embracing Uniquely Talented Problem Solvers
Jodi Asbell-Clarke

Coaching Math Workshop
Nicki Newton

Fluency Doesn't Just Happen in Multiplication and Division:
Strategies and Models for Teaching the Basic Facts
Nicki Newton, Ann Elise Record and Alison J. Mello

High-Impact Tutoring in Math and ELA:
An Evidence-Based Approach to Help All Students Succeed
Nicki Newton

Math Problem Solving Through Small Group Instruction

A Guide to Increasing Proficiency in Grades K–5

Dani Fry Jackson

Routledge
Taylor & Francis Group
NEW YORK AND LONDON

Designed cover image: © Getty Images

First published 2026
by Routledge
605 Third Avenue, New York, NY 10158

and by Routledge
4 Park Square, Milton Park, Abingdon, Oxon, OX14 4RN

Routledge is an imprint of the Taylor & Francis Group, an informa business

© 2026 Dani Fry Jackson

The right of Dani Fry Jackson to be identified as author of this work has been asserted in accordance with sections 77 and 78 of the Copyright, Designs and Patents Act 1988.

All rights reserved. No part of this book may be reprinted or reproduced or utilised in any form or by any electronic, mechanical, or other means, now known or hereafter invented, including photocopying and recording, or in any information storage or retrieval system, without permission in writing from the publishers.

Trademark notice: Product or corporate names may be trademarks or registered trademarks, and are used only for identification and explanation without intent to infringe.

ISBN: 978-1-032-83988-2 (hbk)
ISBN: 978-1-032-83987-5 (pbk)
ISBN: 978-1-003-51070-3 (ebk)

DOI: 10.4324/9781003510703

Typeset in Palatino
by KnowledgeWorks Global Ltd.

Access the Support Material: https://resourcecentre.routledge.com/books/9781032839875

Dedication

To my parents, who taught me how to work hard and pursue my dreams.

To all the teachers in my life; you are the reason this book exists. I learn more from you with every encounter, and you are changing the lives of children every day.

Contents

	Meet the Author	x
	Acknowledgments	xi
	Introduction	1
1	What Is Problem Solving and Why Do Students Struggle with It?	8
2	How Can I Break Down the Behaviors That Drive Mathematical Problem Solving?	38
3	How Do I Pinpoint the Needs of Each Student?	102
4	How Can I Effectively Organize Groups for Differentiated Learning?	141
5	How Is Small Group Instruction Implemented in the Classroom?	155
6	What Strategies Can I Use to Foster Productive Struggle in My Students?	178
7	What Other Small Adjustments Can I Make in My Classroom to Help My Students Develop Problem Solving Skills?	200
	Conclusion	215

Meet the Author

Dani Fry Jackson is an elementary math curriculum coordinator in Frisco, TX. She works with administrators, teachers, and students at 43 elementary schools and one intermediate campus, providing diverse job-embedded professional development and support on all things teaching and learning math. She also co-leads elementary math curriculum development and serves on many district committees. Dani's writing about math instruction has been featured on Edutopia and highlighted within the Marshall Memo, Education Slice, and K–12 Dive. She is a frequent speaker at national, regional, and local conferences and is finishing her doctoral degree in elementary curriculum and instruction. Dani's website is www.danijacksonmath.com, and you can find her on X (@danijacksonmath).

Acknowledgments

To my husband; I couldn't have done this without you. You push me to be the best version of myself and never make me small. I love you.

To all six of my sweet kids; thank you for your patience with me throughout writing this book. You have been my biggest cheerleaders and have given me so much grace.

To my team; you make me love what I do. I never have a day that I don't want to come to work. I am so blessed to work with people who are not only passionate about teaching and learning but also about the people we serve.

To Katie Stafford; you grow my thinking every single day. Thank you for being the yin to my yang. I wouldn't rather be partners with anyone else. Everyone who works with you is blessed to know you.

Introduction

I am a data enthusiast. To me, data is like a puzzle that takes shape as you fit the pieces together. Using data to tell a story creates a clear pathway toward a solution. The right data doesn't just illuminate the problem; it shines a spotlight where effort can meet impact. In education, data can take many forms: spreadsheets with percentages, student work, time on task, reading level, fluency... when put in different combinations, they can help teachers focus their efforts where they will have the greatest impact on student achievement, rather than spreading their energy across broad areas with less effect.

About five years ago, I became captivated by the data surrounding complex math problem solving. Specifically, I was drawn to how students represent and solve problems in various ways. Locally, statewide, and nationally, the data revealed poor performance in this area. This sparked a personal mission to make sense of the numbers and find ways to address the gaps.

My work began in partnership with campus leaders who reached out for help. I introduced labsites, a job-embedded professional development model where teachers engage in a learning cycle: explicitly learning about a concept, observing a modeled lesson, and then trying the approach with their own students. Together with teachers, I analyzed student work on open-ended math tasks, brainstorming and testing a variety of instructional strategies.

What stood out most was the consistency of the challenges across grade levels. From kindergarten to fifth grade, similar patterns emerged. This work became a process of refining actions, focusing on what worked best, and adjusting along the way to maximize effectiveness. Through this hands-on collaboration, we uncovered powerful strategies to address the persistent issues in math problem solving.

Learn more about Labsite Learning here, where I was a guest on Steve Barkley's podcast: https://barkleypd.com/blog/podcast-engaging-teachers-in-labsite-learning/.

When I was a teacher, I primarily taught fifth grade. I started as a departmentalized reading, writing, and social studies teacher. Almost every year, I was reassigned to a different content area—whatever was left after hiring was done. Although this constant shifting was challenging, it gave me the opportunity to deeply develop my understanding of reading comprehension skills. This experience has proven invaluable because I've drawn on it throughout my work with teachers to make connections between deep reading comprehension and the comprehension demands of challenging math word problems.

In addition to my love of data, I have a passion for research that can provide answers as to why data is the way it is. During this time, I have been pursuing my doctorate, allowing me to focus almost exclusively on understanding how students learn and the factors that impact their ability to solve complex problems. Through action research with teachers and students, I had the unique opportunity to try new strategies, immediately review related research, and apply findings in real time.

I am not a neuroscientist, but I'm writing a book about students learning how to think and teachers setting up the conditions for it. My love of data needed to find reasoning behind why certain things that I was seeing work and understand why some outdated practices don't work. In essence, I worked backwards from the data to see what was working in classrooms, then I found the research that explained why it was working in relation to how the brain learns and processes information.

This combination of practice and research has allowed me to design the progression you'll find in this book. It's a culmination of years of collaboration, reflection, and continuous improvement—grounded in what truly works for students and teachers alike.

Why Do Students Need to Learn How to Solve Problems?

Instructional strategies for teaching math have evolved significantly over the years. Most adults grew up learning math through a procedural lens—memorizing steps and rules for solving problems. Although this approach may have produced correct answers, it often left learners unable to explain why their solutions worked or understand the mathematical concepts behind them. Students knew one way to solve problems, and student work likely all looked the same. Research suggests that this method aligned with the needs of the economy at the time, which favored workers who could efficiently follow directions and perform repetitive tasks in industries like factory work, data entry, and other fields requiring precision and attention to detail (Darling-Hammond, 2024).

However, the rapid advancement of technology has transformed the skills required in the modern workforce. Computers and automation now handle many of the routine processes once performed by humans. As a result, today's workforce must be equipped with higher-order thinking skills, such as the ability to analyze, create, and approach complex tasks from multiple perspectives. Workers need to represent their ideas clearly and use their cognitive abilities to process information, develop innovative systems, and solve problems creatively.

The careers that dominate today's economy require a vastly different skill set than those of the past. According to the World Economic Forum (2020), the top ten skills needed for jobs in 2025 related to math problem solving include analytical thinking, learning strategies, complex problem solving, critical thinking and analysis, resilience, flexibility, and reasoning. These transferable skills are woven throughout this book, reflecting the importance of preparing students for a future that demands more than rote memorization or procedural efficiency. An article on the *Fortune* website states that companies are describing a gap in skills in the workforce. When companies were polled about the most in-demand soft skills right now, problem solving landed in the number one spot (Leonhardt, 2023).

To thrive in this rapidly changing world, students must practice and develop these skills across disciplines. They need to be capable of doing what computers and artificial intelligence cannot: thinking creatively, reasoning critically, and approaching challenges with adaptability and innovation.

The National Council of Teachers of Mathematics (NCTM) outlines specific process standards designed to emphasize the importance of these skills and encourage their use in classrooms.

NCTM Process Standards

Problem Solving

Instructional programs from prekindergarten through grade 12 should enable each and every student to do the following:

- ★ Build new mathematical knowledge through problem solving.
- ★ Solve problems that arise in mathematics and in other contexts.
- ★ Apply and adapt a variety of appropriate strategies to solve problems.
- ★ Monitor and reflect on the process of mathematical problem solving.

Reasoning and Proof

Instructional programs from prekindergarten through grade 12 should enable each and every student to do the following:

- ★ Recognize reasoning and proof as fundamental aspects of mathematics.
- ★ Make and investigate mathematical conjectures.
- ★ Develop and evaluate mathematical arguments and proofs.
- ★ Select and use various types of reasoning and methods of proof.

Communication

Instructional programs from prekindergarten through grade 12 should enable each and every student to do the following:

- ★ Organize and consolidate their mathematical thinking through communication.
- ★ Communicate their mathematical thinking coherently and clearly to peers, teachers, and others.
- ★ Analyze and evaluate the mathematical thinking and strategies of others.
- ★ Use the language of mathematics to express mathematical ideas precisely.

Connections

Instructional programs from prekindergarten through grade 12 should enable each and every student to do the following:

- ★ Recognize and use connections among mathematical ideas.
- ★ Understand how mathematical ideas interconnect and build on one another to produce a coherent whole.
- ★ Recognize and apply mathematics in contexts outside of mathematics.

Representation

Instructional programs from prekindergarten through grade 12 should enable each and every student to do the following:

- ★ Create and use representations to organize, record, and communicate mathematical ideas.
- ★ Select, apply, and translate among mathematical representations to solve problems.
- ★ Use representations to model and interpret physical, social, and mathematical phenomena.

(National Council of Teachers of Mathematics, 2024)

Many states have adopted their own versions of these standards, laying the groundwork for students to build a strong foundation in thinking, reasoning, and communicating complex mathematical ideas throughout their education. However, several challenges have contributed to ongoing issues, including low mastery of complex problem solving. The primary obstacle lies in the intricate nature of understanding what effective problem solving looks like and how to achieve it, both for students and teachers.

Although classroom practices have evolved to support this shift, the data consistently highlights that students struggle with complex math problem solving skills from an early age. Addressing these challenges requires a deeper understanding of how to develop these skills effectively and how to support both teachers and students in this critical area.

What Does the Data Say?

When we look at the data surrounding complex math problem solving, we can see right away that there is a gap in learning that needs to be addressed. For students at age 9 in fourth grade, there is only 37% mastery of numerical operations and beginning problem solving (The Nation's Report Card, 2024). They define beginning problem solving as having an initial understanding of the operations to solve one-step problems.

This data is a little misleading. Thirty-seven percent is especially low for fourth graders because this data reflects only their performance on one-step word problems – skills they began learning in kindergarten and are assessed on third- and fourth-grade state tests. These are foundational skills that states deem essential for success in subsequent grade levels.

Even more troubling is the data for eighth graders in the same category. After years of instruction and exposure to increasingly complex problem solving, their performance on one-step word problems only rises to 71%. This highlights significant gaps in student understanding and mastery, even with years of additional instruction.

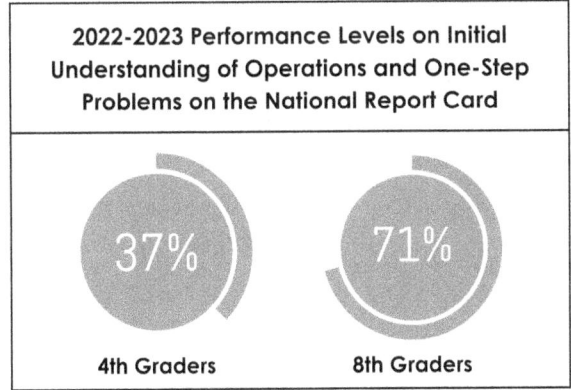

(The Nation's Report Card, 2024)

Figure I.1 The Nation's Report Card, 2024.

At this rate, more intentional work needs to be started at a much younger age to lay a strong foundation for critical thinking in math. In this book, I will clarify what it means for students to be proficient problem solvers at each grade level from K to 5.

Who Is the Audience for This Book?

This book is designed for educators who are passionate about helping students develop strong problem solving skills in mathematics and beyond. Whether you are a classroom teacher, instructional coach, administrator, or curriculum specialist, this guide will provide practical strategies and insights to enhance your approach to problem solving, not only in small group instruction but as a whole.

It's also a valuable resource for the following:

- **New teachers:** Looking for a structured, student-centered way to introduce math problem solving
- **Experienced teachers:** Hoping to refine or refresh their strategies for building mathematical proficiency in diverse classrooms
- **Special education teachers:** Searching for targeted techniques to support a variety of learning needs that will benefit multiple concepts
- **Administrators:** Seeking to guide or support teachers in adopting effective small group instructional practices
- **District curriculum specialists:** Looking for ways to build a cohesive approach to problem solving teaching and learning

Whether you teach in a traditional classroom, a specialized setting, or a remote learning environment, this book offers tools to meet students where they are and help them grow. It bridges the gap between theory and practice, showing how small group instruction can create a space for deeper thinking, equity, and future-ready learners.

How to Read This Book

This book follows a carefully crafted progression, designed to guide you step by step through a coherent and effective approach to math problem solving in small group instruction. To fully grasp the framework and its application, it is essential to read the book in its entirety.

The journey begins with addressing the components of problem solving and how the brain processes them. Then foundational lessons set the stage for analyzing student work. From there, you'll learn how to organize and interpret data to make informed instructional decisions. The focus then shifts to implementing small group instruction that is responsive to students' needs.

The final chapters delve into deeper insights and essential research, addressing the interconnected work that completes the approach. These chapters tie together key elements and provide the tools and understanding necessary to create a truly transformative math learning experience. I'm sure you will recognize some of the moves in this book. I'm hoping you will be as excited as I was to get to know the research behind why they work, so you can use your new knowledge to convince students and other teachers of their importance.

I am excited about the continued collaboration that will follow the completion of this book, with the goal of helping students grow in this critical area – an effort that will have a lasting impact on their futures.

This book is truly for educators to get to know the K–5 progression. Even if you are a grade-level teacher, the intent is for you to understand how your grade level impacts the grades below you and above you in understanding complex problems. I encourage you to complete the tasks for each grade level and pause at the examples provided to think about how that could look for your students. I tried to give a mix of examples to provide a wide-ranging look at how this applies to all elementary students.

References

Darling-Hammond, L. (2024) Reinventing systems for equity. *ECNU Review of Education*, 7(2), 214–229.

Leonhardt, M. (2023). There's a big skills gap at work right now. These are the top 10 skills employers are looking for. https://fortune.com/2023/01/24/top-skills-employers-are-looking-for/

National Council of Teachers of Mathematics. (n.d.). *Principles and standards: Process standards*. Retrieved January 9, 2025, from https://www.nctm.org/standards-and-positions/principles-and-standards/process/

The Nation's Report Card. (2024). *Long-term trend assessment: Mathematics performance, age 9*. U.S. Department of Education, Institute of Education Sciences. Retrieved January 9, 2025, from https://www.nationsreportcard.gov/ltt/mathematics/performance/?age=9

World Economic Forum. (2020). *The future of jobs report 2020: Infographics*. Retrieved from https://www.weforum.org/publications/the-future-of-jobs-report-2020/in-full/infographics-e4e69e4de7/

1

What Is Problem Solving and Why Do Students Struggle with It?

Math problem solving, often referred to as "word problems," involves presenting complex math problems in text form. Students must first comprehend the text, retrieve relevant knowledge from memory, and construct a model to represent the situation. Afterward, they determine the most appropriate method to solve the problem using the necessary computations (Li et al., 2023).

So often, problem solving is equated with just calculation. So much more goes into comprehending the situation and then knowing how to connect the reading and math to solve correctly. Not only do students have to understand how to solve it correctly, but they also need to have the number sense to be able to choose an operation and accurately solve it. Phew! That seems like a lot, especially when you add multiple steps to the same problem. If you dissect a problem, it is easy to see that there is a list of behaviors a student might struggle with, and even if they make only one mistake, it can cause them to get the wrong answer.

It is important to recognize that much of the cognitive work occurs before computation. When problems are complex, students must spend significantly more time thinking through and processing the problem upfront. This is followed by a shorter period of computation, with an even smaller amount of time dedicated to revisiting the solution in relation to the original problem to ensure its reasonableness. The initial phase involves understanding the problem's context. As students work through the problem, they temporarily "decontextualize" – shifting focus from the real-world scenario to the mathematical elements. However, effective problem solvers always return to the original context afterward, rechecking their solution to ensure it aligns with the problem at hand. This final step is known as recontextualization.

What Is Problem Solving and Why Do Students Struggle with It? ◆ 9

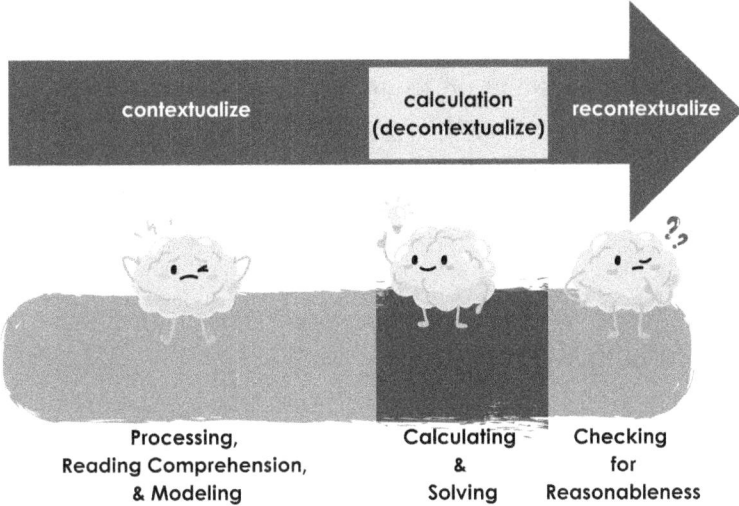

Figure 1.1 The reading and math relationship in problem solving.

This book explores several components that are essential for addressing complex math problem solving: reading comprehension, math computation, and self-efficacy. Also sprinkled throughout is information on how the brain learns and how it processes these components.

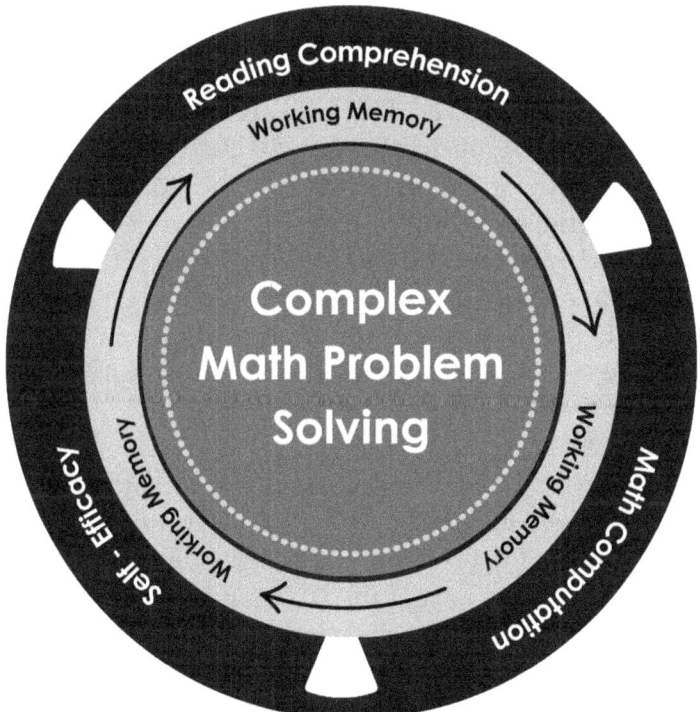

Figure 1.2 The components of math problem solving working together.

These components are woven together in many ways, which validates why students and teachers struggle with this topic. Let's unpack them and learn what happens in the brain to understand why this is so complicated. Don't worry. We won't admire the problem past this chapter. We are just setting the stage with some learning, and the rest of the book will give concrete tools to take away for responding to the needs of your students tomorrow and beyond.

The Role of Working Memory

Working memory is a cognitive system that temporarily holds and processes information required for complex tasks such as reasoning, decision-making, and learning (Gathercole & Alloway, 2008). When students are solving a complex math problem, their working memory plays a crucial role in organizing and manipulating the various pieces of information they need to complete the task. These problems often involve multiple steps, each requiring the application of different mathematical concepts or operations. Students must continuously update and retrieve information from their working memory to keep track of results along the way, adjust their strategies, and manage the different variables of the problem presented. Additionally, the complexity of the problem may introduce variations in the types of operations, such as addition, subtraction, multiplication, and division, each of which requires a unique set of mental processes. The limited capacity of working memory means that students must efficiently manage this information, or they risk becoming overwhelmed or making errors. As the difficulty of the problem increases, the demand on working memory intensifies, requiring greater attention, focus, and cognitive effort to navigate through the solution process successfully (Friedman et al., 2018).

The three parts of working memory that help this process are the phonological loop, the visuospatial sketchpad, and the central executive system.

The Phonological Loop

This part of the working memory processes the verbal and acoustic information. For math problem solving, this could mean that the phonological loop temporarily stores the text from the problem, and it holds onto partial solutions as you solve. This part of the working memory is associated with the development of vocabulary in children (Baddeley, 2000).

For example, while solving a multi-step math problem, a student might need to remember a specific formula, the steps they've already completed,

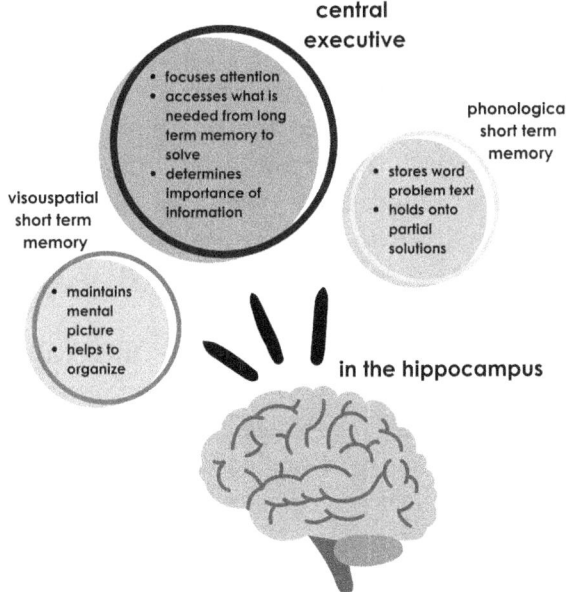

Figure 1.3 The parts of working memory.

or important numerical values as they progress toward a solution. The phonological loop helps store and rehearse this information briefly, so the student doesn't forget it while they continue to work through the problem. This allows them to effectively manage the flow of information without losing track of any key details. When a person repeats something to themselves to remember it, this is called the articulatory rehearsal system (Baddeley, 2000).

The Visuospatial Sketchpad

The name of this part of the working memory gives away its job. This part processes the information in visual or spatial form and contributes to students' mathematical performance through those aspects of solving, such as pictorial representations of numbers, number alignment, and regrouping. Younger students (preschool–8 years of age) have been found to rely more on the visuospatial sketchpad than older math students. Students older than this rely more on verbal strategies and retrieval (DeSmedt et al., 2009). This makes sense because in primary grades, they don't yet have a strong foundation of conceptual knowledge of mathematics. We are building their foundation and "math memories" through the use of manipulatives and drawing pictures so they have images stored in their mind for retrieval later. You will learn more about retrieval in Chapter 7.

The Central Executive System

The central executive system is the most crucial component of the working memory in terms of mathematical performance. This is where the brain determines the importance of the text a student encounters. This system maintains the overall understanding of the text/problem, focuses attention, and removes unnecessary parts. The central executive system also pulls information from long-term memory and integrates it with what is being processed by the other two parts (Friedman et al., 2018; Li et al., 2023).

When students solve complex math problems, their working memory can become quickly overwhelmed due to the simultaneous need to comprehend the problem text, retrieve relevant strategies, and manage multiple steps in the problem solving process. This is called coginitive overload. This occurs when the demands of the task exceed the brain's capacity to process and store information efficiently (Sweller, 2011). It is one of the primary reasons many students struggle with problem solving because the mental resources required to hold and manipulate information can become stretched too thin. The mental strain can lead to mistakes, confusion, or a lack of progress toward a solution, making it difficult for students to navigate more challenging problems successfully.

Together, these components of working memory – the central executive system, the phonological loop, and the visuospatial sketchpad – work in concert to help students manage the cognitive load associated with complex problem solving tasks. Understanding the roles of each system can help educators develop strategies to reduce overload and support students in managing the cognitive demands of math problem solving.

The best way to address and improve working memory can be boiled down to a few simple tasks that address each part of working memory. Helping students learn these tips will clear their minds to process, sort the information, and take the necessary steps to solve.

Offload Information

Teachers have had a longstanding issue with some students wanting to solve problems in their head or only show the least amount of thinking possible on paper. Students might see it as a weakness to have to write everything down. Complex problems take up a lot of space and function in the working memory, so "showing your work" is a practical solution for students to keep track of their thinking and reduce the chances of mistakes. Their working memory cannot hold an infinite amount of information. Hence, students need to learn how to "offload" information in an organized way to keep them on track and use their working memory to its fullest capacity.

An effective strategy to "offload" is for students to learn how to create a model to bridge between the reading of math word problems and the computation. Because math problem solving involves understanding the problem, creating or analyzing a model, and solving, students with stronger working memory will likely be more successful (Li et al., 2023). This would explain why students who suffer from impairments that impact the central executive part of the brain, such as attention deficit hyperactivity disorder (ADHD) and dyslexia, struggle even more with complex math problem solving because attention is essential for learning (Friedman et al., 2018). Many students require accommodations such as small-group administration, oral administration, or preferential seating to boost attention and mitigate the impairment that impacts their working memory.

If we can teach students to offload some of the heavy lifting within a complex math problem and why they need to do that, we can get more buy-in with representation and showing their work. This is a way to help students become independent problem solvers and advocate for their learning. We can equip them with the knowledge to decide how they best learn. For example, if a fourth grader goes to solve this problem:

> **Jamie is traveling to his grandparents' house in Maine. It will take him 1,298 miles to get there by car. On the way, they stop to get gas every 243 miles. How many times will they need to stop for gas?**

If we teach them about their working memory and how a strip diagram or quick sketch helps them offload information so that they have more "thinking space," they can then make a representation like the ones below that will keep the information organized so they can think more deeply about what to do next.

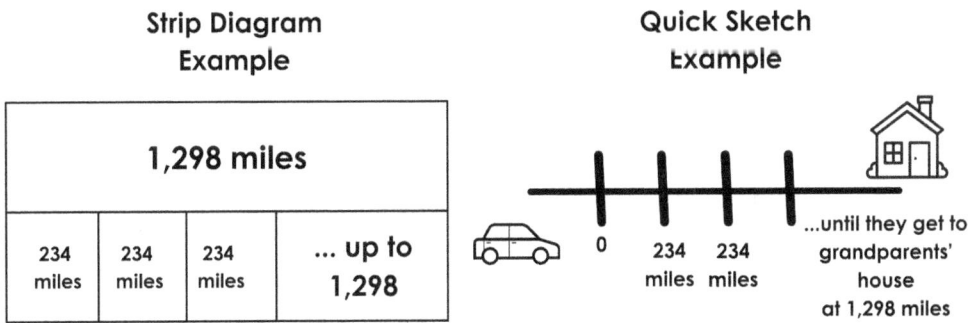

Figure 1.4 Offloading information in an organized way to maintain context.

When students read the problem text, they develop visualization in their minds. A visual model can help them connect their visualization to the relationship with the numbers (Li et al., 2023). It allows students to move from a contextualized real-world problem to a mathematical relationship that they can then represent as an equation.

Refresh Through Rereading

Another way to help students use the knowledge in their working memory is to help them understand that the information they read doesn't stay within their working memory for very long. This is why they must reread problems often, as they need more clarity to refresh the information for processing. This is their main avenue for monitoring their comprehension as they solve, and after they solve, to check for reasonableness.

After students represent the problem, rereading can check that their understanding was correct and pull out anything else missed. Asking a student to reread is one of the easiest ways to get students to do the thinking themselves.

A common thinking routine that emphasizes rereading is the 3 Reads Routine (Kelemanik et al., 2016). In the 3 Reads Routine, students look through specific lenses as they read each time.

- The first time they read the problem, the goal is to understand the context.
- The second time they read the problem, the goal is to interpret the question.
- The third time they read, the goal is to identify the important information.

In addition to using rereading in a thinking routine, it is so important for students to utilize this strategy any time their thinking isn't clear or they lose their train of thought as a check on understanding.

Master Foundational Representations in Primary Grades

Every grade level has standards that dictate the knowledge and skills that students need to learn. Standards do not dictate all the representations that students need to master, and teachers end up choosing what they think works best for their students. We can step back and take a vertical look at which representations will have longevity throughout elementary school and beyond.

To support the capacity of working memory, students need to learn early on how to represent problems with number lines, ten frames, and part-part-whole mats. Many students come into kindergarten already knowing how to add and subtract, write their numbers, and count beyond what is expected.

The part all students must learn is the representations. Suppose students can use these models effortlessly before problem solving turns into multiple steps with more reading comprehension involved. In that case, it can maximize the capacity of the working memory for more efficient solving.

Improving Working Memory for Students	
Teach Students to…	**So They Can…**
Draw a quick sketch or part-part-whole mat/strip diagram.	Offload information in an organized way to have more "thinking space."
Reread the problem.	Refresh their working memory with the task at hand.
Create and use representations in ALL grades with a vertical alignment through the grade levels.	Use more working memory to work on the problem solving piece without the burden of also learning how to create the representations in older grades.

These skills can be taught as early as kindergarten so that students see the value in the process and know how to do it when problems are not as complex. These skills will help them as the problems increase in complexity of steps and mathematical content, where they will need more access to their working memory as they solve. Having a representation also allows students to think flexibly about how they want to solve.

There is not one right way to solve a problem. When they can see the big picture clearly, they won't need to take shortcuts like finding keywords to know what to do. They will have several options and can spend more of their thinking capacity on choosing which strategy from their long-term memory will be the most efficient.

The Role of Reading Comprehension

Reading comprehension goes hand in hand with math problem solving and is processed similarly within the working memory (Friedman et al., 2018). Students need to be able to visualize, make connections, retell, and monitor or adjust their comprehension, among other reading skills. This requires critical thinking and organizing thoughts about the story while connecting it to the computation that can answer the question within context. No wonder students struggle with complex math problem solving! It requires a methodical attack and a toolkit of strategies, while also taming math anxiety to avoid becoming overwhelmed.

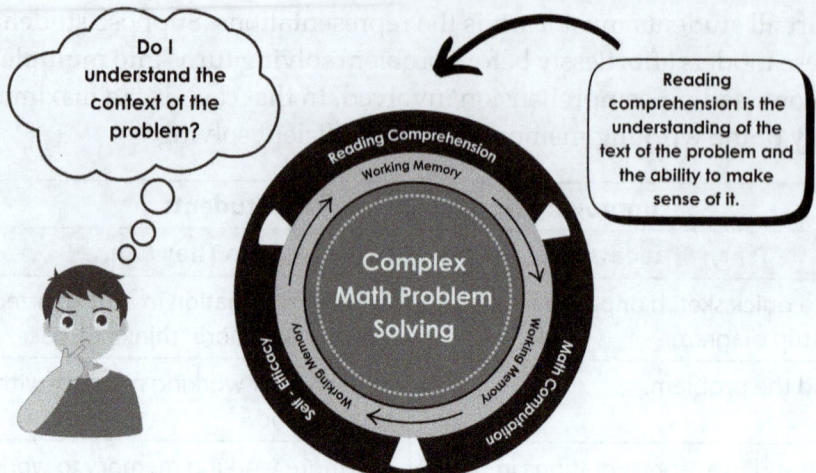

Figure 1.5 The components of math problem solving working together.

When students first read a problem, they can visualize it and treat it like any other story they read. This can help students keep track of reasonableness when solving problems. As students monitor their comprehension and process the story in their working memory, they can do several minor things to offload information to make more "thinking space."

Create Meaning With Color and Context

As discussed in the working memory section, they can draw a quick sketch or a representation, but what is essential for the reading comprehension piece is for students to label the numbers they put into the representation with the context of the problem. Another consideration here is to choose a representation that matches the story. For example, the quick sketch shown in Figure 1.5 was drawn with a number line within the sketch. When a problem includes distance or length, this representation makes sense and adds more relationship to the quick sketch for deeper understanding. Another example would be if a problem said:

> **The orchestra was setting up chairs in the auditorium for a performance. They had 2 rows of green chairs with 6 chairs in each row and 3 rows of blue chairs on the other side with 5 in each row. How many chairs did they set up for the performance?**

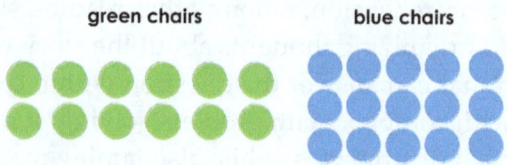

Figure 1.6 Using color to show context.

Using even a bit of color can add context to the problem and help you understand it more quickly than holding this visualization in your head. An array lends itself to representing the visualization of the chairs and linking the reading to the math.

Remove the Numbers or Make Them Smaller

Another strategy to improve reading comprehension is to remove the numbers and replace them with the word "some" so that students are not tempted to solve them before truly understanding the context; this approach is also known as numberless word problems (Bushart, 2012). An additional spin on this strategy is to adjust the problem with smaller numbers so that students don't get overwhelmed by the large value of the numbers (Taylor & Holton, 2022). This helps students feel as though they can solve a complex problem while they gain an understanding of the context and mathematical relationship.

Original Problem	Adjusted Problem
There were 19 ducks at the pond in the morning. In the evening, there were 6. How many ducks left the pond during the day?	There were <u>4</u> ducks at the pond in the morning. In the evening, there were <u>2</u>. How many ducks left the pond during the day?

If a first grader is confident with numbers up to 5, the adjusted problem doesn't seem overwhelming. The student can work up to the original numbers after finding the relationship between the context of the problem and the math content.

Ask Questions to Monitor Comprehension

Students should ask themselves questions as they solve to ensure they are on the right track. While reading the problem, they should be monitoring that their visualization is on point, how many steps they are noticing, and if the question being asked matches what they are seeing in their mind. Some questions they might ask themselves are as follows:

Before Solving
- What do I know?
- What am I trying to find out?
- Who are the characters?
- What are they doing?
- How many steps do I see?
- Draw a model. What is the relationship in the problem?
- About what do I predict the answer to be?

During Solving

- Can I organize my workspace so I can follow how my math matches the story?
- What do these numbers represent?
- Is my calculation accurate?

After Solving

- Does my answer match what I visualized?
- Does my answer match my prediction?
- If not, did I perform all the steps of the problem?
- If not, can I find a mistake in my calculation?

When students develop this skill, their confidence builds. They realize they can answer their own questions about the problem and make sense of tricky situations independently.

Recontextualize After Solving to Check for Reasonableness

After students solve, they have to develop the habit of going back into the problem to see if their answer makes sense and that their answer still aligns to the context of the problem. This is not a natural move for them to make. If students are struggling to do this, a teacher might notice that students are only answering one step of the problem. The teacher might also notice that an answer is unreasonable or that the student didn't actually answer the question from the problem.

When students are able to do this independently, it solidifies their understanding of how the math and reading interact and work together as they solve complex problems.

Improving Reading Comprehension for Students	
Teach Students to...	**So They Can...**
Label the numbers within the context.	Keep the story in mind to find the relationship.
Make the numbers smaller or remove them altogether.	Focus on the story of the problem.
Ask themselves questions about what they know and how that will help them solve the problem.	Build self-efficacy and keep track of what information is important.
Go back into the problem to monitor their comprehension after they solve it.	Check for the reasonableness of their answer within the context of the problem.

The Role of Math Computation

The goal of learning math is to get the answer correct, and ultimately, students have to be strong in math computation to do that. You'll find that computation is woven throughout this book, even though it is not the main focus. The nuance you will see with computation is that it will always be presented with context interwoven. People most likely aren't out in the real world thinking of numbers to add and subtract for no reason.

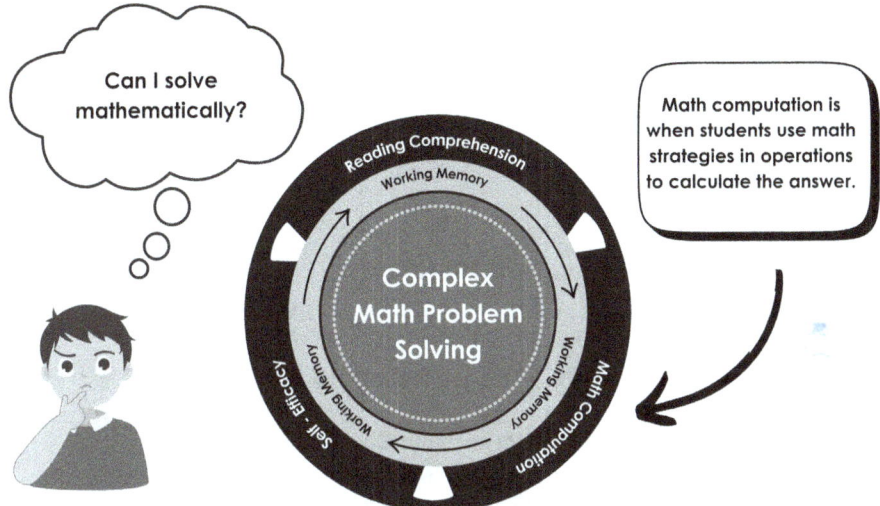

Figure 1.7 The components of math problem solving working together.

Create Connections Through Concrete, Representational, Abstract

You will see computation presented in this book through the concrete representational abstract approach. A researcher named Jerome Bruner came up with an approach in the 1960s that outlined three stages of learning, where students need to experience three representations on a progression to more abstract learning. In math, this equates to students using manipulatives to represent their thinking and drawing models before doing abstract algorithms (Bruner, 1964).

Since the early days of this approach, teachers have found success using this progression to teach math. Recently, teachers have helped students to progress by using the three stages as an intertwined approach. This approach allows students to see their learning not as different strategies but as connected stages of the same operation.

A version of this approach is called the "Build It, Draw It, Write It, Say It" approach, in which students use the representations simultaneously to understand how they are connected. So, instead of a linear, disjointed progression like this:

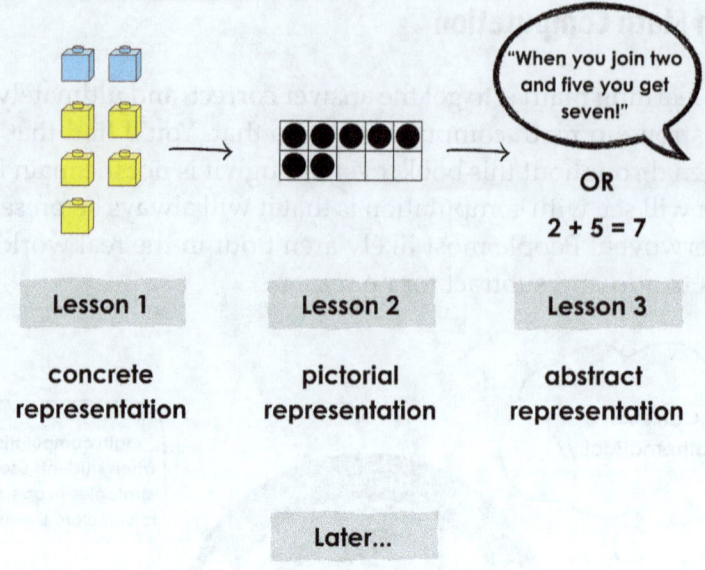

Figure 1.8 Concrete, representational, abstract approach in a linear presentation.

It could look like this….

Nora went fishing with her sister Chloe. Nora caught two blue fish, and Chloe caught five yellow fish. How many fish did they catch together?

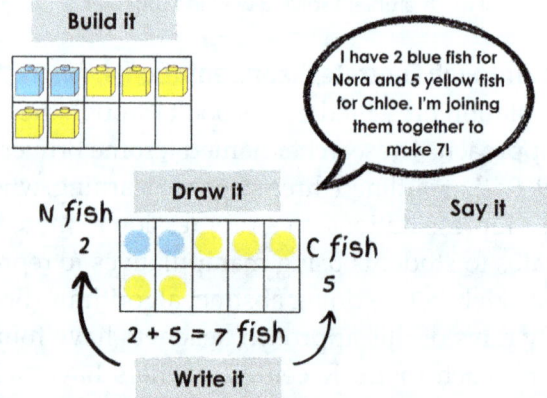

Each day throughout concept

Figure 1.9 Concrete, representational, abstract approach in a connected presentation.

With some concepts, the Build It, Draw It, Write It, Say It approach might be too much for every lesson, but the goal is for students to be able to make connections and do them simultaneously.

Focus Learning Through Side-by-Side Strategies

One way to achieve this is for the teacher to have one of the representations visually available for students to see while they engage with the next strategy that builds upon previous learning.

Let's say the lesson focuses on students practicing the pictorial form of an area model. The teacher gathers students in a circle around a prebuilt tangible version of this using base 10 blocks, and the problem is projected on the board.

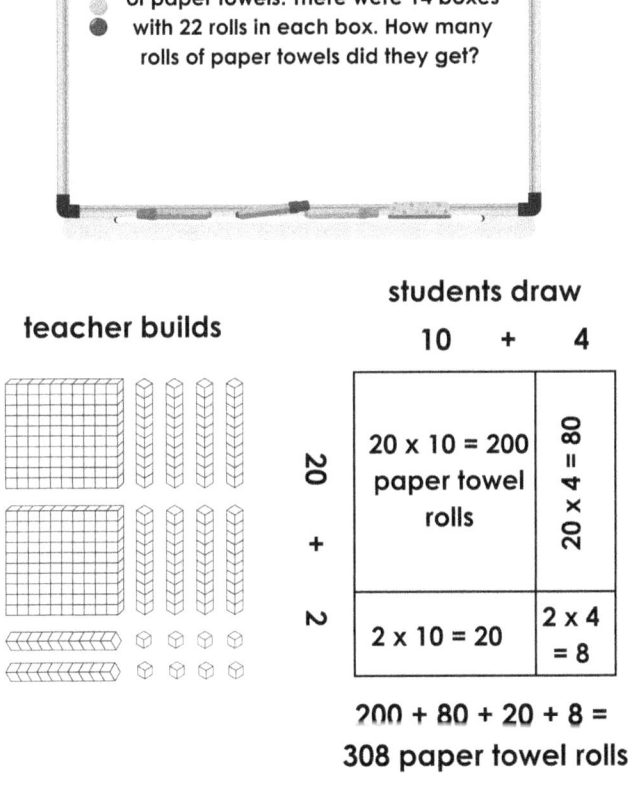

Figure 1.10 Side-by-side math.

This can help keep the lesson focused, remind students of the connections they can make to past math experiences, and help them make sense of their new learning more quickly. However, this should not replace students' regular hands-on experiences in math. Repeated exposure to all types of representations is significant for students' mathematical processing as they build upon their math memories throughout elementary school. As students do mathematical calculations, understanding the context will help them determine if their answer is reasonable and when to use it in their lives.

Keep the Context at the Forefront While Solving

Part of solving is, of course, the mathematical calculation portion. When teachers do teach the calculation piece with math strategies, it is crucial not to have students practice equations in isolation. Students need exposure to numbers in context, even if the context is not the complete focus of the lesson. The context helps students understand the math. Read through both examples carefully to see the moves made by the teacher to establish the context throughout the strategy to maximize understanding.

Fourth-Grade Example	
Problem: At Winston Farm, chickens laid 6,435 eggs last month. They were evenly packaged up and sent to the market in five trucks. How many eggs were transported in each truck?	
Conversation	**Work**
"Today we are going to learn how to divide using partial quotients. I want you to visualize as I read the problem." Read problem. "Turn and retell the problem to a partner." Partners retell. "This is what this problem would look like set up. Our dividend is what we are dividing. In this problem, the dividend is the 6,435 eggs. The divisor is how many groups we have or how many are in each group, depending on the context of the problem. In this problem, the divisor tells us how many groups there are. The five represents the number of trucks. We are (motion to distribute into 5 groups) putting eggs evenly into 5 trucks. Alongside our partial quotients, we are going to see how this is visually represented with the circles representing the trucks."	eggs ↘ 5 ⟌ 6,435 ↗ trucks truck 1 truck 2 truck 3 truck 4 truck 5

Fourth-Grade Example

Problem: At Winston Farm, chickens laid 6,435 eggs last month. They were evenly packaged up and sent to the market in five trucks. How many eggs were transported in each truck?

Conversation	Work
Note: Instead of saying, "How many times does 5 go into 6?" we will lean on the context and talk about the context and the place values. "There are more than 6,000 eggs to put into 5 trucks. We want to break down the dividend by the place value. How many thousands of eggs could we put into each truck? I know that 5 groups of 1,000 is 5,000, so we could put 1,000 eggs into each truck." Write down 1,000 in each circle with the label of "eggs." "So, 5,000 eggs are in the trucks. If we take that out of our total number of eggs we were putting in trucks, there are 1,435 eggs that still need to go into the trucks evenly." Write down the calculation in partial quotients as shown here.	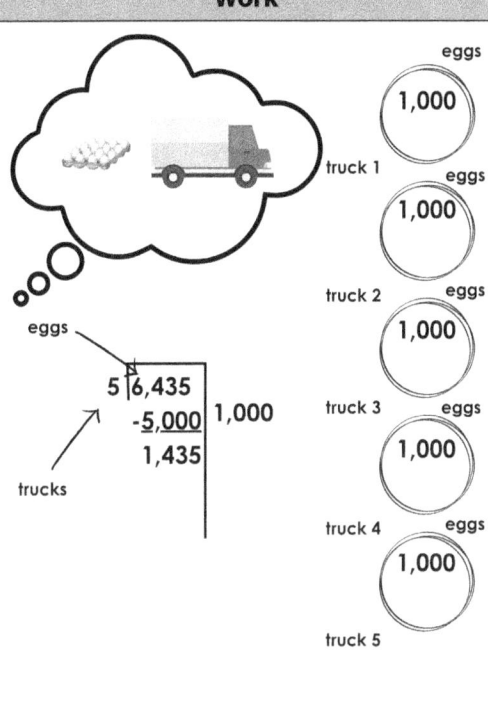
"If I am thinking about how much is left, and we are thinking about it in hundreds, I see in my mind 14 flats of eggs in base 10 blocks. If I have 14 flats or 14 hundreds, how many eggs could I put into each truck? I know that if I put 2 flats in each group, or 200 eggs, that would equal 1,000." Write 200 in each circle, then subtract from the dividend in partial quotients. "When I distribute those eggs, I have 435 left to put into the trucks."	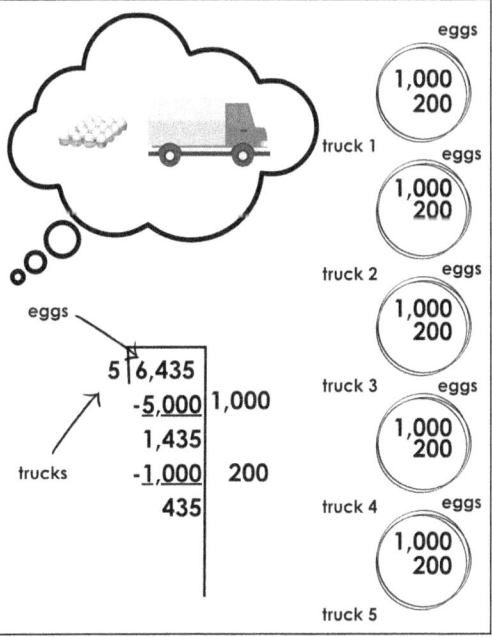

| **Fourth-Grade Example** ||
| Problem: At Winston Farm, chickens laid 6,435 eggs last month. They were evenly packaged up and sent to the market in five trucks. How many eggs were transported in each truck? ||
Conversation	Work
"I know that I can't put another hundred eggs in each truck because that would be 500 eggs, and I don't have that many left. If I put 80 eggs in each truck, that uses 400 of them out of the 435." Write 80 in each circle, then subtract 400 from the eggs remaining. "Now there are only 35 eggs left to put into the trucks."	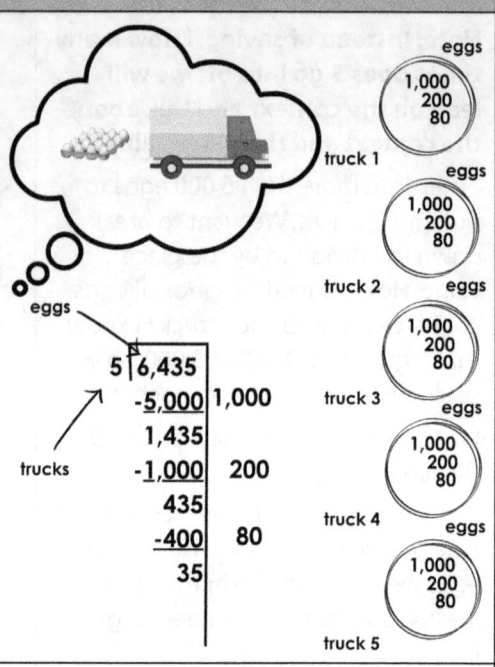
"To evenly divide them, I could put 7 more into each truck, and there is no remainder." Write 7 in each circle. "When we do division, we have to remember the context of what we are talking about to make it make sense and monitor our comprehension. Now we know it makes sense that there are 1,287 eggs in each truck because we can see it. Don't forget to think about how the base 10 blocks regroup and break down as you move into the smaller place values."	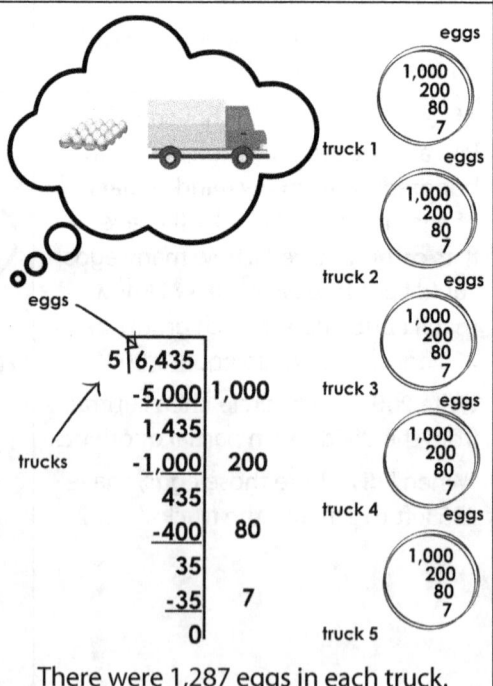 There were 1,287 eggs in each truck.

First-Grade Example
Problem: There were some cows in the field that were spotted and 8 that were not. When Samuel counted all the cows, there were 14. How many were spotted?

Conversation	Work
"Today we are going to practice counting on. One of the ways we can do that is with a part-part-whole mat. Close your eyes and picture this as I read." Read problem. "Turn and retell the problem to a partner." Partners retell. "Let's set up our part-part-whole mat to show what's happening in the problem. I'm also going to represent it with our equation to show the story of the cows in the problem for the beginning, middle, and end."	 ___ + 8 = 14 spotted not total spotted cows
Note: Instead of saying, "When we have the total and a part, we subtract," we will lean on the context and show a way that we can use this representation to solve using the counting on strategy. "We know that Samuel counted a total of 14 cows. Some of them were spotted, and some of them were not. We can use the number we know to count on to the total using our part-part-whole mat and subitizing. Let's count on from 8." Draw circles organized like a ten frame as you count on to 14. "9, 10, 11, 12, 13, 14. At a glance, I can see that there are 6 spotted cows. When I organize them like a ten frame, I don't have to recount. Then I can label the dots with a 6. After that, I can put my answer into my equation and read it to make sure my answer is reasonable or makes sense. Does 6 + 8 equal 14? Yes! I can see in my mind the 6 spotted cows and the 8 that were not spotted. That gives me a total of 14 cows, just like Samuel counted!"	 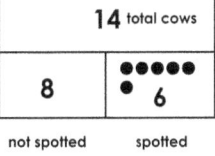 6 + 8 = 14 spotted not total spotted cows

As mentioned earlier, doing math side by side helps students connect what they are learning with what they already know and strengthens connections to previous learning for deeper understanding. Talking through the calculation with context also links the abstract calculation with its actual life application. Hence, the context stays alive throughout the solving, and students can more easily monitor their comprehension and the reasonableness of their answer.

Improving Math Computation for Students	
Teach Students to...	**So They Can...**
Build It, Draw It, Write It, Say It.	Make connections with the concrete, pictorial, and abstract representations with the context.
Make connections by presenting strategies side by side.	Build on their learning in a targeted way, where they can focus on the strategy at hand.
Keep the context at the forefront even when performing the calculation.	Visualize the amount in context to understand.

The Role of Self-Efficacy in Students

Self-efficacy is one's belief that they can or cannot do something, which impacts their ability to do so. This metacognitive component in math is where students decide if they can or cannot solve a problem. It is how people view themselves as competent mathematicians. They will quickly determine if a problem is too tricky, which indicates how motivated they will be to solve it. They will display more effort and determination if they believe they can solve the problem. Then, they will decide whether to try multiple strategies or give up. Along the way, they will monitor if they are making progress and evaluate how accurate they think their answer is. If a student does not believe they can solve a problem, even if they genuinely have the ability, it can create math anxiety (Scheibe et al., 2023).

Math anxiety is when students feel anxiety toward math that interferes with their ability to manipulate numbers or think deeply about mathematics. It can be debilitating to the working memory, leaving competent students unable to show what they know in a complex math problem. Math anxiety is different from generalized anxiety. It is specific to math situations and is likely to be caused by prior negative experiences while learning math (Cuder et al., 2023).

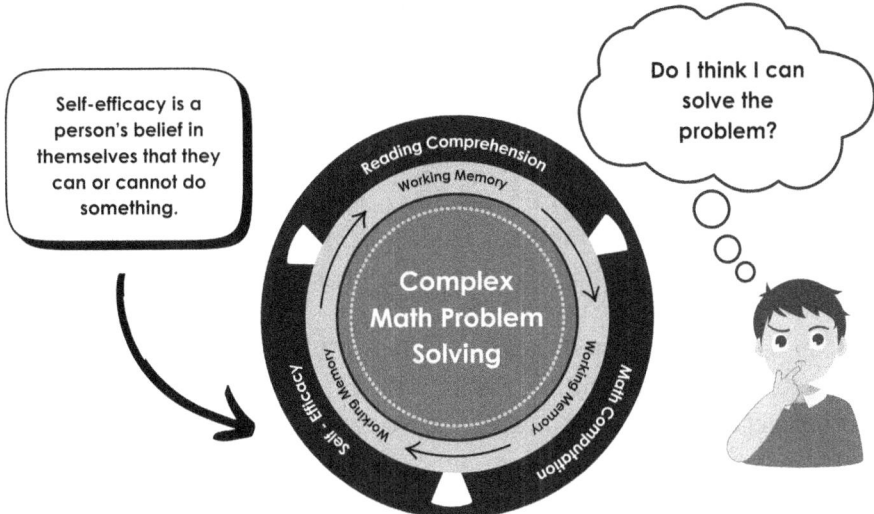

Figure 1.11 The components of math problem solving working together.

It takes time and patience to mitigate math anxiety and negative attitudes toward math. Productive math struggle is vital in helping students become independent doers of math. Productive struggle is when students grapple with a difficult task that is just out of their reach, but not so far that it brings about high frustration. Teachers provide scaffolds and just-in-time questioning to encourage students to persevere. Students need to feel safe taking risks and making mistakes, and see them as a part of learning. Students need to be able to see themselves as mathematicians and succeed in the classroom to build their math identity (Sangiovanni et al., 2020).

Develop a Growth Mindset

A classroom is filled with students who are either learners or nonlearners. Students with a growth mindset are the learners. They believe that they get smarter through hard work, persistence, and effort. They understand that no one is set as smart or unintelligent, and they have the power to change the outcome of their learning experience. These students understand the value of learning from others.

The opposite of this is the fixed mindset of the nonlearners. A fixed mindset is believing that intellectual abilities cannot be changed. Students with a fixed mindset believe they were born with a certain amount of intelligence. They may think they are "good at math" or "bad at math," and nothing they do will change that. For students with this type of mindset, it is tricky to get them to put forth extra effort because they don't see a reason to do so. Students who believe they were born bright must prove they are smart and protect their identity. So they may choose the easiest route to avoid making mistakes in front of anyone. The ones who believe they were born without good math abilities may exhibit low confidence, lack of effort, and aversion to anything difficult (Dweck, 2006).

Some ways to develop a growth mindset include celebrating mistakes as part of the learning process. Students need to see that when they encounter a mistake, it is growing their brain, teaching them new ways to get better. We can also help students see that people they admire who are famous encountered many hurdles to learn their craft. If a student loves basketball, remind them that Michael Jordan did not make his high school basketball team at first. He had to go and practice even more to get better and then try again.

Strategically complimenting students by acknowledging their effort and how it impacts their learning can validate that it is not their ability that is growing their math skills. It is their hard work. There is a difference between telling a student, "Wow, you are so smart!" and saying, "Wow! I see how you took your time to organize your thinking, and you reread the problem multiple times to check your understanding. That is what helped you get the answer correct. That is what good mathematicians do." One makes them want to protect their image and replicate exactly what they did, reinforcing the need for a fixed mindset. The other one motivates students to keep working hard and showing effort to learn.

Take Breaks That Improve Thinking

Sometimes, students can get stuck, and their working memory gets overwhelmed, unable to get back on track. Especially if students have math anxiety, this makes the working memory even less able to process complex problems. Students can learn more about their brain to make decisions about what they might need to ease their anxiety or clear their mind.

One option to get students back on track is for them to lay their heads down and do some breathing exercises. Students can develop math anxiety, the feeling of tension when solving math calculations or problem solving that can cause low math performance or an aversion to it (Shimizu, 2022). When we get anxious, our nervous system can send our heart racing and speed up our breathing. We have what is called a "relaxation response" that lowers stress, and blood flow and oxygen come back down to normal ranges. Deep breathing can help students achieve this (Cedars-Sinai, 2023). Breathing exercises can also improve focus and emotional regulation.

Another way to help students think more clearly is to have them drink water. In studies with children, even mild dehydration was linked to lower academic performance and reduced attention (Khan et al., 2019; Edmunds & Burford, 2009). In adults, dehydration has also been shown to increase the perception of task difficulty (Armstrong et al., 2012).

In addition, when students take a walk or have increased physical activity, it increases blood flow to the brain and allows more oxygen to travel through the bloodstream. When the brain receives more oxygen, cognitive function increases, such as attention, memory, and emotional regulation (Donnelly et al., 2016). Teaching students about this helps them understand why it works. There is a classroom management aspect to this one. Students will need to know the parameters of where they can walk, the time limit they are allowed, and when are appropriate times to use this strategy.

Get Unstuck Using Available Resources

To take ownership of their learning, students need to get themselves unstuck instead of relying on others, especially the teacher. Students have many resources to guide them as they encounter obstacles while solving. When teachers answer students questions about content, students can develop learned helplessness, thinking that if someone isn't available to answer their question, they will remain stuck. This could create a belief that they are incapable of doing math, lowering their confidence and belief in themselves as mathematicians. Instead, they should be pointed to manipulatives, anchor charts, or their math journal to gain understanding and confidence that they can access the knowledge they seek.

Avoid Perfectionism Through Flexibility

Often, students feel their work needs to look just like the teacher's. They are anxious about putting anything on paper, fearing that it might be incorrect. To avoid this, teachers must create a safe space for students to make mistakes and take risks. Student work should be celebrated when they think creatively, and teachers can intentionally show examples of different ways students solve the same problem. This one goes right along with a growth mindset.

Say Positive Affirmations

Students need a positive inner voice to motivate them to keep going when problems are challenging. A considerable part of self-efficacy is self-doubt. Many of my students who did not believe in themselves were the ones who had great number sense, worked hard, and knew what to do to solve. They just didn't believe in themselves. Teaching students phrases they can say to themselves to keep going and reminding them that you know they can do it will grow their confidence in continuing to try. Then, the more they can overcome that voice that says they can't, the more they will realize they can.

Improving Self-Efficacy for Students	
Teach Students to…	**So They Can…**
Have a growth mindset.	Realize that mistakes are part of the learning process.
Take a break when they get overwhelmed.	Get more oxygen to their brain to be able to think more clearly by taking a quick walk, drinking water, or taking deep breaths.
Find resources to use when they get stuck.	Get themselves unstuck and grow confidence and independence.
Be flexible in their thinking and solving.	Overcome perfectionism in their work.
Say positive affirmations to themselves.	Build self-confidence and keep trying.

You will find lessons to build these skills in Chapter 6.

The Role of Self-Efficacy in Teachers

Another aspect of self-efficacy is for teachers. Teachers need to know their content well to respond to student needs. The Common Core Initiative introduced new math standards in 2010 to get students involved in their education (National Governors Association Center for Best Practices & Council of Chief State School Officers, 2010). In our changing education climate, more teachers are entering the profession without a teaching education background. This leads to students being in classrooms with educators who have yet to learn new pedagogy and have likely not seen a teaching model since they were in a classroom as elementary students. In addition, math is not always taught in college teacher preparatory programs, even if teachers did go to college for the profession. Preservice teachers are predominantly procedural learners in math. Learning math conceptually supports procedural learning, but not vice versa (Ozpinar & Arslan, 2022). This creates an even more significant margin for teachers to gain self-efficacy.

Last school year, a new teacher asked me bluntly, "Why can't we just teach kids like we learned?" This teacher had been trying that approach, but it wasn't working. Usually, my explanations of what is best for kids will suffice, but this teacher wanted a deep understanding. I loved this conversation because it pushed my thinking, and I couldn't shake it for weeks. I kept pushing myself to get to the root cause of why we cannot do that. I went back to the purpose of schools in the first place. Schools were created, so people could contribute to society with what was needed. When I was in elementary school, cell phones weren't widely spread, and there was no Google. People didn't have calculators in their hands at all times. Technology has advanced so much that people need to be able to think the way computers cannot. We need students to solve problems creatively, persevere, communicate, and collaborate with others. Teachers teach soft skills through the content and teach students the "why" of math instead of following procedures. This can be daunting for a new teacher, especially if they've never experienced it.

Research shows that when teachers feel confident in their teaching and believe their students can master the material, they have higher student outcomes in achievement and engagement. They also have higher teacher outcomes in job satisfaction, lower rates of burnout, and higher commitment to the work (Perera & John, 2020).

So, how do teachers build self-efficacy?

Attend Professional Development Opportunities

New research is constantly emerging on what works best for student learning. Teachers need to attend professional learning, no matter how many years they have worked with students in schools. Teachers may be changing grade levels or content each year, which can create a gap in teacher knowledge. They need time to learn the content they will be delivering to students so they can feel confident and build self-efficacy.

Some primary considerations need to be made to support new teachers in understanding the why of conceptual learning and process standards to build their self-efficacy. The time to help teachers learn their content and the best instructional strategies is tricky to find with all that is expected of educators. According to the Center for Public Education, it takes educators up to 20 times practicing a complex skill to implement it and use it well, or up to 50 hours of practicing and getting coaching and feedback (Gulamhussein, 2013). That is a lot of time, and many campuses and districts need to find a way to provide this time, so teachers can learn and practice. This learning should be job-embedded and learning that is easy to implement quickly, not just sitting and getting information. Quality professional learning is an investment that will increase teacher retention and student achievement.

Partner Math and Reading Teachers for Learning

Because of departmentalization, upper-grade math teachers have a gap in knowledge for teaching reading comprehension. Deep comprehension is engaged when the problems get complicated and multiple steps and operations are involved. I have also found that most curriculum resources don't include specifics about reading comprehension within problem solving. When I was a teacher, I taught fifth grade. I always struggled more with reading comprehension as a child. One year, I switched to teaching reading after I had taught math for several years in a row. Reading felt so abstract to me. I learned so much that year about reading comprehension that when I taught all subjects the following year, I had found the missing piece to help students understand problem solving!

The more we can integrate learning for students and show them that they can use skills in multiple settings, the more they can remember. When subjects are kept in isolation, short-term solutions are often employed. Teachers must avoid low-level thinking acronyms such as CUBES, where students:

    C – Circle the numbers
    U – Underline the question
    B – Box the keywords
    E – Evaluate (what operation to use) or Equations
    S – Solve and check using keywords to solve problems.

Teachers must also avoid teaching short-term tricks, such as the following:

- If you see these keywords, you do (operation).
- You always divide the bigger number.
- You subtract from the bigger number.
- If you are multiplying by 10, just add a zero.
- If you have the total, you are going to subtract or divide.
- If you don't have the total, you will add or multiply.
- When you add or multiply, the numbers always get bigger.
- When you subtract or divide, the numbers always get smaller.
- If you have a change-unknown problem, you always _____.

These might seem related only to math computation and not problem solving, but they keep students from thinking deeply about the situation. Eventually, these tricks expire, and key words appear in problems just to trick students. Most word problems test how students think and visualize, not solely their math computation ability.

Create Consistency Through Vertical Collaboration

Teachers need time with colleagues in a vertical setting to understand how they can support success in the next grade level. When teachers unpack process standards together, they can form a cohesive, collective understanding and commitment to the following:

- Expectations to embed the process standards within all content standards.
- A common problem solving thinking routine, such as the 3 Reads Routine, involves students reading problems three times to understand them and identifying certain aspects during each reading. Although this routine has many different versions, students must have a consistent one (Kelemanik et al., 2016).
- Common vocabulary; for example, one team of teachers might use the word "regrouping," whereas another team uses the outdated term carrying.
- Common representations. (Do some teachers draw base 10 pictorial models as sticks and dots? Do some draw small, vertical rectangles for them?)
- High expectations for communication in math through speaking and writing

These may seem nitpicky, but when students spend less time learning different ways to do the same things, the things that matter become habitual, and they can focus more on the new content being presented. When teachers can unpack process standards at each grade level, they build collective teacher efficacy. Collective teacher efficacy is the overall belief of the staff that they can positively impact student achievement when they work together (Visible Learning, 2018).

Improving Self-Efficacy for Teachers	
Provide Teachers Opportunities to…	**So They Can…**
Participate in professional learning opportunities that are job-embedded and personalized to their needs.	Learn how math has changed and why it is important to teach differently than they learned as children.
Partner with reading teachers in upper grades when math teachers have little experience with teaching reading comprehension.	Understand the strategies that will help students in math problem solving that students have already learned.
Meet as vertical teams on campus to discuss what problem solving looks like and sounds like at each grade level.	Create consistency for students and understand their contribution to the vertical progression of problem solving.
Learn about how to break down problem solving behaviors into a progression of skills.	Target specific skills through intentional, differentiated small groups.

Break Down Problem Solving Into a Progression of Skills

In the next chapter, you will learn more about how problem solving can be broken down into phases of understanding. There will be a progression with lessons to support student learning. When looking at specific student behaviors, we can identify the strengths they have and what they are ready for next on their journey to being outstanding mathematicians.

Chapter 1: Reflection

What are three things you learned from reading this chapter?

1
2
3

What are two questions that you still have?

1
2

What is one thing you want to examine more deeply and learn more about?

1

Apply Your Learning

- Identify the complex problem solving standards in your grade level. (Go to the standards that are followed in your state or school. Find the standards for representing and/or solving single- or multi-step problems. In grades 3–5, there should be standards for both addition/subtraction and multiplication/division.)
- Identify the aligning standards that occur vertically (in the grade level before and after) in your state that apply to your school or district.
- Collect data on how your students have performed recently on these standards. (This would be based on either current assignments or assessment data housed in a data management system.)

What do you notice?

What do you have questions about?

References

Armstrong, L. E., Ganio, M. S., Casa, D. J., Lee, E. C., McDermott, B. P., Klau, J. F., Jimenez, L., LeBellego, L., Chevillotte, E., & Lieberman, H. R. (2012, February). Mild dehydration affects mood in healthy young women. *The Journal of Nutrition Ingestive Behavior and Neurosciences*, 142(2), 382–388.

Baddeley, A. (2000). The episodic buffer: A new component of working memory? *Trends in Cognitive Science*, 4(11), 417–423.

Bruner, J. (1964). The course of cognitive growth. *American Psychologist*, 19(1), 1–15.

Bushart, B. (2012). Numberless Word Problems. https://numberlesswp.com/introduction/

Cedars-Sinai. (2023). *Five deep breathing exercises for kids and teens*. Cedars-Sinai. https://www.cedars-sinai.org/blog/five-deep-breathing-exercises-for-kids-and-teens.html

Cuder, A., Zivkovic, M., Doz, E., Pellizzoni, S., & Passolunghi, M. C. (2023). The relationship between math anxiety and math performance: The moderating role of visuospatial working memory. *Journal of Experimental Child Psychology*, 233, 105688. https://doi.org/10.1016/j.jecp.2023.105688

DeSmedt, B., Janssen, R., Bouwens, K., Verschaffel, L., Boets, B., & Ghesquiere, P. (2009). Working memory and individual differences in mathematics achievement: A longitudinal study from first grade to second grade. *Journal of Experimental Psychology*, 103, 186–201.

Donnelly, J. E., Hillman, C. H., Castelli, D., Etnier, J. L., Lee, S., Tomporowski, P. Lambourne, K., & Szabo-Reed, A. N. (2016, June). Physical activity, fitness, cognitive function, and academic achievement in children: A systematic review. *American College of Sports Medicine*, 48(6), 1197–1222.

Dweck, C. S. (2006). *Mindset: The new psychology of success*. Random House.

Edmunds, C. J. & Burford, D. (2009). Should children drink more water?: The effects of drinking water on cognition in children. *Appetite*, 52(3), 776–779.

Friedman, L. M., Rapport, M. D., Calub, C. A., & Eckrich, S. J., (2018, November). ADHD and core foundational learning: Working memory's contribution to reading comprehension and applied math problem-solving abilities. *ADHD Report*, 26(7), 1–3.

Gathercole, S. E. & Alloway, T. P. (2008). *Working memory & learning: A practical guide for teachers*. Sage Publishing.

Gulamhussein, A. (2013). Teaching the teachers: Effective professional development in an era of high stakes accountability. *Center for Public Education*.

Kelemanik, G., Janssen Creighton, S., & Lucenta, A. (2016). *Routines for reasoning: Fostering the mathematical practices in all students*. Heinemann.

Khan, N. A., Westfall, D. R., Jones, A. R., Sinn, M. A., Bottin, J. H., Perrier, E. T., & Hillman, C. H. (2019). A 4-d water intake intervention increases hydration and cognitive flexibility among preadolescent children. *The Journal of Nutrition Ingestive Behavior and Neurosciences*, 149(12), 2255–2264. https://doi.org/10.1093/jn/nxz206

Li, T., Sun, G., Zhou, X., & Wang, T. (2023). Controlled attention, but not temporal storage of working memory correlates to math problem solving. *Educational Psychology*, 43(8), 895–913. https://doi.org/10.1080/01443410.2023.2254522

National Governors Association Center for Best Practices, & Council of Chief State School Officers. (2010). Common Core State Standards for Mathematics. Retrieved from http://www.corestandards.org/Math/

Ozpinar, I.& Arslan, S. (2022) Investigation of basic mathematical knowledge of preservice maths teachers: Procedural or conceptual?. *International Journal of Mathematical Education in Science and Technology*, 53(8), 2115–2132. https://doi.org/10.1080/0020739X.2020.1867915

Perera, H. N. & John, J. E. (2020). Teachers self-efficacy beliefs for teaching math: Relations with teacher and student outcomes. *Contemporary Educational Psychology*, 61, 101842. https://doi.org/10.1016/j.cedpsych.2020.101842

Sangiovanni, J. J., Katt, S., & Dykema, K. J. (2020). *Productive math struggle: A 6-point action plan for fostering perseverance*. Corwin.

Scheibe, D. A., Was, C. A., Dunlosky, J., & Thompson, C. A. (2023). Metacognitive cues, working memory, and math anxiety: The regulated attention in mathematical problem solving (RAMPS) framework. *Journal of Intelligence*, 11(6),117. https://doi.org/10.3390/jintelligence11060117

Shimizu, Y., (2022). Relation between mathematical proof problem solving, math anxiety, self-efficacy, learning engagement, and backward reasoning. *Journal of Education and Learning*, 11(6), 62–75.

Sweller, J. (2011). Cognitive load theory. In J. P. Mestre & B. H. Ross (Eds.), *Psychology of Learning and Motivation* (Vol. 55, pp. 37–76). Academic Press.

Taylor, W. & Holton, D. (2022). Enabling problem solving in the primary maths classroom. *APMC*, 27(3), 17 23.

Visible Learning. (2018, March). *Collective teacher efficacy according to John Hattie*. Retrieved from https://visible-learning.org/2018/03/collective-teacher-efficacy-hattie/

2

How Can I Break Down the Behaviors That Drive Mathematical Problem Solving?

I have heard over and over throughout my experiences in education that math is very black and white, right or wrong. Teachers can immediately look at their students' work and see if their answers are correct or incorrect. Most can even name where a student's mistake occurred and the misconception in their calculation. Although this may be true, there is still a tricky part of addressing math data, including when the students' answers are not anywhere near accurate, when students don't know where to start, or when they only complete part of the problem.

Contributing to the problem, here are four of the most common ways student work has been sorted:

- Grouping students into three groups: a group that "got it," a group that "almost got it," and a group that "didn't get it"
- Grouping students in a general range of scores: a common percentage on a standard or an assessment
- Grouping students by their ability in math: high learners, medium learners, striving learners
- Grouping students into general buckets: "my problem-solving group" and "my computation group"

Grouping students in these ways causes frustration for teachers and students, and these methods will not get the desired results. When students are grouped broadly or by general overall math proficiency, there is no specific

DOI: 10.4324/9781003510703-3

aim for instruction. This can cause students in a group to have very different needs, and the groups last way too long trying to navigate where to go with a "level" of instruction. Categorizing students into a singular group limits a teacher's ability to see them flexibly for all of their needs.

When personally grading papers or looking at student work in collaboration with other teachers, I have noticed that many students who got the correct answer were not doing deep thinking work and that getting the correct answer as quickly as possible had become a primary goal. As a teacher, this is both validating and frustrating. Trying to grow students who are already getting the answer correct is a tough battle to fight. In contrast, many of my students who did not get the answer correct showed a lot of understanding and exhibited many strengths. I also noticed commonalities in misconceptions students across the class were having or mistakes they were making. I would never have put these students into the same group by merely looking at data in a spreadsheet.

My approach to sorting students into small groups needed to change. I needed to identify specific learning targets to make my lessons shorter and more strategic to grow every student. As I started this work, diagnosing a problem within their computation or specific content-related material was reasonably straightforward. Still, it was harder to identify what to do if a student didn't understand the problem at all or if they got off track in that process. I started to break down those skills as a teacher, but the real breakthrough happened when I realized this was a problem with students everywhere, and I could partner with teachers to see what was working.

As I started working with teachers on small-group instruction, we found that there were concrete skills that could be built upon each other to help create independent, successful problem solvers and critical thinkers. Still, there were no resources we could find that fit our observations of the impact of low self-efficacy, low reading comprehension, high math anxiety, and students not using their working memory to its highest capacity.

To increase proficiency in math problem-solving, we must consider two buckets: problem-solving behaviors and mathematical computation. We must also be careful not to separate them. Brain research says that breaking down complex tasks into small steps can improve performance, boost confidence, and deepen learning (Cooney Horvath, 2019). This chapter's progression will help break down complex math problem solving into small steps so that students and teachers can feel more successful with a clear pathway to proficiency. Because teachers can already tell when a student computes correctly or incorrectly, we will not focus on that in this progression. Still, my philosophy on mathematical computation will be shared throughout this book, when applicable.

Figure 2.1 Math problem solving in two buckets.

Process Standards vs. Content Standards

In the 1990s, the New Standards Project was initiated to set up a consistent set of high standards for learning and related assessments that would be tied to them. This is how the Common Core standards were named to create college and career readiness in students across the United States in 2010. States were not forced to use these specific standards, but it was a step toward creating a set of "fewer, clearer, higher" standards for learning. This meant that math standards became more conceptual and less procedural.

Process skills were added and meant to be embedded within all content standards (Parkay et al., 2014). These skills directly impact complex problem solving, where students apply mathematics to everyday problems, learn to use a problem-solving model, create and use representations, and analyze mathematical relationships.

Different states use different standards to dictate what students learn at each grade level; however, a common idea remains. Two types of standards are taught across grade levels in math: content standards and process standards. Content standards define the knowledge and skills students are expected to learn in a given grade level. Process standards describe the skills and practices students should develop and use while engaging with the content standards. One issue with how some of the standards are presented in documents for teachers is that they are divided into two sets, which can unintentionally separate process standards from content standards. You can't teach process standards without the content standards, and you can't teach content standards without the process standards. It is not one or the other. It's both. The tricky part is that to analyze student behaviors, you have to be able to separate them to determine where the breakdown occurs for each student. For example, if teachers are looking at a scope and sequence and see this Common Core standard:

> CCSS.Math.Content.3.OA.D.9 - Identify arithmetic patterns (including patterns in the addition table or multiplication table) and explain them using properties of operations.
> (National Governors Association Center for Best Practices & Council of Chief State School Officers, 2010a)

They might teach these skills in isolation, showing students what it's like to calculate patterns on a table without considering the Mathematical Practices.

Students should have opportunities to think more deeply using real world application and the process standards for the Common Core standards shown here.

	Standards for Mathematical Practice
MP1	Make sense of problems and persevere in solving them.
MP2	Reason abstractly and quantitatively.
MP3	Construct viable arguments and critique the reasoning of others.
MP4	Model with mathematics.
MP5	Use appropriate tools strategically.
MP6	Attend to precision.
MP7	Look for and make use of structure.
MP8	Look for and express regularity in repeated reasoning.

(National Governors Association Center for Best Practices & Council of Chief State School Officers, 2010b)

The process standards allow students to learn soft skills needed throughout life and other disciplines. If we want to know how to help students grow through engaging with the math content and thinking deeply, we need to make their thinking visible. To get this required evidence, it is imperative to have a task with the appropriate rigor and structure to bring out the deep thinking to find where each student needs instruction. The task cannot be so easy that students can complete it quickly, but it also cannot be so complex that students shut down out of frustration before they even begin. As the process standards portray, when students are learning, they need to spend a lot of time thinking, processing, and communicating. They will need to experience struggle and perhaps approach the problem from different angles. They may start and then erase or cross through their original work. Math tasks must be open-ended. Students need to be free to make sense of the problems for themselves with flexibility. Such skills are very abstract and complex.

A Progression for Problem Solving

As we start to look at the heart of this issue, the problem-solving progression in this chapter was created, so teachers can walk away from this book and have a tool to help them analyze students' strengths and determine next steps. This tool and the targeted lessons can be used for differentiation in tierone instruction, for students being served through special education settings, for students that are served through Multi-tiered Systems of Support (MTSS), or any other program or tier. It should be used as a guide to get students to high levels of proficiency in math problem solving, regardless of where they fall in the beginning.

Teachers will use student work as a guide to place students on the progression so they can learn skills to progress all the way through. In the next chapter, we will look at student work to practice noticing student behaviors and see what they are ready for but not yet doing. You will see that many of these strategies are based on comprehension and thinking skills. Students already use many of these strategies as they solve problems without paying attention to them.

An example is when you have students who know the answer but struggle to work it out on paper. Or when you have students who can work out the problem mathematically, but they are confused when you ask them what the numbers in the problem represent. We have to help students acknowledge the parts of their thinking to which they need to pay more attention. Students must be taught the strategies, informed of their importance, and shown how these skills will enhance their understanding of math problems (Willingham, 2024).

Missing guidance of this kind could explain why students struggle with comprehension, especially in math. Students need to be told which behaviors and strategies they are already using mentally that are essential when solving complex math problems. Connections need to be made that the skills they are using to understand books in reading are important and are the same skills they can lean on for comprehension in math. Comprehension in math must be an intentional focus for teachers to learn and model so they can transfer that focus to student work and practice.

Research says that to facilitate learning of such complex tasks, teachers need to break down the task into smaller, more achievable tasks, especially for students learning something new (Ashman, 2023). As you read this chapter, you will find an overview and background for each phase. Then, you will see how each phase is broken down into those smaller, more achievable tasks. Sample lessons with anchor charts are provided to showcase what this learning could look like for students.

The progressions here show the strategies students must understand and the behaviors that teachers might notice that signal a student's need to develop specific skills. Take a moment to study the progressions and internalize how to read them.

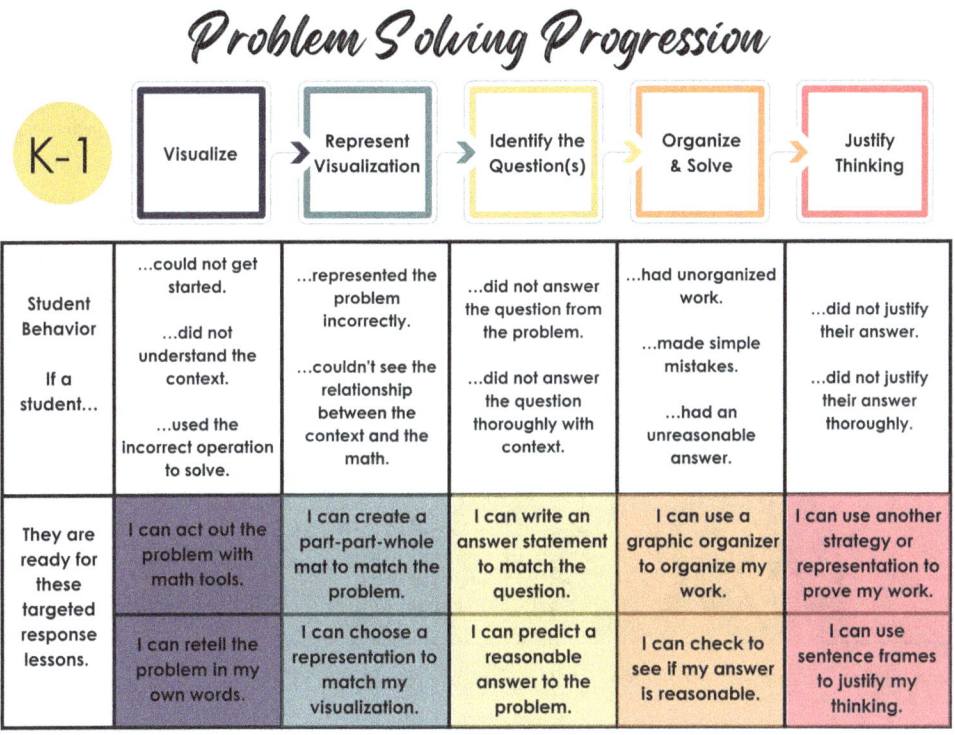

Figure 2.2 Kindergarten and first grade problem-solving progression.

To create meaningful learning experiences for students, the data must come from their independent work. Observations from their written work will guide teachers to look in the first row of the progressions to identify where each student may need to enter this progression of skills based on the skills they need to develop next. These noticings can help the teacher refer to the Targeted Response Lesson section for the teach points to help students master that progression phase. For example, suppose a student doesn't even know where to start, their paper is blank, or what they wrote down doesn't make sense. In that case, they can be put in a group that only focuses on those skills in the first column in small-group instruction until they are ready for the next part of the progression of representing what they see in their mind on paper.

Problem Solving Progression

2-5	Visualize	Represent Visualization	Identify the Question(s)	Organize & Solve	Justify Thinking
Student Behavior **If a student…**	…could not get started. …did not understand the context. …used the incorrect operation to solve.	…represented the problem incorrectly. …couldn't see the relationship between the context and the math.	…did not answer the question from the problem. …did not answer the question thoroughly with context. …only completed one step of a multi-step problem.	…had unorganized work. …made simple mistakes. …had an unreasonable answer.	…did not justify their answer. …did not justify their answer thoroughly.
They are ready for these targeted response lessons.	I can act out the problem with math tools.	I can create a part-part-whole mat/strip diagram to match the problem.	I can write an answer statement to match the question.	I can use a graphic organizer to organize my work.	I can use another strategy or representation to prove my work.
	I can remove the numbers or make them smaller to understand the context.	I can label the numbers with context to show meaning.	I can predict a reasonable answer to the problem.	I can monitor my comprehension as I solve the problem.	I can use sentence frames to justify my thinking.
	I can retell the problem in my own words.	I can choose a representation to match my visualization.	I can set up a workspace for each part of the problem.	I can check to see if my answer is reasonable.	I can write a justification that includes my math and reading comprehension.

Figure 2.3 Second grade to fifth grade problem-solving progression.

If a student knows the right steps, but their work is unorganized and spills all over the page, causing them to make simple mistakes, that student would need to be in a group where they learn to be more organized. Based on their work, once students are sorted, they may have missed entirely different questions on an assignment or assessment, but they need to learn the same skill to progress in their level of thinking.

This progression includes five phases:

1 **Visualize:** Students make meaning out of text by using their reading skills to make a movie in their minds.
2 **Represent Visualization:** This phase is the bridge from reading to math. Students use the problem context to choose a way to model in order to make the relationship visible.

3. **Identify the Question(s):** Students sometimes read the context of the problem, and when they go to solve it, they forget to go back to check that they have done and that their answer makes sense. In this phase, they will learn how to make moves to keep their eye on their purpose for solving.
4. **Organize and Solve:** Oftentimes, the highest achieving students can make simple mistakes because they are not organized in their work. They might get lost in the steps of the problem or need a tool to learn how to stay on track.
5. **Justify Thinking:** Every student deserves to grow and deepen their thinking. When students justify their thinking, they learn to analyze their thinking processes and communicate them thoroughly.

The progressions are broken down by kindergarten and first grade on one, and then grades 2–5 on the other because the complexity of the problems that students experience in these grade levels varies greatly. In kindergarten and first grade, students have only one-step problems. Their content standards keep them within 20 for problem solving. When students get to second grade, the rigor of the comprehension required rises substantially, increasing to 99 in some states and to 1,000 in others. In addition, second grade is where multi-step problems begin.

Visualize

The first skill that students need to solve complex problems is visualizing them. This can also be called mental imagery, where students make a movie of what is happening in their minds. One way to help students bring the problem to life is to use objects to see the action and talk about what is happening in the problem, like a story.

Consider this: you are assembling furniture without a picture. Imagine you have a box of furniture parts and an instruction manual.

The manual just lists the steps:

1. Insert bolt A into panel D
2. Attach bracket C
3. Tighten with a wrench
4. etc....

You might follow every step perfectly, but still feel uncertain. Are you building it right? Is that piece supposed to look like that?

Consider a different manual. It has the same steps but includes pictures along the way, and the cover has a picture of what it looks like completed. Now you can compare your work to the image and see where you're headed. If something looks off, you can spot it early and adjust.

Visualization in math works the same way. You need to build a mental picture of what's happening. Like those furniture pictures, visualization lets you check if you're on the right track and spot when something doesn't look quite right.

Students struggle with this skill because they may lack experiences that help them relate to specific contexts, or they may lack experiences with math manipulatives. When students learn to read, visualizing becomes more manageable because, often, students see what they are reading about in movies or real life. I love how math guru Christina Tondevold explained that when students hear the word "cat," they immediately see a furry animal that meows, not the letters c-a-t. When we ask them what they see when we say "37," they would most likely say the digits 3 and 7, not the value. When students visualize math, those memories are created in the classroom with manipulatives and drawing models that bridge from the concrete to the abstract (Tondevold, 2019). Students build numbers and manipulate them to compare, add, subtract, and so on, building math memories. When students lack experience and confidence with manipulatives, it can hinder them as they move through upper grades in elementary school.

Represent Visualization

This progression section goes back to working memory and how it functions. When students read through a complex problem, the brain tries to understand it. As this occurs, the working memory becomes full of information. To create more space, information can be "offloaded" and organized to aid in a deeper comprehension of the relationship within the problem. Then, they can reread to catch any of the information they missed and see what should be added to their representation of thinking. The part-part-whole and strip diagram are constructive in understanding the relationships within problems. If students want to focus on getting good at one model, this one has the most significant impact on comprehension.

Another aspect to consider in this part of the progression is matching the context of the problem to the type of representation that best fits the situation. As discussed in Chapter 1, a problem about people running a race would be better understood on a linear model such as a number line or a bar model. A problem about pieces of a puzzle might be better represented by a pictorial model of base ten blocks. If problems have multiple parts, students may use different models to represent each part depending on the context. This part of the progression is where reading comprehension meets the math of the problem. It's the bridge from concrete to getting more abstract.

Models: The Key to Understanding Complex Problems

The word "representation" can be confusing. Representations help offload the problem from the working memory, so students can think through what to do next. Many students will solve the problem and then draw a representation after the fact as a form of compliance because the teacher told them to do so. Once a representation is written down with the context labeled, students can use all of their processing power to make a plan to solve. Representations make relationships visible from the problem. This stage is often the most difficult for high-achieving students, who need to practice slowing down their thoughts and communicating in ways that are not natural to them.

Getting the correct answer is not everything. We need every student to be able to communicate ideas in different ways and learn how to simplify complex ideas on paper. Learning how to do this in elementary school will make it more natural when the ideas that students encounter become more complicated as they grow older.

Students can put context on paper in multiple ways to make the problem visible. They can label the numbers or model with words from the problem they represent, or draw a quick sketch that makes the problem come to life. Below, you will see an example of two ways to show context.

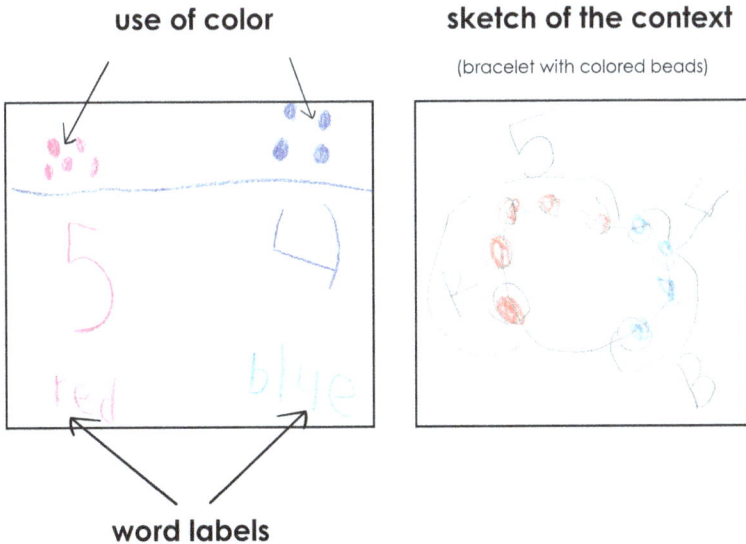

Figure 2.4 Context shown in student work.

One of my very favorite things is to analyze data. Data leads to answers and tells a story. In my work with teachers, the data that kept arising was that students struggled with complex problem solving. When I looked into statewide data, almost every problem-solving standard had less than 50% mastery. This piqued my curiosity and drive to find answers. So, I dove into third- and fourth-grade problem-solving items from state tests and started working them out myself. I wanted to see what the misconceptions were. My common noticings were as follows:

- Students tried using keywords to help them understand the operation instead of visualizing it. The test creators included keywords to confuse students.
- The problems where students were meant to divide for both steps were exceptionally low.
- The problems were not overly complicated. If students could "see" the context, they should be able to solve them quickly or at least know if their answers are reasonable.

I needed to know more. I started noticing phrases that really stuck out to me in classrooms: "What operation is this?" or "What operation is first?" When I solved the problems in these grade levels, I noticed that I did not typically use the operations most teachers expected if they presented one of these questions. I often represented the problem with a quick sketch or a strip diagram, leading me to skip count, count on, or create a table to find a pattern. Students were trying to go straight to solving.

To see for yourself, take a moment and solve the problem below. It came from the third-grade test in my state. As you solve it, ponder these things:

- How many times did you need to read it to understand it?
- What feelings did you have as you were solving? Excitement? Anxiety? Frustration? Accomplishment?
- Third graders have been doing multiplication and division for less than a year.
- Did you feel a sense of mental relief or the ability to think more clearly once you offloaded your thinking into a representation?

A group of people bought tickets for a roller-coaster ride.

- The group spent $4 for each ticket.
- Altogether the group spent $48 on tickets.
- Each person in the group got 2 tickets.

How many people were in the group?

3rd Grade Released STAAR Test Question
(Texas Education Agency, 2022)

Solve here:

What operations did you use to solve? Did you draw a quick sketch or jot down some notes to remember? Over the last few years, I've presented this problem to hundreds of administrators and teachers and have seen a lot of variation in understanding this problem. In addition to a handful of people who did solve using the standard algorithm for division, I have provided some of the most common creative ways in Figure 2.5. We cannot box students into one way of solving or a specific operation as the only way to enter a problem. We need them to have habits and tools that allow them to think deeply and learn how to think more clearly in complex situations. As stated by Elena Aguilar and Lori Cohen (2022), "Habits are behaviors that you enact so often that you internalize them and they become routine… Once a behavior is a habit, it doesn't take as much cognitive, physical, or emotional energy as when you started."

In addition, teachers have to remember that students are novices in the math they are learning each year. Teachers have had time to process and master the content already. Students need to have the opportunity to slow down, make connections, and create mathematical memories that can anchor their habits for thinking deeply. A vital part of this is that we must be on board to push students beyond solving for the correct answer.

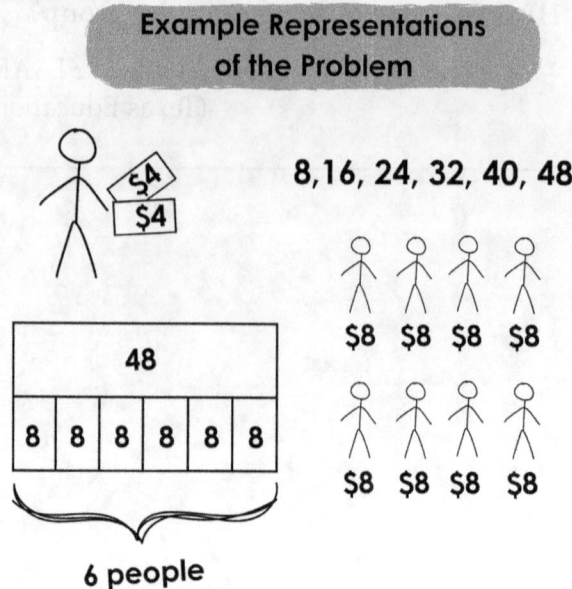

Figure 2.5 Ways students may solve the problem.

As you look at the models above, you will see that multiplication is even more visible than division. When students create representations, often they build up to the whole. This may explain why students see addition and multiplication more easily. Oftentimes, students can't even name what operation they are trying to do, but they can solve and name it afterward once they can see the patterns presented.

Part-Part-Whole to Strip Diagrams
Do you notice that you read out loud to yourself when texts get complex? Or perhaps you reread or slow down? That is a strategy your brain uses to help you understand and process. Representing with models is much the same for math. Students don't need to represent every problem they encounter, just like we don't need to read out loud to ourselves or reread every text. It is a skill we need to acknowledge that can be used when things are complex and help students know how and when to use these strategies. In elementary school, teachers build the foundation for students and the habits they will use throughout their lives as they encounter problems of many types and in many settings.

The first lesson in this phase concerns representing with a part-part-whole or strip diagram. You might wonder why there is a specific lesson for this particular representation. When I first got intrigued by strip diagrams, only 8% of students in Texas got an answer correct on a problem from our state test where students had to choose a matching strip diagram on a multi-step addition problem. That wasn't the only problem that had dismal scores. If we can give students one representation to master that makes sense to use almost every time, it is this one. Students struggle more with subtraction and division than with addition and multiplication. This part-to-whole representation magnifies the relationship between the numbers in the problem and gives a way to offload in an organized way. This step needs to come before writing an equation. This is the step that HELPS students write the equation. It also removes the need to name an operation because this visual opens multiple ways to approach the problem. Students will not be solving during this phase of the progression. They will only be creating a model to match the math situation. The founder of Math is Figureoutable, Pam Harris, writes about the difference between models and strategies. You use a model to show the relationship you see on paper. The strategy is how you manipulate the numbers to answer the problem (Harris, 2020).

For example, consider the following problem::

> **There were 303 songs recorded at a studio last month.**
> **97 were rap, 89 were pop, and the rest were jazz.**
> **How many jazz songs were recorded in the studio last month?**

To represent this problem, you can easily find the parts and the whole to see the relationship in the problem. Students in grades K–2 need to master the part-part-whole and students in grades 3–5 move on to strip diagrams. The difference between a part-part-whole and a strip diagram is that the parts of the strip diagram move with the size of the number. This can help students estimate the value of parts they don't know to ensure their answer is reasonable..

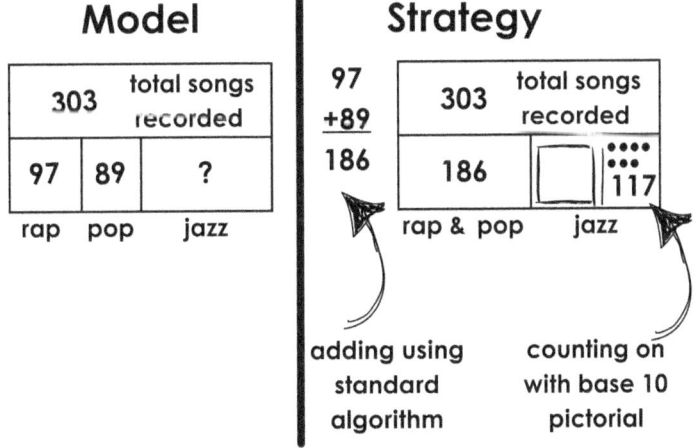

Figure 2.6 Using a representation as a model vs. a strategy.

Taking Your Mind Movie to Paper

As you look at another lesson included in this progression phase, the focus is, as it says, "Representing Visualization." This phase was my biggest "aha" in my work with students and my quest to find answers to low problem-solving mastery. As a teacher, I always wondered why we must teach students so many representations. I've also heard other teachers ask, "Why can't we just let them use the one they like?" or "If they would just use (favorite strategy), they would be able to get the answer right and not be confused by all of these representations!" I always felt that the reason was that certain kids would understand using certain representations, so we had to expose students to all of them until they found their fit. I have since adjusted my thinking. Visualize this problem in your head.

> **Damion walks dogs for his neighbors to earn extra money. First, he goes to Mrs. Jensen's house, which is 0.4 miles away. He walked her dog 1.7 miles. Then he walked 0.4 miles home. How far did Damion walk?**

Visualizing that in your head makes sense as a bar model or a number line as you see Damion walking distances. Representing as base 10 or as a table does not make as much sense.

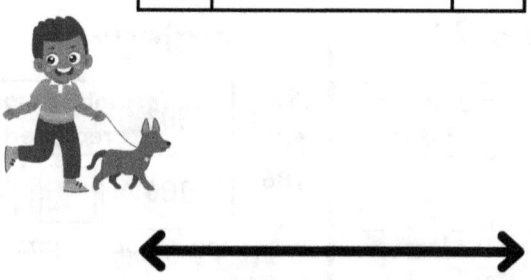

Figure 2.7 Visualization to a representation on paper.

Choosing the representation that makes sense with the context helps students to offload the problem onto paper in a way that maintains meaning. Students think we ask them to show their work on paper to control or keep them from cheating or guessing. We need to help students understand that we are showing them how to communicate their thinking on paper and how to maximize the use of their brains in processing information.

Students must still represent with concrete and pictorial models in the fourth and fifth grades. Some students may have mastered using models, but not with the new content they are learning. Upper-grade students need to create the meaning of decimals and fractions to communicate about them well and make connections to what they already know about whole numbers. Too often, teachers assume that students should move quickly to the abstract phase of concepts, which hinders students' ability to learn the content deeply and discover connections themselves. Students must be able to represent problems independently and efficiently as part of demonstrating mastery of each concept. In primary grades, this might feel repetitive or unnecessary since many students are able to solve more easily, sometimes even in their heads. As problems progress in complexity, their foundational knowledge of how to represent problems that were easy for them to solve will allow them to use those same tools to make complex problems easier to understand. They will be able to connect what they know already to form new Pictorial Representations Appropriate for Each Grade Lavel knowledge and understanding. Below, you will find appropriate pictorial representations for each grade level as a progression through fifth grade.

	Pictorial Representations Appropriate for Each Grade Level			
	Vertical Alignment for Part to Whole	**Vertical Alignment for Base 10**	**Vertical Alignment for Linear Models**	**Other Representations Needed**
Kindergarten	• Part-Part-Whole Mat	• Five Frames • Ten Frames	• Number Line to 10 (could be printed)	• Quick Sketch of Context • Table to Organize • Equation
First Grade	• Part-Part-Whole Mat • Part-Part-Part Whole Mat	• Double Ten Frames	• Number Line to 20 (could be printed) • Bar Model	• Quick Sketch of Context • Table to Organize • Equation
Second Grade	• Part-Part-Whole Mat (might use two different ones for multi-step problem) • Part-Part-Part Whole Mat	• Base 10 Pictorial • Place Value Chart	• Open Number Line • Bar Model	• Quick Sketch of Context • Table to Organize • Equations

| Pictorial Representations Appropriate for Each Grade Level |||||
	Vertical Alignment for Part to Whole	Vertical Alignment for Base 10	Vertical Alignment for Linear Models	Other Representations Needed
Third Grade	• Strip Diagram (lines adjust based on values)	• Base 10 Pictorial • Place Value Chart	• Open Number Line • Bar Model	• Quick Sketch of Context • Table to Organize or Find Pattern • Area Models • Equations
Fourth Grade	• Strip Diagram (lines adjust based on values)	• Base 10 Pictorial • Place Value Chart	• Open Number Line • Bar Model	• Quick Sketch of Context • Table to Organize or Find Pattern • Area Models • Equations
Fifth Grade	• Strip Diagram (lines adjust based on values)	• Base 10 Pictorial • Place Value Chart	• Open Number Line • Bar Model	• Quick Sketch of Context • Table to Organize or Find Pattern • Area Models • Equations

In primary grades, teachers can have a significant impact by ensuring students can use all representations independently and effectively. Students may come into kindergarten and first grade knowing how to add and subtract well. Teachers and parents often ask how they can challenge these students. The time can be used with students mastering the representation of problems on each model for their grade level. At first, students might need to use printed versions as they polish their fine motor skills. Teachers can set up an area of the classroom where students can choose which representation they want to use with stacks of different representations on small pieces of paper to staple to their work. I have also seen teachers print representations on labels that students can just peel and put on their page based on which one they want to use. Throughout the school year, students can work toward creating the models themselves.

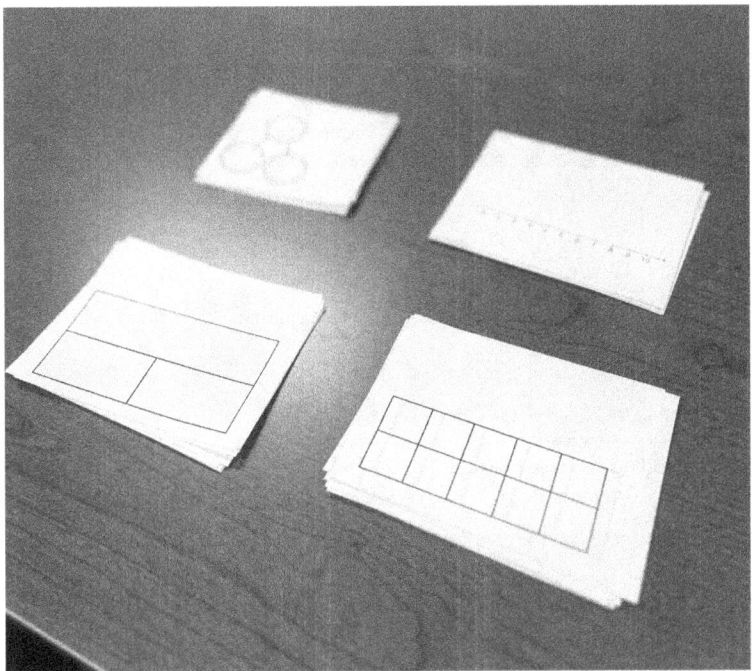

Figure 2.8 Representations printed for student independence and choice.

Identify the Question(s)

Throughout my work in schools, I have encountered students who don't solve the whole problem, don't answer the correct question, or don't even acknowledge the question throughout the problem-solving process. This is where there is a difference between math and reading. When reading a book, students know their goal is to understand and think about what they are reading. When students are reading a math problem, they are reading the context of the story or situation. Then, students go into math mode and do what is called decontextualization. Decontextualizing is when students come out of the context of the problem to solve and perform calculations with the numbers involved (CCSSI, 2010). This is where many students think they are done. They believe that the goal of solving a math problem is to do the calculation to get the answer. A lot of students do this and arrive at an accurate calculation.

When we *do not* ask students to answer the complete question, we create a habit of making them think they are done when they arrive at a completed calculation. Depending on the assessment structure, it is often accepted as correct, but is that the end goal for students? There is a step that is sometimes overlooked by students, especially if they are getting the correct calculation most of the time. The accurate calculation and the correct answer are not

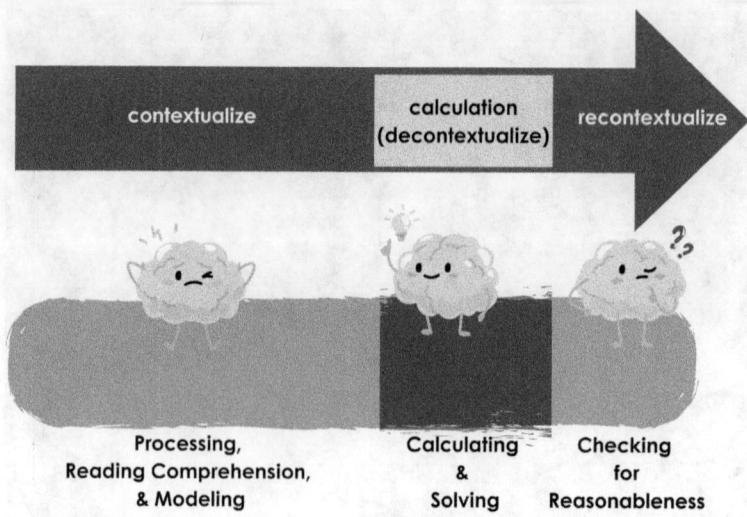

Figure 2.9 Students need to learn to recontextualize after solving.

necessarily the same thing. Students must return to the problem or recontextualize to ensure their answer makes sense. They need to think about what their answer represents within the problem – was it apples, how much money someone made, the number of dogs at a dog park?

Often, problems require students to decontextualize and recontextualize multiple times as they solve different steps and check their understanding. This habit is especially apparent when students go from solving one-step problems to multi-step problems. To build this habit, students can practice some concrete actions to get them to recontextualize after solving. This phase of the progression helps students set up their workspace to build some accountability for slowing down and ensure they prioritize what they understand as readers and mathematicians.

Organize and Solve

There is great value in having organized work. Having organized work is not necessarily about having neat work. It is about making thinking visible, lowering the cognitive load, and creating clarity. Cognitive load is the amount of information that the working memory can process at any given time (Medical College of Wisconsin, 2022). If we overwork our working memory, little can be learned (Ashman, 2023).

Students in this progression phase usually understand the problem, but their work is all over the page. They may make simple mistakes or get lost in their work along the way to solving complex problems. Comprehension and organization go hand in hand. Comprehension guides the organization. If any confusion

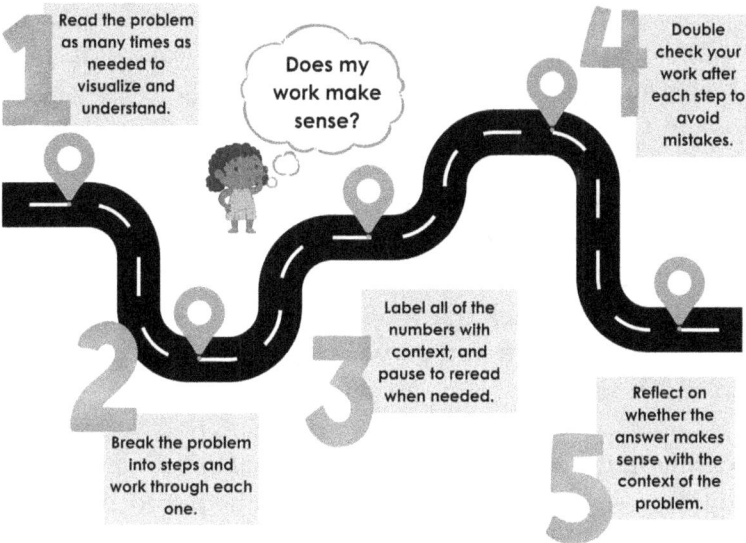

Figure 2.10 A pathway to monitoring comprehension.

arises, organized work provides a place to go back and easily find a mistake. The organization offers a roadmap. Monitoring comprehension assists students in following the road map correctly and noticing when they go off course.

When students learn to use graphic organizers and ask themselves questions to monitor their comprehension, it gives them a plan and a path to get started. The goal is to help students find a structure that works for them that they can replicate and internalize as a habit of thinking beyond just math. Some teachers may worry that some students who need this don't have access to accommodations, so they shouldn't get to use them in class. Graphic organizers are not meant to be used forever. Students don't need to have an accommodation to use a graphic organizer. It is a tool to help students experience organization so they can replicate it on their own.

Justify Thinking

Communication about our thinking is a crucial life skill. However, this skill can be difficult for all students, including our high achievers or gifted students. When students justify their thinking, they must verify whether they are correct and whether their answer is reasonable considering the context. Writing about one's thinking can be very time-consuming at first, which can deter teachers from having students do it. However, the time is well spent because it creates deep thinking habits for students. As the quote at the beginning of this chapter says, *"Habits are behaviors that you enact so often that you internalize them and they become routine …. Once a behavior is a habit, it doesn't take as much cognitive, physical, or emotional energy as when you started."* In my experience, students struggle more emotionally with writing. They become more confident when we give them structure and more positive experiences. The more experience they have with it, the less energy and time it will take to do it.

In my last year of teaching fifth grade, I would ask my students to justify their thinking, and I would get responses like, "I'm right because I'm correct," "I'm right because I solved it," or "I'm correct because I multiplied." I was frustrated because I felt like students would just give up. So, I had to create ways to support them in their writing as they connected to what they already did in other subjects. Here are a few ideas.

- **"Writing in the air":** I was in a professional development session once, and the presenter talked about how it can help students get started by communicating out loud what they want to write before they get it down on paper. This is so true even as adults. Many students must process out loud to organize their thoughts and be ready to write.
- **Sentence stems or sentence frames:** When students can see the direction their writing needs to take, it can ease their anxiety and help them get started. For examples, see the lesson "I can use sentence frames to justify my thinking."
- **Justification wall:** When students had great examples of justifications, they got to add them to our justification wall, a space in the classroom where student examples were displayed. This gave students the motivation to try their best to be showcased, the opportunity to be celebrated, and it also created a wall of examples that students could use to help them with their own.
- **Routine practice:** Making justifying student thinking an expectation in class helped students improve quickly. Differentiating in small groups based on what justifications are lacking can help students gain momentum through clarity of expectations.
- **Connection to other subjects:** In science, students may be used to using CER (claim, evidence, reasoning) to justify their thinking. In literacy, they may use a short constructed response with evidence from the text to prove what they have inferred. Helping students to see connections to other subject areas can make it less daunting to try.

Reasoning and proof are among the process standards the National Council of Teachers of Mathematics named. Critical thinking about problems is not only for high-achieving students. It is essential for all. In some classrooms, only the students who solve their work correctly have

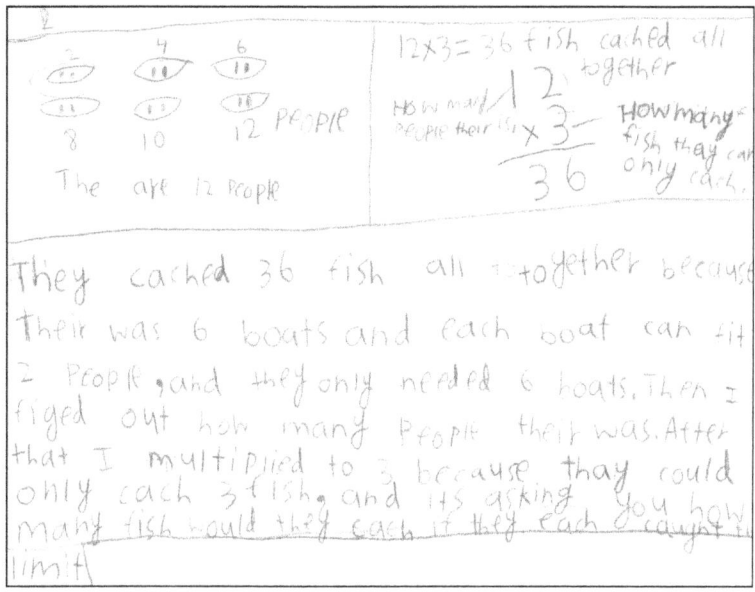

Figure 2.11 An example of a third grade Justification.

to prove their answers. However, we must be careful not to make it an extension activity.

On the other hand, sometimes, students who get the correct answer are just left alone by the teacher because they have mastered the computation required for the concept being learned. It is vital to ensure that *all* students get the opportunity to grow. High-achieving students need to be pushed to their instructional level within the classroom, just like every other student. Process standards are a great way to ensure those students have access to deep learning opportunities.

What Does This Learning Look Like for Students?

The goal is for this type of thinking to become habitual. As we fill in gaps in problem-solving behaviors and encourage students to use their working memory to its fullest capacity, they will become faster and more proficient at solving complex problems. As you explore the lessons, remember these are examples. There are many ways to present this learning to students in a way that meets their specific needs.

Each lesson contains four components: Intro, Teach, Try it, and Send off. These components are explained in more detail in Chapter 5. As you read through these lessons, reflect on how these lessons are similar and different from what you do in small-group instruction or general problem-solving instruction already. Envision which students you think might benefit from these lessons and which behaviors you are already seeing in action.

Visualize
Kindergarten and First-Grade Lessons

Lesson 1: I can act out the problem with math tools.

Intro: *Sometimes math problems can feel tricky when it's just numbers and words on a page. One way we can bring it to life is to use our math tools to act it out like we are the main character in the story! This helps our brain to understand what is happening so we can figure out how to solve.*

Teach: Show the anchor chart. *When we act out the problem with math tools, we can make it come to life. This can help us understand what is happening as mathematicians. Let's try it out together.* Show a chosen problem. You could act it out with exact amounts or just show the action. The goal is not to name an operation or do the problem to completion. *I'm going to talk about these math tools like they are the subjects of the problem. I'm labeling this part as (noun or name) and this as (noun or name). The goal is not to solve. The goal is to understand. By acting out this problem, I can see how (describe the relationships you are able to see because of acting out the problem).* The next stage of the progression will have students draw a representation of what they visualize, and then they will decide how to solve.

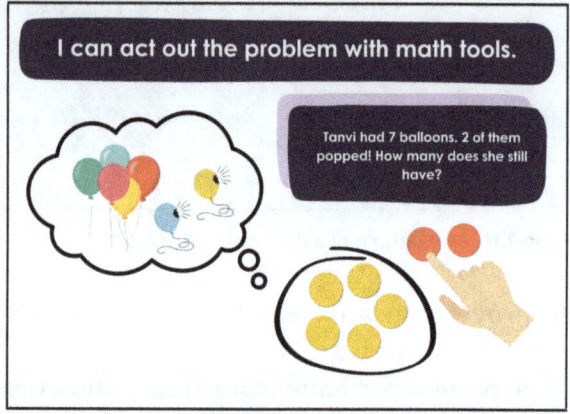

Figure 2.12 Anchor chart for acting out the problem with math tools in kindergarten.

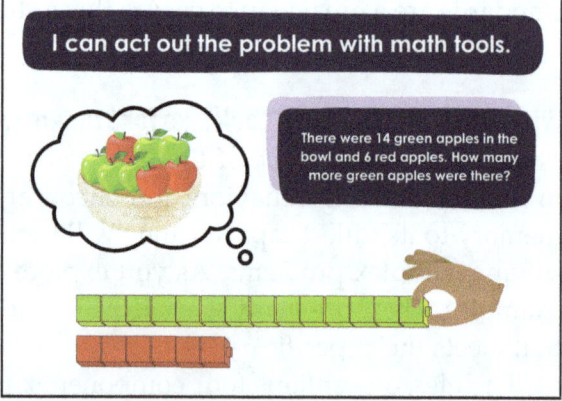

Figure 2.13 Anchor chart for acting out the problem with math tools in first grade.

Try it: Give students another problem. They will now try it out on their own. Encourage them to label their parts with a dry-erase marker with names or nouns related to the problem. Remind them they are not solving.

Send off: *Remember that acting out the problem with math tools can help the problem come to life when you are struggling to see what is happening in your mind. This is a strategy you can use when you don't understand a problem right away.*

Lesson 2: I can retell the problem in my own words.

Intro: *Math problem solving is like reading a story, only it also has numbers and a question to answer. To solve it, we must first be able to visualize what is happening. One way we can do that is by retelling the problem in our own words.*

Teach: Show the anchor chart. *When we retell in our own words, it can be helpful to think about the characters in the story or what it is about, what is happening, and anything else we might be thinking or seeing in our mind. When we can visualize the story and talk about what we see, it makes it easier to solve the problem.* Read a chosen problem aloud. You might want to have students close their eyes as you read. Model a think-aloud that tells everything you see in your mind. Then retell the problem, talking about the characters or thing, what is happening, and other conclusions you may be drawing based on what you read. You can use the anchor chart to model how to follow it with your finger as you answer the different parts and use the question prompts.

Figure 2.14 Anchor chart for retelling the problem in my own words in kindergarten and first grade.

Try it: Have students try it out with a new problem, sharing with a partner, and referring back to the anchor chart if needed. Students may need to reread or hear the problem several times. Students can trace the anchor chart with their finger from dot to dot to add a kinesthetic component.

Send off: *As you visualize, you can always retell the story to help you understand what is happening in the problem. I can't wait to see you try this in your work as mathematicians.*

Visualize
Second- to Fifth-Grade Lessons

Lesson 1: I can act out the problem with math tools.

Intro: Sometimes math problems can feel tricky when it's just numbers and words on a page. When we can see and touch the problem, it can make the problem easier to understand so you know how to solve.

Teach: When we act out the problem with math tools, we can make it come to life. This can help us understand what is happening as mathematicians. Let's try it out together. Show the anchor chart. You could act it out with exact amounts or just show the action. The goal is not to solve or do the problem to completion. *I'm going to talk about these math tools like they are the subjects of the problem. I'm labeling this part as (noun or name) and this as (noun or name). The goal is not to solve. The goal is to understand. By acting out this problem, I can see how (describe the relationships you are able to see because of acting out the problem).* The next stage of the progression will have them draw a representation of what they visualize, and then they will decide how to solve. It will be important to try out this skill with single-step problems and multi-step problems so that

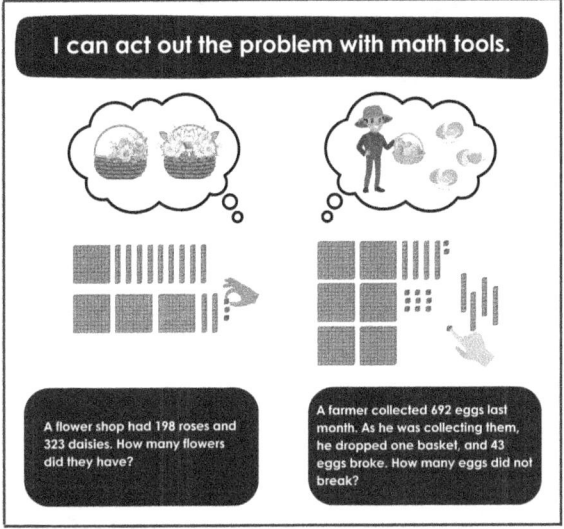

Figure 2.15 Anchor chart for acting out the problem with math tools in second grade. To view this anchor chart in color, access the online Support Material: https://resourcecentre.routledge.com/books/9781032839875

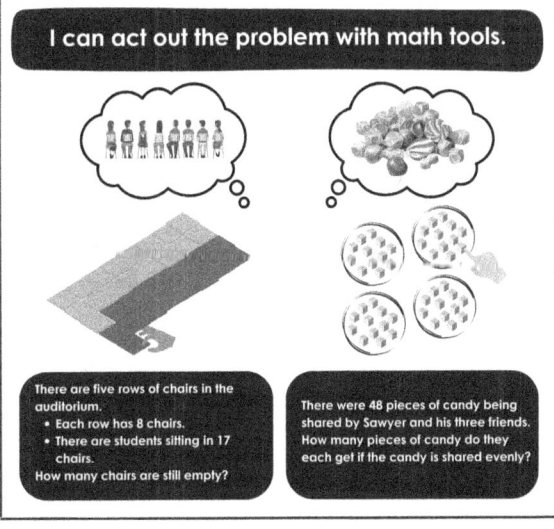

Figure 2.16 Anchor chart for acting out the problem with math tools in third grade. To view this anchor chart in color, access the online Support Material: https://resourcecentre.routledge.com/books/9781032839875

students can see how to break individual steps into separate actions.

Try it: Give students another problem. They will now try it out on their own. Encourage them to label their parts with a dry-erase marker with names or nouns related to the problem. Remind them they are not solving, and they only need to act it out until they can explain what they would do to solve each step.

Send off: *Remember that acting out the problem with math tools can help the problem come to life when you are struggling to see what is happening in your mind. This is a strategy you can use when you don't understand a problem right away.*

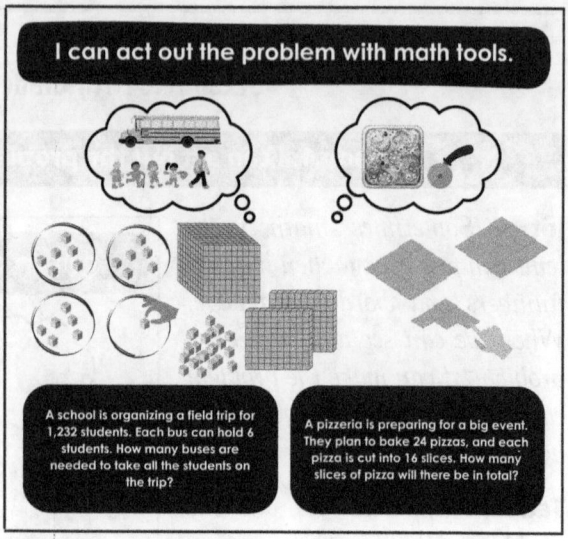

Figure 2.17 Anchor chart for acting out the problem with math tools in fourth grade. To view this anchor chart in color, access the online Support Material: https://resourcecentre.routledge.com/books/9781032839875

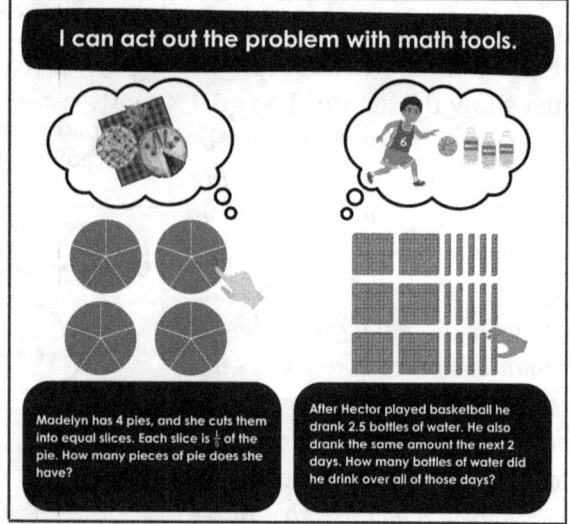

Figure 2.18 Anchor chart for acting out the problem with math tools in fifth grade. To view this anchor chart in color, access the online Support Material: https://resourcecentre.routledge.com/books/9781032839875

Lesson 2: I can remove the numbers or make them smaller to understand the context.

Intro: *Have you ever looked at a word problem and felt overwhelmed by all the numbers, and you didn't know where to start? Today we're going to learn a powerful strategy that master problem solvers use so they don't get distracted or tricked. Think of it like turning down the volume on the numbers so we can hear the mathematical story more clearly.*

Teach: *We'll learn how to temporarily remove the numbers or make them simpler so we can focus on understanding what's really happening in the problem. Show students the anchor chart and walk through the process with a problem of your choosing. We can cover the numbers with sticky notes here. As we read, we can use the word "some" where the numbers used to be. Then we want to think about the picture we see in our mind. As I ask myself the questions that are on the anchor chart, I am see-ing (describe your visualization) in my mind. I can see that the amount of ___ is (getting bigger or smaller). Let's check this other strategy of making the numbers smaller to see if it validates what I was visualizing before. When we make the numbers smaller, we*

Figure 2.19 Anchor chart for removing the numbers or making them smaller to understand the context in second grade. To view this anchor chart in color, access the online Support Material: https://resourcecentre.routledge.com/books/9781032839875

Figure 2.20 Anchor chart for removing the numbers or making them smaller to understand the context in third grade. To view this anchor chart in color, access the online Support Material: https://resourcecentre.routledge.com/books/9781032839875

need to make sure that the greater number still stays a greater number and smaller numbers stay smaller. Try it with numbers less than 20 to see if that helps you to get a grasp on what you see in your mind on a more manageable scale.

Try it: Give students another problem. It would be helpful if it was a problem they struggled to understand before. Let them use sticky notes to cover up the numbers and tell a partner what they see in their minds.

Send off: *Remember that when problems get tough, you can use the strategy of removing the numbers or making them smaller to help you visualize the mathematical story.*

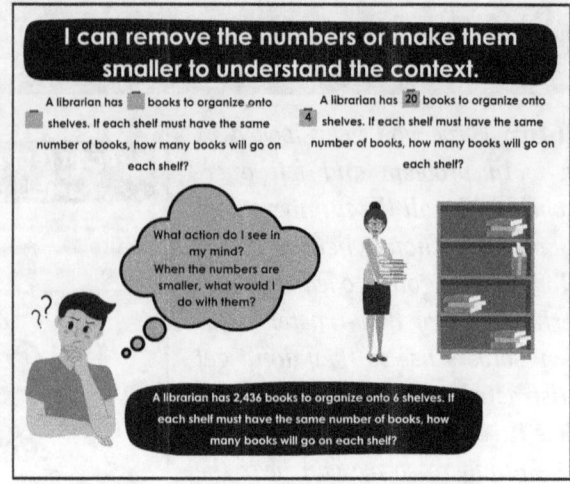

Figure 2.21 Anchor chart for removing the numbers or making them smaller to understand the context in fourth grade. To view this anchor chart in color, access the online Support Material: https://resourcecentre.routledge.com/books/9781032839875

Figure 2.22 Anchor chart for removing the numbers or making them smaller to understand the context in fifth grade. To view this anchor chart in color, access the online Support Material: https://resourcecentre.routledge.com/books/9781032839875

Lesson 3: I can retell the problem in my own words.

Intro: *As you get older, the math problems become longer and longer with more and more details. It's important to be able to read them like a story so we can replay them like a movie in our mind to make sense of them.*

Teach: *Today we are going to work on retelling the problem in our own words. This can help us focus on the most important information we need from the problem so we know how to get started with solving. We can focus on the information like it is a story we are reading. We can think about the characters or what the story is about; we can think about what happens to the characters, and we can think about what other details we need to know or describe what happens next! You can even follow along the dots on the anchor chart and use the sentence stems as you retell to keep you on track.*

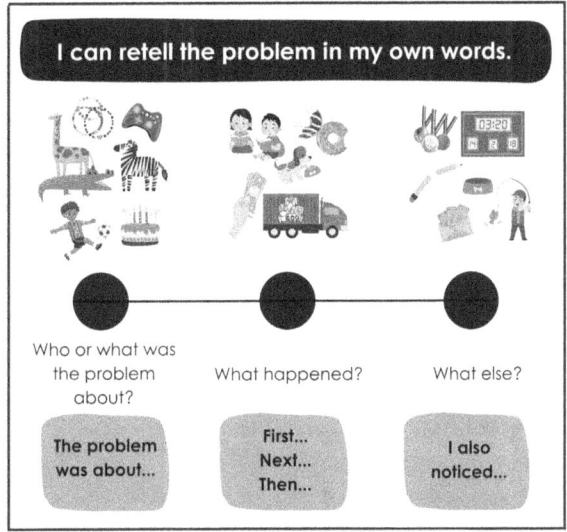

Figure 2.23 Anchor chart for retelling the problem in my own words in second–fifth grades. To view this anchor chart in color, access the online Support Material: https://resourcecentre.routledge.com/books/9781032839875

Model this with a problem. Depending on the needs of your students, you might want to do this lesson with a single-step problem first, then later repeat with a multi-step problem. Make a connection to a read-aloud that has been done in class or a relevant movie to your class.

Try it: Put students in partners and give the partnership two problems. Each student will try it out with their given problem. Each partnership will need its own anchor chart to follow along.

Send off: *Remember that retelling the problem in your own words can help you visualize it in your mind. You can think about the characters or what the problem is, what is happening to the characters, and anything else relevant to the problem to help you focus on what is most important.*

Represent Visualization
Kindergarten and First-Grade Lessons

Lesson 1: I can create a part-part-whole mat to match the problem.

Intro: *Today we are going to be math detectives. In math, we are going to encounter lots of problems to solve. Sometimes they will get tricky, and you might need some special tools to help you.*

Teach: *When we use a part-part-whole mat, it can help us know exactly what is missing so we know how to solve.* Show the anchor chart. *It looks like this, where the top part equals the bottom part. The top is called the whole or the total, and the bottom boxes hold the parts. There could be even more than 2 parts, but they always have to equal the whole on top. You can also put the whole on the bottom and have the top with the parts. The important thing to remember is that the parts have to equal the whole. If there are 10 hats at a store and 6 are blue and the rest are green, I could put a question mark for the green hats. So, 6 blue hats + some green hats = 10 hats. The whole is the total number of hats. The parts are the blue hats and the green hats. We want to remember what we are solving for as we work, so mathematicians also label their work with what the numbers represent.*

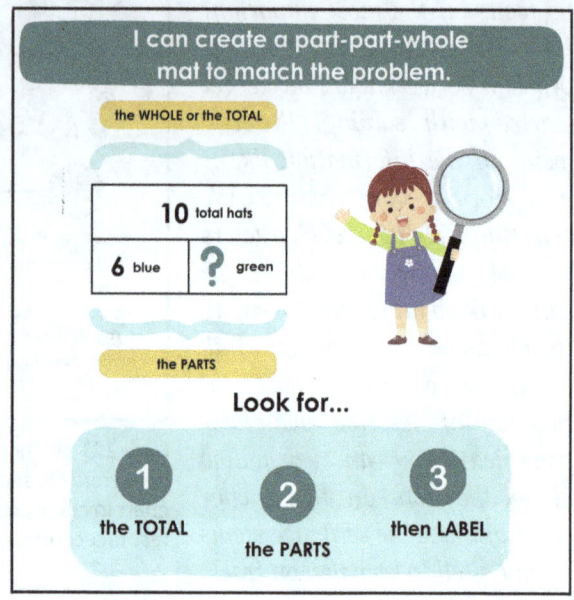

Figure 2.24 Anchor chart for creating a part-part-whole mat to match the problem in kindergarten and first grade.

The part-part-whole mat leads into strip diagrams as students get older and is one of the most helpful tools for students to use in solving complex problems. That is why this representation is so important for students to learn and use well.

Try it: *It's your turn to solve a mystery! Look for the total or the whole, the parts, and label your numbers!* Give students a problem to try out. Point them back to the anchor chart as a reference. You may need to help students draw the part-part-whole mat, but the goal is for them to use it correctly, not focus on drawing it. Feel free to draw it for them at first or give them one that is printed.

Send off: *When you need to understand how to solve a math problem, it is helpful to identify the parts and the whole to know what to do next!*

Lesson 2: I can choose a representation to match my visualization.

Intro: *Did you know that math isn't about just getting the correct answer? In kindergarten and first grade, the biggest job of a mathematician is to learn how to use all the representations to show your thinking!*

Teach: *Mathematicians have many representations, so they can match what they are seeing in their mind to a math tool they can draw on paper. Sometimes certain representations don't make sense for what is in the problem. Let me show you what I mean. It is so important to not just choose your favorite way to show your work and only do that one. Mathematicians have to get really good at all of them, and it takes practice. Show the anchor chart and name each representation. You might want to focus only on the top three in the first lesson and add on more later. If I have the problem, "A frog hops 4 times. Then it hops 3 more times. How many times did it hop?" When I look over the anchor chart, one of them really matches what I see in my mind when the frog hops and then hops further. I see that on a number line! Here is how I can represent it. If it were a problem about 2 black cats and 6 white cats, I might use a ten frame to show the cats and use color or a part-part-whole mat. There could be more than one that works based on what you see in your mind.*

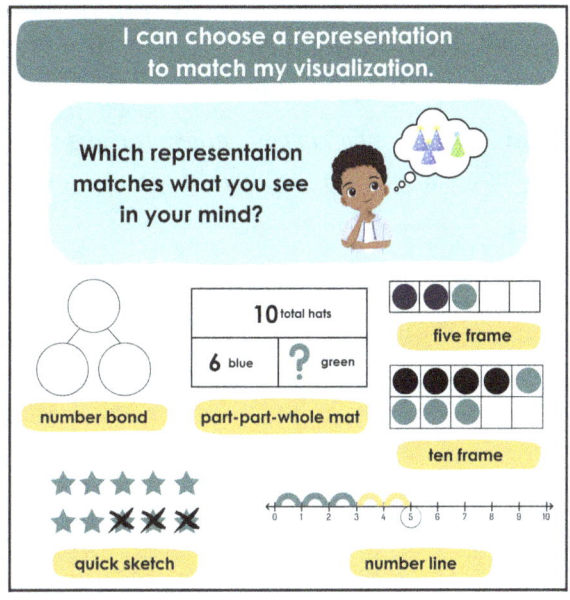

Figure 2.25 Anchor chart for choosing a representation to match my visualization in Kindergarten.

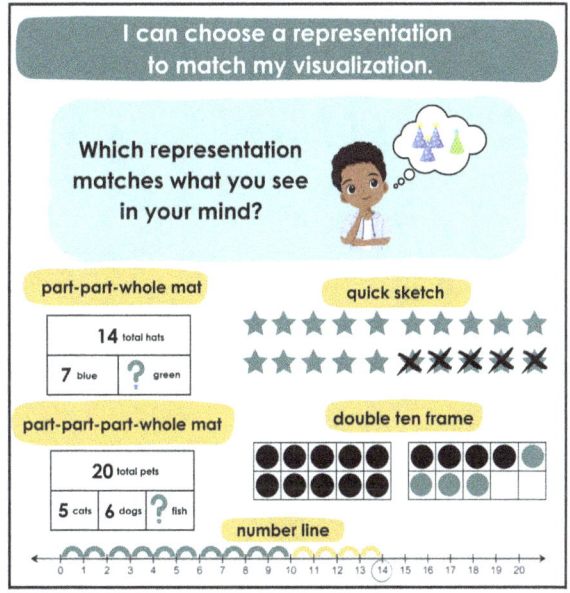

Figure 2.26 Anchor chart for choosing a representation to match my visualization in first grade.

Try it: Have students try it out with a new problem. You may need to break it into two steps. First, have them choose the representation they want to use after you read the problem. Then have them create it or give them a paper copy of it to use. The focus is not on drawing the representation itself, but on representing the problem on it.

Send off: *Remember, when mathematicians represent a problem, they choose the one that makes sense with the problem to show their thinking.*

Represent Visualization
Second- to Fifth-Grade Lessons

Lesson 1: I can create a part-part-whole mat/strip diagram to match the problem.

Intro: *One of my favorite things to do when I have free time is put together puzzles. Every puzzle is different, and I like to lay out all of the pieces so that I can plan how I might put them together. This is what a part-part-whole mat or strip diagram can do for you.*

Teach: *Today, we are going to find the pieces of our puzzle, the problem, and see how it can help us to come up with a plan to solve our math problems. When we read complex problems, it is important to have a way to get the information on paper in an organized way so that we can think more clearly about what to do next. Here are the steps we need to take to create this representation.* Show the anchor chart. Use a problem to model how you would decide the parts and the whole, how you would label them with context, and model your thinking about different ways you could approach the problem.

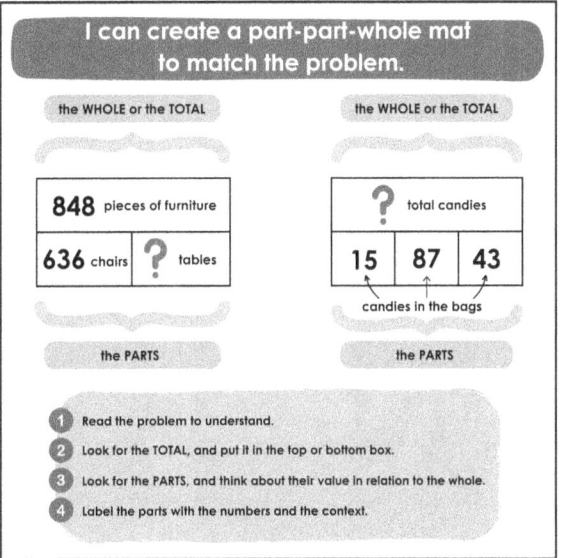

Figure 2.27 Anchor chart for creating a part-part-whole mat to match the problem in second grade. To view this anchor chart in color, access the online Support Material: https://resourcecentre.routledge.com/books/9781032839875

(Strip diagrams are different because the value of the number in the box changes where the parts are separated. This can be particularly difficult for students and may need to be a lesson on its own.) You might want to start with a single-step problem, then show in a later lesson how you could use one to represent multiple steps for some problems, and for other problems, you might need to create two different representations. In the third grade, it is appropriate to keep the strip diagrams separate for each step. In the fourth grade, students need to eventually combine the whole problem into one strip diagram where there may be multiple parts on the top and bottom of the model.

Try it: Give students another problem. They will now try it out on their own. Refer them to your example and the anchor charts if they struggle.

Send off: *When we can lay out all the pieces of the problem like a puzzle, we can make a plan to solve. This tool can help you see the big picture within complex problems.*

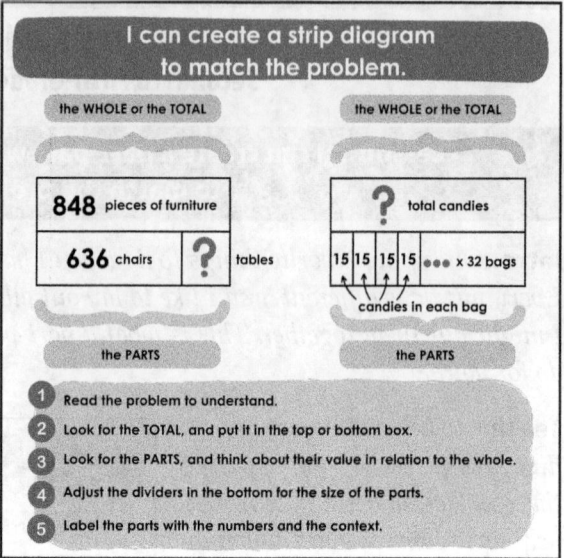

Figure 2.28 Anchor chart for creating a strip diagram to match the problem in third–fifth grades. To view this anchor chart in color, access the online Support Material: https://resourcecentre.routledge.com/books/9781032839875

Lesson 2: I can label the numbers with context to show meaning.

Intro: *Imagine looking at a map or graph with no labels, just lines and shapes. It would be really confusing, right? That's what math problems can feel like when you are solving, and you don't have any labels on any of the numbers. It can make the problem feel tricky.*

Teach: *Numbers are more than just digits on a page; they have meaning and represent things such as pencils, apples, or people. As you get older, the problems get more and more complicated. To help us stay on track, we can use labels with our numbers, and even color sometimes, to magnify the meaning of what we are putting on paper to keep us on track. Model with a problem and show how to keep labels on the numbers as you solve. You might want to make this into two lessons where you can show how color brings meaning to a different problem, depending on the needs of your students.*

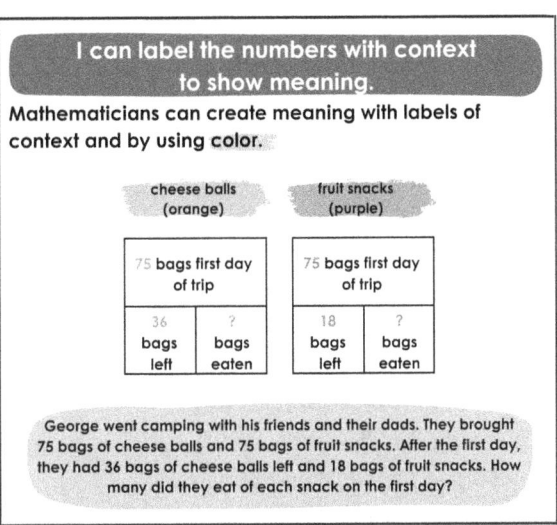

Figure 2.29 Anchor chart for labeling the numbers with context in second grade. To view this anchor chart in color, access the online Support Material: https://resourcecentre.routledge.com/books/9781032839875

Try it: *You might want to give students a problem they worked on previously, where they got lost in the problem, so they can try again with labels to see how it helps them maintain meaning as they solve.*

Send off: *When you use labels or even color on your work as you solve, it helps you keep visualizing throughout solving. This can help you maintain the context of the problem to know you are on the right track.*

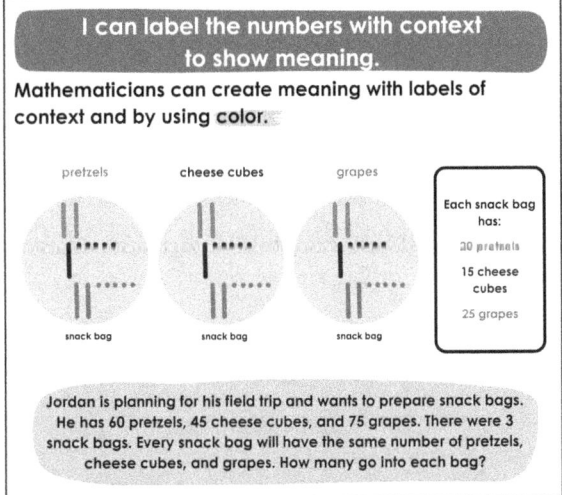

Figure 2.30 Anchor chart for labeling the numbers with context in third–fifth grades. To view this anchor chart in color, access the online Support Material: https://resourcecentre.routledge.com/books/9781032839875

Lesson 3: I can choose and create a representation to match my visualization.

Intro: *One time, a friend of mine asked me to hang out with her at the park with our dogs. It was the summer, so I was wearing my favorite sandals. What I didn't realize was that once I got there, it was a park where you go hiking. I had the worst blisters on my feet by the end of the day. My shoes did not match the situation for our activity.*

Teach: *The same thing can happen when you are solving math problems. We need to choose the representation that matches the situation of the problem. For example, if I have a problem about a race and I see in my mind that one person goes farther than another, it would make sense to represent it with a number line or a bar model. If I have a problem about a person doing chores and making money each day, I might want to organize that on a table. Choosing a representation that makes sense can help us ensure we are on the right track and our answer is reasonable.* Explain the anchor chart and remind them they are not solving today. Remind students that there is more than one way that will make sense, but choosing one that doesn't match can make the problem confusing or cause unneccesary frustration like with the wrong shoes for the situation analogy in the intro.

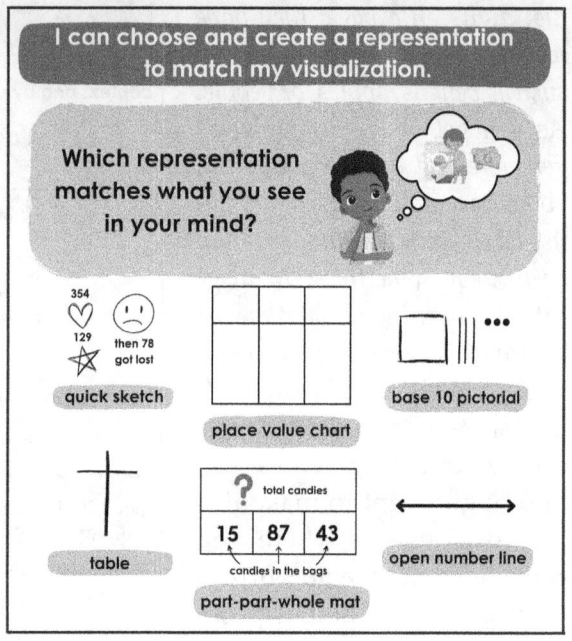

Figure 2.31 Anchor chart for choosing a representation to match my visualization in second grade. To view this anchor chart in color, access the online Support Material: https://resourcecentre.routledge.com/books/9781032839875

Try it: Now students will try it out with a new problem. Give students time to think and decide before they share. Another option could be to provide students with three problems and three representations. They could then match them with the best fit.

Send off: *It's important to use the best match between what you visualize and what you put on paper. This will help you see the relationship more clearly.*

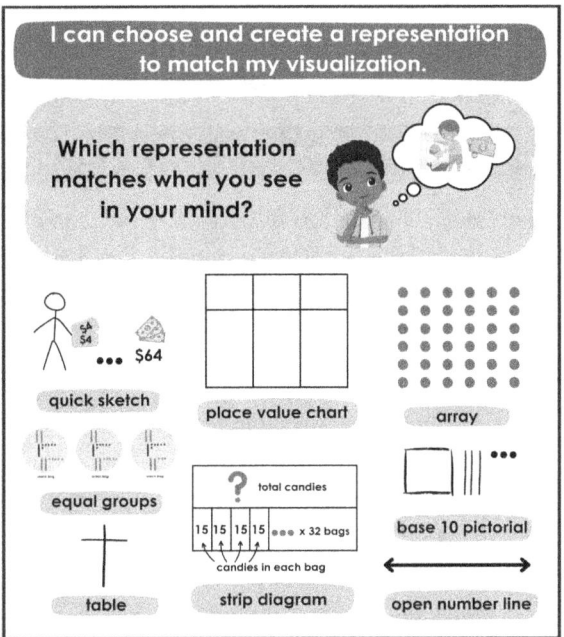

Figure 2.32 Anchor chart for choosing a representation to match my visualization in third–fifth grades. To view this anchor chart in color, access the online Support Material: https://resourcecentre.routledge.com/books/9781032839875

Identify the Question(s)
Kindergarten and First-Grade Lessons

Lesson 1: I can write an answer statement to match the question.

Intro: What if I ask you what kind of pizza you want, and your response is "Soup!"? That would be kind of silly, wouldn't it? Sometimes we get so distracted in math problems that we forget to check what it is really asking, and we answer a question that wasn't asked.

Teach: Today, we are going to work on creating an answer statement for the problem that will help us pay special attention to the question. We can write this after we read the problem a couple of times and before we solve. That way, after we solve, we have a reminder to check that we were answering the right question. Walk students through the anchor chart and the components of a good answer statement. Remind them that if they have trouble spelling the words, they can use the problem for reference. Some students might not be ready to write the whole word. They could write the first letter at first to signify what their answer represents or draw a small sketch to represent the meaning next to the number.

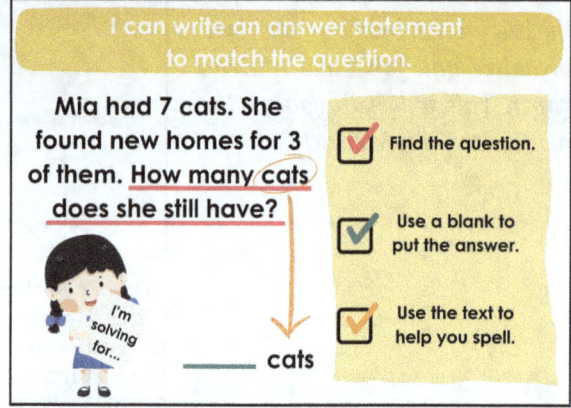

Figure 2.33 Anchor chart for writing an answer statement for the problem in kindergarten and first grade.

Try it: Give students another problem. It would be beneficial to give them back a problem where they did not answer the question, so they can see how useful this strategy can be. Another way to have students try it would be to have them match answer statements with different problems to get practice finding the question and the noun the answer is trying to find.

Send off: As mathematicians, we want to make sure that we are doing the work the problem is asking us to do. When you write an answer statement, it can remind you what you are solving for in the given problem.

Lesson 2: I can predict a reasonable answer to the problem.

Intro: *Have you ever guessed how much more time you have left at recess, or how long a movie will last? That's called making a prediction or a guess about what you think something will be based on what you know. You can also do this for tricky math problems.*

Teach: *When we make predictions in math problems, it can help us stay on track, catch any mistakes, and help us make sure our answer is reasonable after we solve. It can also help us decide which operation we want to use to solve! A prediction should be quick and not very detailed. It's just a quick checkpoint to monitor our understanding of the problem.* Show the anchor chart and focus on using the comparison symbol. Model how to solve the problem and check to see if the prediction was correct. Also, if the student's answer didn't match their prediction, talk through why that happened. You could suggest they go back to reread and check their work to see what happened.

Figure 2.34 Anchor chart for predicting a reasonable answer to the problem in kindergarten and first grade.

Try it: To make this part go quickly, students could make a prediction on a problem they have done before. After their prediction, you could give them their work with their answer to see if it matches their prediction. If it doesn't, have them go back to see if they can find a mistake in understanding or computation.

Send off: *When we make predictions about the answer, it can help us monitor our understanding as we solve the problem.*

Identify the Question(s)
Second- to Fifth-Grade Lessons

Lesson 1: I can write an answer statement to match the question.

Intro: *The other day, I was talking to a student, and I asked her what time it was. She said it was the day we go to music. She did not answer the question I was asking. I think she might have been distracted. Has this ever happened to you?*

Teach: *This happens in math all the time, especially when there are multiple steps in a problem. Today I want to show you a strategy that can keep you from doing this. It's called writing an answer statement. When you get really caught up in solving the problem, you can get distracted and answer the wrong question. The way we can keep from doing this is to find the question and turn it into a phrase or sentence.* Walk students through the anchor chart. This lesson supports the start of a solid justification in the last phase of the progression. This is a task they do before attempting to solve the problem. This will help students focus on the right information.

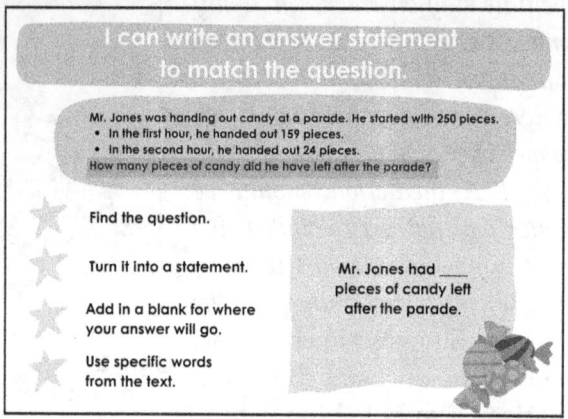

Figure 2.35 Anchor chart for writing an answer statement for the problem in second and third grades. To view this anchor chart in color, access the online Support Material: https://resourcecentre.routledge.com/books/9781032839875

Try it: Students will now practice on their own using another problem. It can be very helpful to give students a problem they did previously, in which they only answered the first part of the problem. This helps them see the value of it and gives

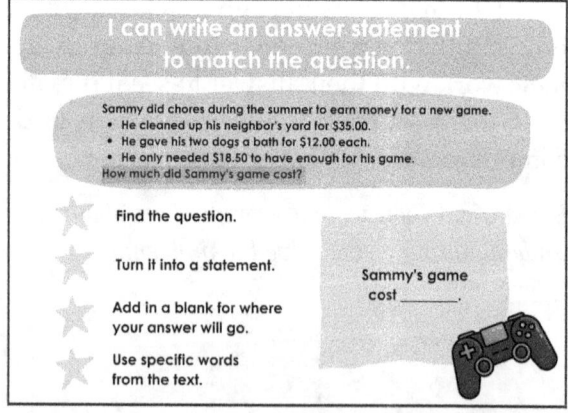

Figure 2.36 Anchor chart for writing an answer statement for the problem in fourth and fifth grades. To view this anchor chart in color, access the online Support Material: https://resourcecentre.routledge.com/books/9781032839875

practical practice. Turning a question into a statement can be tough work for students. As a scaffold, you might have them first match questions with the appropriate answer statement so they can see the correlation in an additional lesson before writing their own.

Send off: *Mathematicians can get distracted from the main purpose of the problem. We can write an answer statement to bring our focus to the right information as we solve.*

Lesson 2: I can predict a reasonable answer to the problem.

Intro: *In reading, you make predictions all the time. You might guess what a character is going to do or what the setting is based on how the author describes what is happening. You can also do this during math problems by making a prediction about what the answer might be based on the context you read in the problem.*

Teach: *As you make predictions in math, they should be quick. This is a bit different than making an estimate, although an estimate is also a type of math prediction. Let's look at this problem together. We are going to think about the numbers in the problem and predict if our answer will be greater than or less than a number presented in the problem. This is just a quick check along the way of solving to make sure our answer is reasonable once we get there.* Present students with a problem and walk them through your prediction and your reasoning to get there. Then show them the answer to show how you would then use your prediction to check if your answer is reasonable.

Try it: Give students a problem that they recently got incorrect. Give them the problem at first to predict. Then give them their original work to see if their answer fell within their prediction. Have them try to find where they

Figure 2.37 Anchor chart for predicting a reasonable answer to the problem in second grade. To view this anchor chart in color, access the online Support Material: https://resourcecentre.routledge.com/books/9781032839875

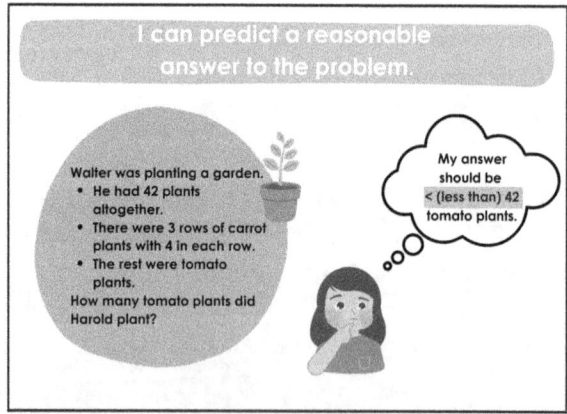

Figure 2.38 Anchor chart for predicting a reasonable answer to the problem in third grade. To view this anchor chart in color, access the online Support Material: https://resourcecentre.routledge.com/books/9781032839875

went wrong. They can correct it at their desk if they would like. The goal here is to talk only about the importance of a prediction.

Send off: *Making a prediction on tricky problems can be a quick way to help us analyze our work. Do this as a strategy in your work this week.*

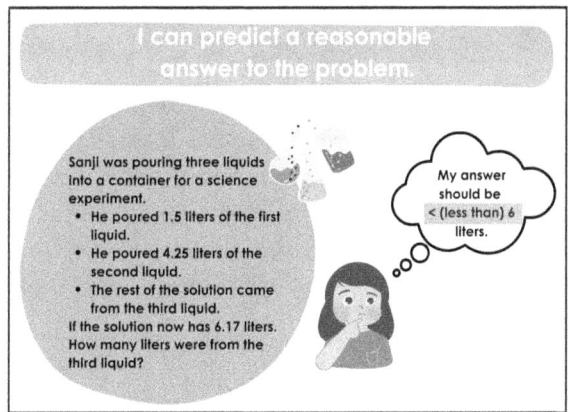

Figure 2.39 Anchor chart for predicting a reasonable answer to the problem in fourth and fifth grades. To view this anchor chart in color, access the online Support Material: https://resourcecentre.routledge.com/books/9781032839875

Lesson 3: I can set up a workspace for each part of the problem.

Intro: *The other day, I was trying to find my favorite shirt. I had just washed it, and it was in this huge pile of laundry. It was so frustrating and difficult! I wanted to just give up. When everything is folded and put away in its place, it's easy to find exactly what you need, and getting ready for school isn't so crazy! When something is a mess, it can be hard to focus. This can also be true in our math work. It can make us have anxiety, frustration, and make it really hard to complete complex problems to the end.*

Teach: *Today we are going to learn how to pay attention as we read so we know how to organize our work and ensure we do all the steps. As I read this problem, I'm going to try to notice when there might be a sign there are different steps to the problem. I'm going to number them as I come across them the second time I read the problem. Then I'm going to set up a place to work out each step, so I don't forget to do any parts. We are not solving today; we are only practicing setting up a workspace. The workspace should have a place for each step and also a phrase for what each step will solve for.*

Figure 2.40 Anchor chart for setting up a workspace for each part of the problem in second–fifth grades. To view this anchor chart in color, access the online Support Material: https://resourcecentre.routledge.com/books/9781032839875

Try it: Give students another problem. They will now try it out on their own. It is helpful to give students a problem where they were unorganized or didn't answer the right question to see how this can help them in the future. Remind them they are not solving.

Send off: As students finish, send them off with this reminder. *Remember that, as you read, pay attention to where you think you might have a new step in the problem. This can help you to set up a workspace to keep your work organized and remind you to solve every part of the problem.*

Organize and Solve
Kindergarten and First-Grade Lessons

Lesson 1: I can use a graphic organizer to organize my work.

Intro: *Yesterday, I went to the grocery store. I only needed a few things, so I was sure I would remember. Once I was shopping, I could not remember the last thing I needed. I should have written a list to be organized. Sometimes, a plan can help us remember what we need to do, even in math problems!*

Teach: *Today I'm going to show you a plan called a graphic organizer. It can help you stay on track to remember what you need to do. You can use this graphic organizer as a tool, then later you can draw what you need on your own! Let me show you how to use it.* Walk students through representing on the part-part-whole and making a prediction with an answer statement. Then tell students they can choose another representation to solve. They don't have to use all of them. They should pick the one that matches how they see the problem in their mind.

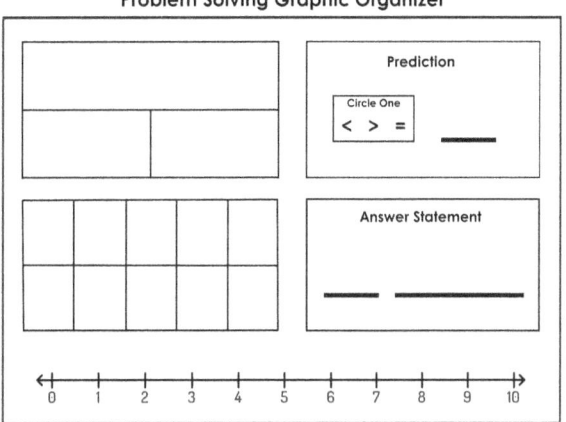

Figure 2.41 Problem-solving graphic organizer: Kindergarten.

Try it: Students can now try it out with a different problem. You could go meet with other students as they practice using the graphic organizer, and then come back to check on their progress. Show students where they can find extra copies of this graphic organizer to use in the future

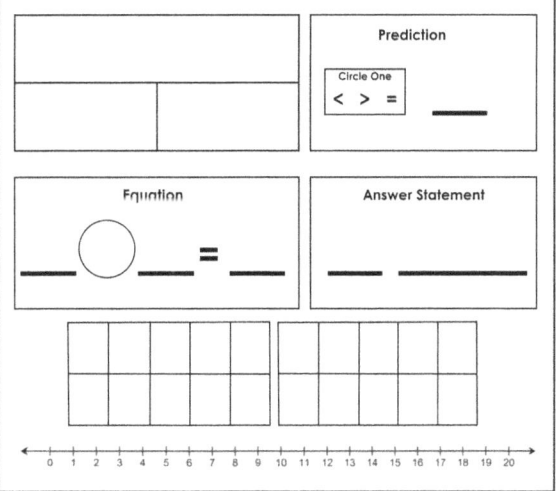

Figure 2.42 Problem-solving graphic organizer: First grade.

when they need it or it could be put into a sheet protector and used multiple times with a dry erase marker.

Send off: *Using a graphic organizer can help mathematicians stay organized and not forget important steps as they solve. When problems are tricky, you can come get one of these to use to keep you on track.*

Lesson 2: I can check to see if my answer is reasonable.

Intro: *Have you ever been to the store to buy a candy bar? What if the cashier told you that your candy bar was $100? Would you pay it? Sometimes when we are solving math problems, we can get to the end and just get to the answer, but we need to make sure it is reasonable, just like you would if you were buying something at the store!*

Teach: *Today, I want to show you some ways that you can check to make sure your answer makes sense. Sometimes we can make mistakes, like subtracting instead of adding or miscounting. We can't just answer a problem and accept that it's the answer without stopping to think about it.* Show the anchor chart and remind students that they can check their work against their prediction and by recounting. If there is a contradiction, they will need to go back to the problem and see where they went wrong. For the teach piece, you could show students a piece of student work with the answer and have them evaluate whether the answer is reasonable or not while you voiceover how you would go through this process.

Figure 2.43 Anchor chart for checking to see if my answer is reasonable in kindergarten.

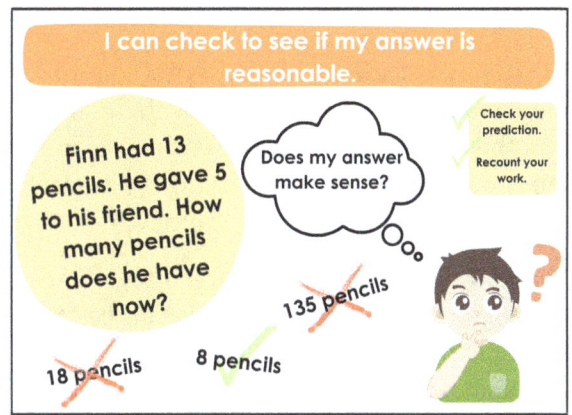

Figure 2.44 Anchor chart for checking to see if my answer is reasonable in first grade.

Try it: You could give students another example of student work to see if they think the answer is reasonable. Have them evaluate a piece of their own student work that has an unreasonable answer, or give them a sort where they have to separate reasonable answers from unreasonable ones.

Send off: *Remember, once you solve, you aren't quite done. You need to check your work and pause to think if your answer makes sense.*

Organize and Solve
Second- to Fifth-Grade Lessons

Lesson 1: I can use a graphic organizer to organize my work.

Intro: *Have you ever read something or listened to a lot of information and thought, "Wait... what did I just learn?" Sometimes our brains get overwhelmed trying to keep track of ideas, facts, or steps all at once. That's where graphic organizers come in. They're tools that help us see how information fits together, like a map for our thoughts. Whether we're reading a story, planning an essay, or trying to solve a problem, a graphic organizer can help us organize what we know – and what we still need to figure out. Today, we're going to explore how these tools can make learning easier, clearer, and even a little more fun.*

Teach: *Today, I want to show you a tool that can help you learn how to organize your math work. Once you get used to using it, you can draw your own with the pieces that help you. Let me show you how to use it.* Show students a multi-step problem to show how to use the organizer. Remind them that they will only use as many of the parts as they need for the steps, depending on the problem. You might want to have copies of a completed example for them to take with them for reference. Tell them where they can find this organizer to use when they need it later.

Try it: Give students another problem or one of their own problems where they were unorganized. Have them transfer their work to the organizer and then discuss how their work is clearer and how it makes them feel to be more organized. While they do the transfer, you can confer with other students or pull another group somewhere else in the classroom.

Send off: *When your work is organized, it can help you be able to think more clearly. Using this tool can help you develop the habits you need to do that and show you how to do this work independently later.*

Problem Solving Graphic Organizer

Who or what is the problem about?	What is happening in the problem?

Change the question into an answer statement.

Step 1	
Solving for:	Solve:
Representation:	

Step 2	
Solving for:	**Solve:**
Representation:	

Step 3	
Solving for:	**Solve:**
Representation:	

Figure 2.45 I can use a graphic organizer to organize my work.

Lesson 2: I can monitor my comprehension as I solve the problem.

Intro: *When I go to my grandma's house, I always have to check the map along the way. I have been there a lot of times, but I need checkpoints along the way to make sure I don't take a wrong turn and make a mistake along the way.*

Teach: *When solving complex math problems, you can check a map along the way too. It's important to check for mistakes early along the way so you can correct the direction you are going to solve. Let's look at our map together.* Show students the anchor chart, and walk them through the questions they need to ask themselves. This is much like what they do as a reader to check on their comprehension to make sure the story makes sense. Model what this looks like with a problem, checking off the steps on the anchor chart as you go. You might make this lesson over two days because the teach may take a little longer.

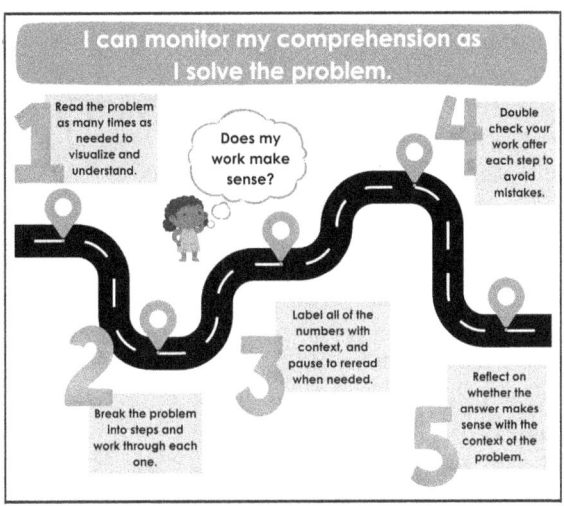

Figure 2.46 Anchor chart for monitoring my comprehension as I solve the problem in second–fifth grades.

Try it: On day two, remind students of the work you did with the anchor chart to check your work along the way. Watch students as they monitor themselves on an old problem to see which checkpoints they missed. Ask open-ended questions if they start to get off-track. Be sure not to jump in too early. Allow wait time to let them check their own work as much as possible.

Send off: *It is so important in any subject to monitor our thinking as we answer problems. We need to always have questions like these in the back of our minds so we don't get too offtrack in the wrong direction as we solve.*

Lesson 3: I can check to see if my answer is reasonable.

Intro: Have you ever been to the store to buy a candy bar? What if the cashier told you that your candy bar was $100? Would you pay it? Sometimes when we are solving math problems, we can get to the end and just get to the answer, but we need to make sure it is reasonable, just like you would if you were buying something at the store!

Teach: Today, I want to show you something you can do once you solve, just to double check if your answer makes sense. Once you work out a problem and have your answer, go back and reread the problem one last time, check your prediction to see if your answer aligns, and check over your calculation to make sure your answer makes sense. Go over the questions on the anchor chart. Analyze a piece of student work with students as you think aloud. First, look at the answer. Then reread to see if it makes sense and check over the prediction and calculation. Make sure there is a mistake in the work that you are going to point out to students.

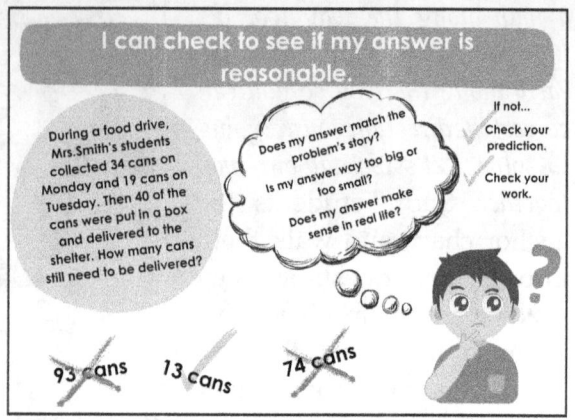

Figure 2.47 Anchor chart for checking to see if my answer is reasonable in second grade. To view this anchor chart in color, access the online Support Material: https://resourcecentre.routledge.com/books/9781032839875

Try it: Now students will try it out. Give them a piece of their own work that has an unreasonable answer so they understand the impact of using this strategy personally. Ask each student which question from the anchor

Figure 2.48 Anchor chart for checking to see if my answer is reasonable in third grade. To view this anchor chart in color, access the online Support Material: https://resourcecentre.routledge.com/books/9781032839875

chart helped them determine that their answer wasn't reasonable. Let students work at their own pace.

Send off: *When mathematicians get to the end of solving, that doesn't mean the work is done. We need to make sure that we go back into the problem to ensure our answer is reasonable and makes sense with the problem.*

Figure 2.49 Anchor chart for checking to see if my answer is reasonable in fourth grade. To view this anchor chart in color, access the online Support Material: https://resourcecentre.routledge.com/books/9781032839875

Figure 2.50 Anchor chart for checking to see if my answer is reasonable in fifth grade. To view this anchor chart in color, access the online Support Material: https://resourcecentre.routledge.com/books/9781032839875

Justify Thinking
Kindergarten and First-Grade Lessons

Lesson 1: I can prove my work another way.

Intro: *Have you ever tried to tell someone a story, and they didn't quite understand what you meant? You might try to explain it another way or draw a picture to help them see what you are trying to say. In math, we can show another way of solving a problem to prove our answer is correct and show another way of thinking!*

Teach: *When you finish solving, you can show that you understand the problem even more by showing another strategy you could have used to solve it or by representing it another way. Here are some of the strategies or representations you might use.* Show the anchor chart, then use a problem you have used in class recently. Show them how you could prove your work with another strategy and representation. You might want to do this lesson over two sessions to focus on strategy one day and representation another day.

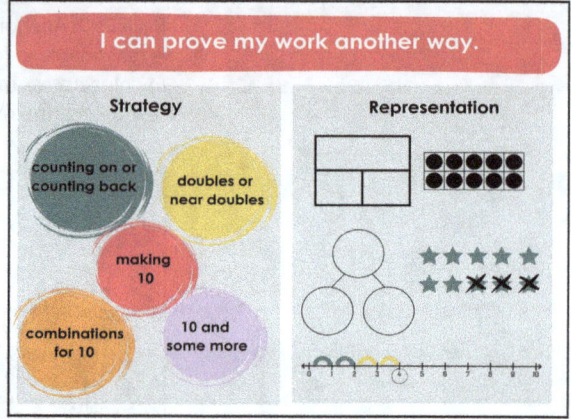

Figure 2.51 Anchor chart for proving my work another way in kindergarten and first grade.

Try it: Give students another problem that they worked out recently. Have them add to their work by proving it with another strategy and/or representation.

Send off: *To push yourself and check your work, you can prove you are correct by using another strategy or representation to show your understanding of the problem.*

Lesson 2: I can use sentence frames to justify my thinking.

Intro: *Have you ever tried to explain your thinking, but it's tricky to get started? You know that your answer is correct, but it's just tricky to explain what you did?*

Teach: *Today, I want to show you something called sentence frames. They can help you get started with explaining your math thinking. Look at this problem we solved recently.* Show the problem. *Explain how you know the answer makes sense, but it was tricky to get started explaining it. Use the sentence frames to justify your answer and how you know you are correct.* At first, you might just have students verbalize their justification. Eventually, students need to practice writing it. Show them how to use the anchor chart as support as they explain their thinking and that they can refer to it anytime they need to be reminded of how to get started.

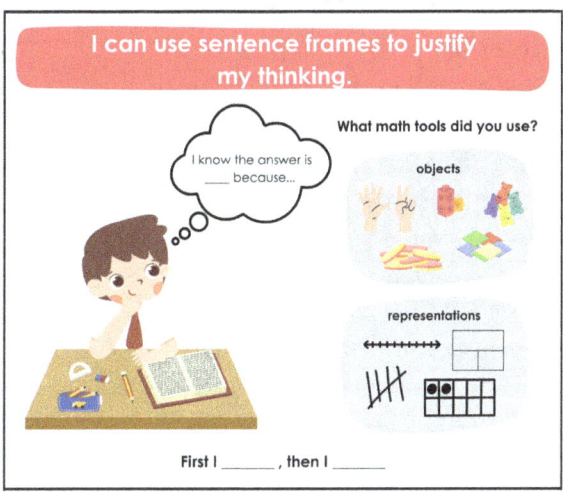

Figure 2.52 Anchor chart for using sentence frames to justify my thinking in kindergarten and first grade.

Try it: Students will now try it for themselves. You might do some shared writing at first or do very small groups to give each student the chance to rehearse saying their thinking out loud. This is a great way to challenge students who get the answer correct regularly. All students need practice communicating their thinking early and often.

Send off: *It is important for mathematicians to explain how they know their answer is correct. Sentence frames can help you get started.*

Justify Thinking
Second- to Fifth-Grade Lessons

Lesson 1: I can prove my work another way.

Intro: *Have you ever been with a friend or sibling, and they claim they are the best at something? Maybe they are "the fastest runner" or they say they are "the tallest"? Would you just believe them, or would you want them to prove it? It's similar in math when we get to an answer. When we solve a problem, we can't just get to the answer and claim it's correct. We need to be able to prove it by explaining how we know by speaking, writing, and other ways we put our thinking on paper.*

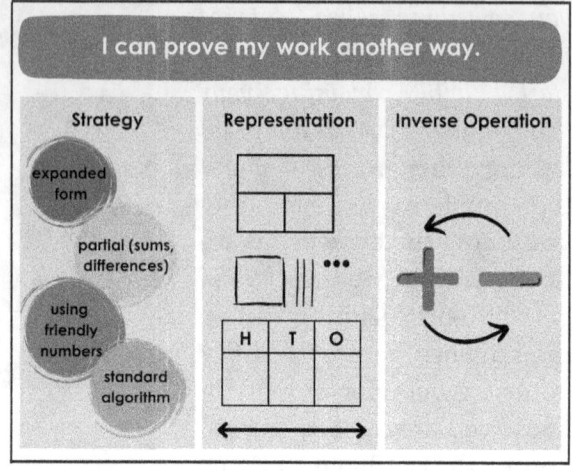

Figure 2.53 Anchor chart for proving my work another way in second grade. To view this anchor chart in color, access the online Support Material: https://resourcecentre.routledge.com/books/9781032839875

Teach: *When mathematicians solve problems, they can use an additional way to prove their thinking.* Show the anchor chart and walk through the meaning of strategy, representation, and inverse operation. *Look at this problem we solved together last week.* Use each way from the anchor chart to elaborate on your answer, so students understand what the terms mean. *I'm going to show you what it would look like to justify my thinking in each of these ways so that you know what they mean. It is important to justify your thinking in each step of a*

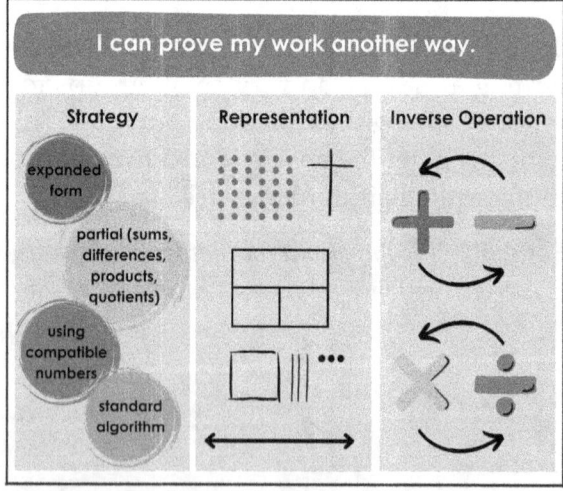

Figure 2.54 Anchor chart for proving my work another way in third–fifth grades. To view this anchor chart in color, access the online Support Material: https://resourcecentre.routledge.com/books/9781032839875

problem, but for the lesson today, I am just going to focus on one step. Walk through an example of each method to justify your thinking. *Doesn't this make you more convinced that my answer is correct? It also helps me as the mathematician to feel more confident that I didn't make any mistakes.*

Try it: Give students their work on a previous problem and have them choose a way to justify their thinking further with another strategy, representation, or inverse operation. Refer them to the anchor chart and your example to find an additional way to show their thinking if they start to struggle.

Send off: *As you solve, remember not to just say what your answer is, but to prove it by using another strategy, representation, or the inverse operation. This will make your answer more credible and also help you to check your work for mistakes.*

Lesson 2: I can use sentence frames to justify my thinking.

Intro: *Have you ever had the right answer in your head but didn't quite know how to explain it? Or maybe you knew why something made sense but couldn't find the words to say it clearly? That's something a lot of people struggle with – and that's where sentence frames can help. Sentence frames give us a starting point to explain our thinking. They're like training wheels for your brain: they help you focus on your ideas instead of getting stuck on how to say them. Today, we're going to learn how sentence frames can help us share our thinking more clearly, sound more confident, and back up our ideas with strong reasons.*

Teach: *I want to show you today how you can communicate your thinking and prove what you know is correct by practicing with sentence frames. We really have to slow down our thinking to explain how we solved it and why.* Use a problem that students are familiar with already to help keep the lesson focused. *The first thing I would want to do is state what the answer is in a sentence, or my answer statement. For this problem, it would say… Then I would want to explain how I know that is true. Here are some sentence frames or stems to choose from. I'm going to choose this one and this one because…* Tell what made you choose those frames based on your thinking process. Circle them to model what students can do independently to avoid getting overwhelmed by the large list. Show one piece at a time to help them see how your thinking progressed so they can replicate it. You might model more than one, just to show there are several different ways you could communicate your thinking.

> **I can use sentence frames to justify my thinking.**
> - "I noticed that the problem is asking me to __, so I __."
> - "I chose to use __ (strategy) because __."
> - "I thought about __, but I realized that __ would work better because __."
> - "(First, Next, Then) I __ because __."
> - "I did __ because I know that __."
> - "My next step was to __ because __."
> - "My solution makes sense because __."
> - "I checked my answer by __, and I found that __."
> - "I know my answer is correct because __."
> - "Another way I could have solved this problem is __, but I chose __ because __."
> - "At first I thought __, but then I realized that __ because __."
> - "The mistake I made was __, so I went back and __."
> - "The challenging part of this problem was __, so I __."

Figure 2.55 Anchor chart for using sentence frames to justify my thinking in second–fifth grades. To view this anchor chart in color, access the online Support Material: https://resourcecentre.routledge.com/books/9781032839875

Try it: Have students try it out with another familiar problem, sharing with a partner, and referring back to the anchor chart if needed. Based on time, you can decide how many stems you want them to choose.

Send off: *Remember, as we communicate, we can't just say we are correct and stop there. We have to justify how we know we are correct, and a way we can do that is through using sentence frames.*

Break Down the Behaviors That Drive Mathematical Problem Solving ◆ 97

Lesson 3: I can write a justification that includes my math and reading comprehension.

Intro: *What if I told you that vanilla is the best ice cream? I bet some of you would disagree with me. BUT, if I said vanilla is the best ice cream because you can add anything to it to make it whatever you want it to be, you might then see my point of view. If your favorite was cookies and cream, my point is still valid because you just added cookies to make your vanilla better. It is important to not only communicate what you think, but WHY you think that. This will help people understand your point of view, just like when you explain why you made certain choices as you solved a math problem.*

Teach: Show the anchor chart. *When justifying your thinking in math, you need to be able to express your math AND reading comprehension. You have to be able to explain what parts of the story helped you know what math computation to do. There are four components to a good justification: your answer statement, your mathematical*

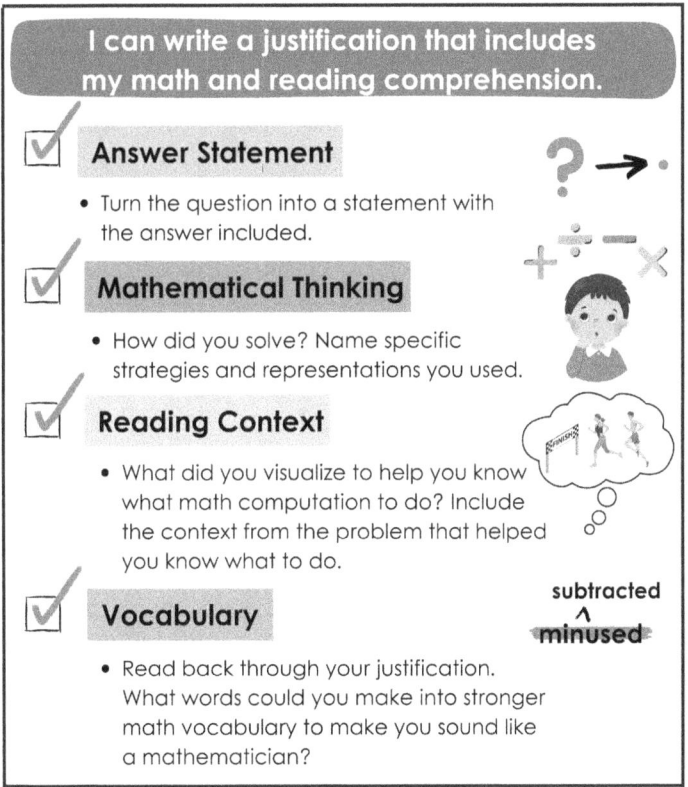

Figure 2.56 Anchor chart for writing a justification that includes my math and reading comprehension in second–fifth grades. To view this anchor chart in color, access the online Support Material: https://resourcecentre.routledge.com/books/9781032839875

Justify Your Thinking			
☐ Answer Statement	☐ Math Thinking	☐ Reading Context	☐ Math Vocabulary

Figure 2.57 Graphic organizer with checklist.

thinking, the reading context, and making sure you use strong math vocabulary. Let me show you what that looks like with this problem we did the other day. Using a problem students are familiar with will help save time and keep the focus clear. Color-code your example so they can see the different parts.

Try it: Have students try it out with a new problem they are also familiar with. They could do this work in partners where one partner says it and the other one writes it down. Feel free to step away as they do this work or pull another group because it will take them some time. Tell them to use the anchor chart and example for support. This lesson might need to be broken up into several different lessons depending on what aspects of justifying students need. A lot of the time, they struggle the most with adding in the reading context. This may need to be a separate lesson to strengthen what they already have in their justification.

Send off: *As you justify your thinking, it is important to explain why. For math problem solving, we include what we did with the math and what from the reading helped us know what to do.*

These types of lessons may be very different from anything you have seen before. You might have some questions swirling in your mind. Here are some that I have encountered when working with teachers and some I have anticipated you might have.

Questions and Answers

I have so much content to teach. When do I have time for this?

The great news is that you can use these lessons with any concept where your students need support. You are exposing students to content standards through the process standards as they were intended. These skills will help students with every math concept they encounter.

These lessons have too much on the anchor charts. What do I do if some of my students aren't ready for all of it?

Sticky notes are great for covering up parts of anchor charts to make the lessons even more targeted. The lessons are meant to be done with students more than once to master the specific skills. In the next chapters, you will learn ways to adjust the components of the lessons to make them work even better for your specific students. Another option is to just create your own anchor chart on a piece of paper with the parts you need. Nothing needs to be fancy to be great for kids.

Chapter 2: Reflection

1. What process standards apply to your state? Print them and read them carefully.
    - Underline the standards that you see students often apply in your classroom.
    - Highlight the standards you want to focus on next with students as a whole group.
    - Put a question mark next to the standards you are curious about. Hopefully, you will develop some clarity throughout the next few chapters.
    - Look at the progressions from this chapter and write down where they align with the process standards you have.

References

Aguilar, E. & Cohen, L. (2022) *The PD book*. Jossey-Bass.

Ashman, G. (2023). *A little guide for teachers: Cognitive Load Theory*. Corwin.

Common Core State Standards Initiative (CCSSI). Common Core State Standards for Mathematics. Washington, D.C.: National Governors Association Center for Best Practices and the Council of Chief State School Officers, 2010. http://www.corestandards.org.

Cooney Horvath, J. (2019). *Stop talking, start influencing*. Exile Publishing Pty, Ltd.

Harris, P. (2020). Strategies vs. Models. MathisFigureoutable. https://www.mathisfigureoutable.com/blog/strategyvmodel

Medical College of Wisconsin. (n.d.). *Cognitive load theory*. Medical College of Wisconsin. https://www.mcw.edu/-/media/MCW/Education/Academic-Affairs/OEI/Faculty-Quick-Guides/Cognitive-Load-Theory.pdf

National Governors Association Center for Best Practices, & Council of Chief State School Officers. (2010a). *Common Core State Standards for Mathematics: Grade 3 – Operations and Algebraic Thinking* (CCSS.Math.Content.3.OA.D.9). http://www.corestandards.org/Math/Content/3/OA/D/9

National Governors Association Center for Best Practices, & Council of Chief State School Officers. (2010b). *Common Core State Standards for Mathematics: Standards for Mathematical Practice*. http://www.corestandards.org/Math/Practice/

Parkay, F. W., Anctil, E. J., & Hass, G. (2014). *Curriculum leadership: Readings for developing quality educational programs* (Custom 10th ed.). Allyn & Bacon.

Tondevold, C. (2019) What is the Concrete Representational Abstract Approach? Build Math Minds. https://www.youtube.com/watch?v=8Kl3CvIKytc

Texas Education Agency. (2022). *2022 STAAR grade 3 mathematics test*. Texas Education Agency. https://tea.texas.gov/student-assessment/staar/released-test-questions/2022-staar-3-math-test.pdf

Willingham, D. T. (2024). Beyond comprehension. *Educational Leadership, 81*(4), 34–43.

3

How Do I Pinpoint the Needs of Each Student?

Teachers ask themselves, "What's the story behind this answer?" as they analyze student work. One of the most complex parts of teaching math is analyzing student responses and identifying what students need next. In this chapter, we examine student work from each grade level to determine their strengths and where their thinking got offtrack.

Gathering Current Reality

Sometimes, you can see exactly what students need to learn next, but sometimes it is not clear at all. Students must have ample practice solving open-ended questions and tasks. Teachers can then see the thinking of a student or lack thereof. Choosing a quality thinking task is key. To be able to see their ability to solve complex problems, the task must do the following:

- ◆ Include multiple entry points where students can solve in a variety of ways.
- ◆ Be challenging. The expectation is not solely to see if students can get the correct answer. We want to see where their thinking breaks down.
- ◆ Be open-ended. The goal is to see how students arrived at their answers. Multiple-choice assessments can give teachers and students a false sense of understanding.
- ◆ In grades 2–5, it is ideal to choose one with multiple operations. This can make the task data last longer, lowering the frequency of assessments.

You might be wondering why multiple choice assessments are not recommended. It is very challenging to group students based on multiple-choice assessments. Although they are easy to grade based on whether they are correct or incorrect, they send the wrong message to students and other stakeholders about what is valued in the classroom. For example, you might have a student who worked diligently to show their work on a problem by representing it, but unfortunately chose an answer that looked like their answer but was incorrect. Another student just guessed because they didn't even know how to get started, but they chose the correct answer. If small groups are organized by who got it correct and incorrect, these students won't be taught the necessary strategies to become better mathematicians. You'll end up with a student who guessed the correct answer not getting instruction on a skill they need, and you'll have a student who knows how to perform the skill in a group working on something they have already mastered. Not to mention, neither of their grades accurately represents their level of knowledge of the skill. (I'll talk more about grading techniques in Chapter 5.) Research shows that multiple-choice assessments end up with three groups of students with correct answers: Students who have knowledge and get the correct answer, students who have partial knowledge and get the correct answer, and students who do not have the knowledge and correctly guess (Abu-Ghazalah et al., 2023). The students with partial knowledge and the guessers still have skills that need to be developed, but this type of assessment may not alert the teacher to those needs.

Anticipating the Negative and Positive

Understanding student thinking requires anticipating potential misconceptions that students may have when solving problems. To do this effectively, it's essential for you to work through the problem yourself using manipulatives and pictorial representations, which can offer insight into the various approaches students might take (Smith & Stein, 2018). Teachers should solve it themselves, using multiple strategies to understand and identify the most efficient ways to solve. This preparation helps teachers anticipate both correct and incorrect interpretations of the problem so that they are equipped to address misunderstandings and guide students toward deeper mathematical understanding. For each grade-level problem in this chapter, there is a dedicated section to do this work.

Next to each sample of student work, you will see the strengths listed and the student's areas for growth. Our brains are wired to have negativity bias or to be drawn to the negative. In this case, that would be the errors or what students do incorrectly. Just as early humans needed to be able to sense threats to survive, teachers are trained to identify threats to learning. Our brains naturally allot more attention to negatives because the incorrect disrupts the expected patterns we seek. It is essential to acknowledge not only what students did wrong or need to do better, but also the behaviors you see that they are doing well. Students need reinforcement of correct strategies and clear next steps to understand the discrepancy between their current and desired understanding (Hattie & Timperley, 2007).

As you examine the student work in this chapter, monitor your focus. Just as we want students to develop thinking habits, we need to grow our own habits as we learn.

Kindergarten

Blue and Red Beads

Taylor has nine beads to make a bracelet. Five beads are red. The rest of the beads are blue. How many blue beads does Taylor have? Show and tell how you know.

Copyright 2018, Exemplars, Inc. All rights reserved. Additional rubrics and task samples may be viewed at www.exemplars.com.

Represent and Solve the Problem	Anticipate Misconceptions

Visualize	
Student Behavior **If a student…**	**They are ready for these targeted response lessons.**
…could not get started. …did not understand the context.	I can act out the problem with math tools.
…used the incorrect operation to solve.	I can retell the problem in my own words.

Strengths: This student is doing a great job representing numbers and labeling them. They even added in color for context.

Areas for Growth: Observe how this student struggles with visualization. They represented the numbers from the problem but did not represent the correct context.

Represent Visualization	
Student Behavior **If a student…**	**They are ready for these targeted response lessons.**
…represented the problem incorrectly. …couldn't see the relationship between the context and the math.	I can create a part-part-whole mat to match the problem.
	I can choose a representation to match my visualization.

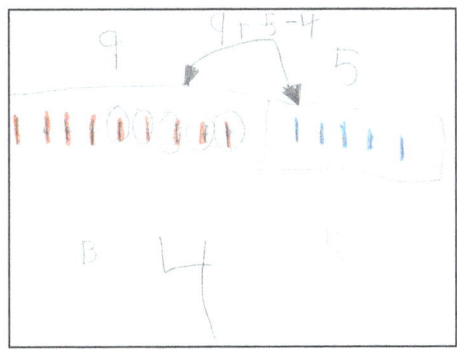

Strengths: This student understood what the problem was asking and got the correct answer. They used color and letters to represent the context. They attempted to write an equation.

Areas for Growth: Although they got the correct answer, the problem was not represented in a way that matched the context.

Identify the Question	
Student Behavior If a student...	**They are ready for these targeted response lessons.**
... did not answer the question from the problem.	I can write an answer statement to match the question.
... did not answer the problem thoroughly with context.	I can predict a reasonable answer to the problem.

Strengths: This work shows the problem represented correctly. They used color to show the correct context of five red beads and four blue beads.

Areas for Growth: They did not pay attention to what the question was asking and circled both numbers as the answer.

Organize and Solve	
Student Behavior If a student...	**They are ready for these targeted response lessons.**
...had unorganized work. ...made simple mistakes.	I can use a graphic organizer to organize my work.
...had an unreasonable answer.	I can check to see if my answer is reasonable.

Strengths: The student correctly represented the problem and labeled the parts with the correct numbers.

Areas for Growth: The work shown is unorganized. The student needs to learn some organizing habits to avoid future mistakes.

Justify Thinking	
Student Behavior **If a student…**	**They are ready for these targeted response lessons.**
…did not justify their answer.	I can prove my work another way.
…did not justify their answer thoroughly.	I can use sentence frames to justify my thinking.

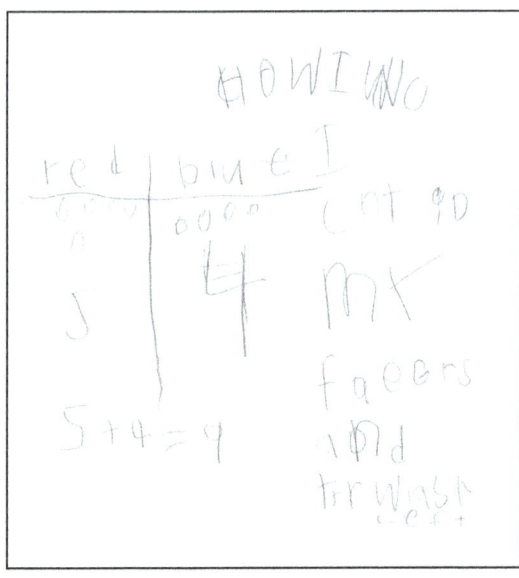

Strengths: The information is organized on a table. There are number and word labels for context, an equation, and even a justification.

Areas for Growth: This student is ready to show their thinking another way and build on their written justification using sentence frames.

First Grade

A Birdbath

Leah counts the birds that come to her birdbath. In the morning, Leah counts six birds that come to her birdbath. In the afternoon, Leah counts fourteen birds that come to her birdbath. Leah says nineteen birds came to the birdbath. Is Leah correct? Show all your mathematical thinking.

Copyright 2018, Exemplars, Inc. All rights reserved. Additional rubrics and task samples may be viewed at www.exemplars.com.

Represent and Solve the Problem	Anticipate Misconceptions

Visualize	
Student Behavior **If a student…**	**They are ready for these targeted response lessons.**
…could not get started. …did not understand the context. …used the incorrect operation to solve.	I can act out the problem with math tools.
	I can retell the problem in my own words.

Strengths: This student shows an understanding of how to make 14. They have represented and labeled the two numbers from the problem. They also answered one of the questions.

Areas for Growth: This student's work does not visualize the situation in this problem. Instead of adding six and fourteen together, they found a missing addend to get the sum of 14.

Represent Visualization	
Student Behavior **If a student…**	**They are ready for these targeted response lessons.**
…represented the problem incorrectly. …couldn't see the relationship between the context and the math.	I can create a part-part-whole mat to match the problem.
	I can choose a representation to match my visualization.

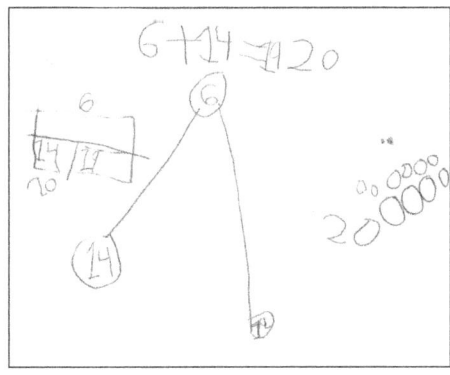

Strengths: This student tried to represent in multiple ways. They were able to get to 19 as the sum.

Areas for Growth: The models were used incorrectly, and the student didn't answer the question. The student will also need to develop the habit of revisiting the problem and answering the question.

Identify the Question	
Student Behavior **If a student…**	**They are ready for these targeted response lessons.**
…did not answer the question from the problem.	I can write an answer statement to match the question.
…did not answer the problem thoroughly with context.	I can predict a reasonable answer to the problem.

Strengths: This student not only had a correct representation of both sets of birds but also recounted to check their work.

Areas for Growth: The question was not answered. Even though the student showed some understanding of it, there was no clarification of whether Leah was right or wrong.

Organize and Solve	
Student Behavior **If a student…**	**They are ready for these targeted response lessons.**
…had unorganized work. …made simple mistakes.	I can use a graphic organizer to organize my work.
…had an unreasonable answer.	I can check to see if my answer is reasonable.

How Do I Pinpoint the Needs of Each Student? ◆ 111

Strengths: Twenty birds are represented and labeled with the quantity. The student also answered the question from the problem that Leah was incorrect.

Areas for Growth: The representation in this work is unorganized. There are no labels for the context of the problem. When the student learns to organize their work, it will be easy to monitor their thinking as they solve and justify their work thoroughly.

Justify Thinking	
Student Behavior If a student…	**They are ready for these targeted response lessons.**
…did not justify their answer.	I can prove my work another way.
…did not justify their answer thoroughly.	I can use sentence frames to justify my thinking.

Strengths: Notice how the sketch of work is organized in groups of five, as in ten frames. They have a correct equation and correct answer statement.

Areas for Growth: This student is ready to communicate how they solved through writing. They could also show another way to solve and include the context within their work.

Second Grade

Feather Collection

Hannah collects feathers. Hannah's aunt gives Hannah forty-two feathers to add to her collection. Hannah says now she only needs twenty-three feathers and she will have a total of one hundred fifty feathers! How many feathers did Hannah have before her aunt gave her more feathers? Show all your mathematical thinking.

Copyright 2018, Exemplars, Inc. All rights reserved. Additional rubrics and task samples may be viewed at www.exemplars.com.

Represent and Solve the Problem	Anticipate Misconceptions

How Do I Pinpoint the Needs of Each Student? ◆ 113

Visualize	
Student Behavior If a student…	**They are ready for these targeted response lessons.**
…could not get started. …did not understand the context. …used the incorrect operation to solve.	I can act out the problem with math tools.
	I can remove the numbers or make them smaller to understand the context.
	I can retell the problem in my own words.

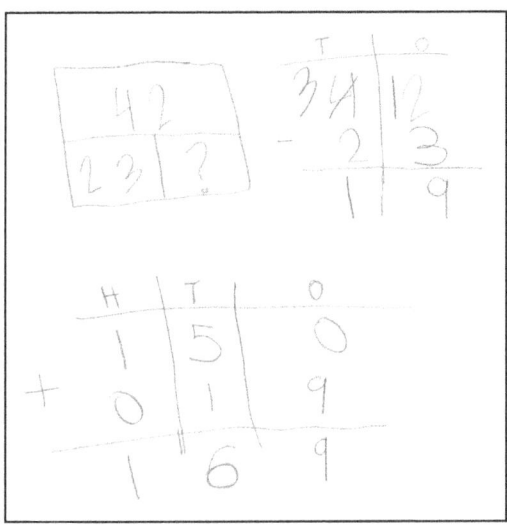

Strengths: A part-part-whole mat was attempted. The student solved using the standard algorithm in a place value chart beautifully for addition and subtraction. The work is organized well and easy to follow.

Areas for Growth: The part-part-whole mat in this problem is incorrect because the student could not appropriately identify the parts and whole from the context.

Represent Visualization	
Student Behavior If a student…	**They are ready for these targeted response lessons.**
…represented the problem incorrectly. …couldn't see the relationship between the context and the math.	I can create a part-part-whole mat to match the problem.
	I can label the numbers with context.
	I can choose a representation to match my visualization.

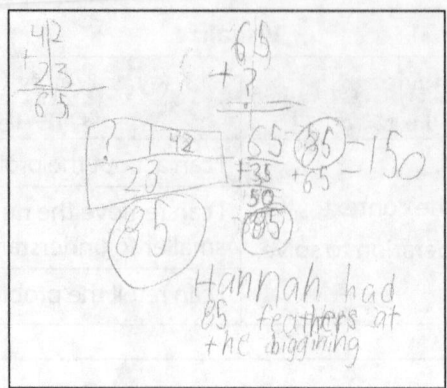

Strengths: The answer in this work is correct, and the student even included an answer statement in a complete sentence. The student has excellent calculation skills and number sense for addition.

Areas for Growth: This student does not use the part-part-whole mat correctly. I also noticed that the student did bridge to 100 to find the missing part. This would have been a perfect place to use an open number line to make the calculation easier.

Another thing I noticed is that the student didn't subtract to find the missing piece. This would cause me to look at other work samples to see if they are proficient at subtraction. I might save this work to highlight to the rest of the class that there is more than one way to solve a problem.

Identify the Question	
Student Behavior **If a student…**	**They are ready for these targeted response lessons.**
…did not answer the question from the problem.	I can write an answer statement to match the question.
…did not answer the problem thoroughly with context.	I can predict a reasonable answer to the problem.
	I can set up a workspace for each part of the problem.

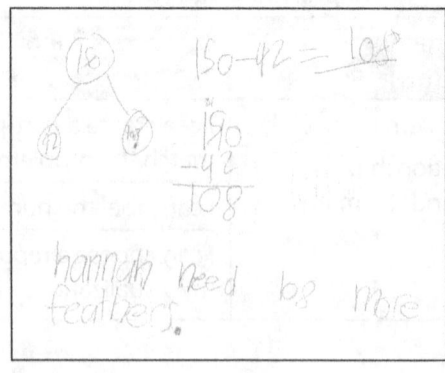

Strengths: The number bond was used correctly, and their subtraction with regrouping was done well. The student wrote an answer statement using the context of the problem.

Areas for Growth: A part of the problem was missed. An answer statement was written, but it does not match the question. This student will need to develop the habit of rereading the problem and monitoring for the steps to ensure they solve all parts.

Organize and Solve	
Student Behavior If a student…	**They are ready for these targeted response lessons.**
…had unorganized work. …made simple mistakes. …had an unreasonable answer.	I can use a graphic organizer to organize my work.
	I can monitor my comprehension as I solve the problem.
	I can check to see if my answer is reasonable.

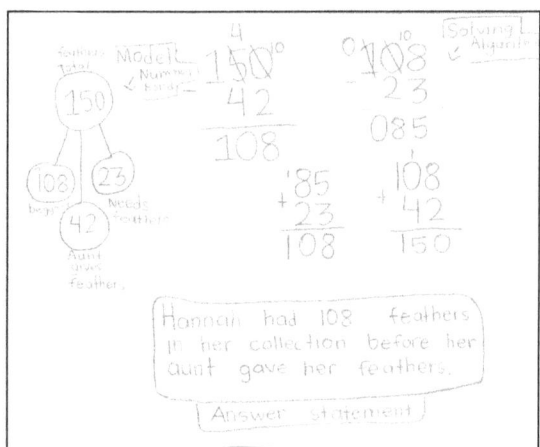

Strengths: The work here is so neat. The student even named their model, strategy, and answer statement. Their calculations for addition and subtraction were done well.

Areas for Growth: Even though the student solved the problem correctly, they got lost in their work and used the wrong part of it as the answer. Setting up a workspace for each part of the problem would help them separate their work for the different steps. They would also benefit from practicing to check if their answer is reasonable.

Justify Thinking	
Student Behavior **If a student…**	**They are ready for these targeted response lessons.**
…did not justify their answer.	I can prove my work another way.
…did not justify their answer thoroughly.	I can use sentence frames to justify my thinking.
	I can write a justification that includes my math and reading comprehension.

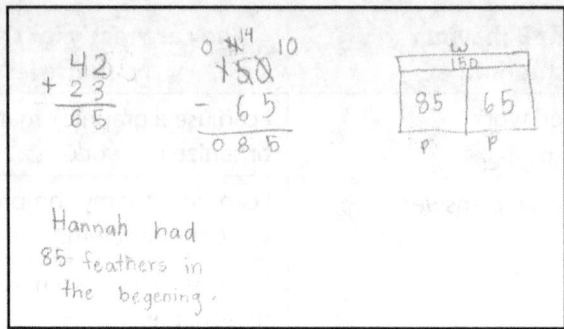

Strengths: Notice how the student's work is separated by step. They also represented their thinking in a part-part-whole mat and provided an answer statement that matched the question from the problem.

Areas for Growth: To grow this student further, have them practice writing about their thinking. Their work is all present, but it would be great to see more context and evidence that they checked their work to ensure they did not make mistakes.

Third Grade

Fishing With Friends
Some friends are camping near the shore. One friend suggests that they go fishing. Six boats are available at the campsite. Each boat holds two people and the friends are excited because that is exactly how many they need. The rule on this lake is that each person can catch only three fish. How many fish did the friends catch that day if each friend caught the limit? Show all your mathematical thinking.

Copyright 2018, Exemplars, Inc. All rights reserved. Additional rubrics and task samples may be viewed at www.exemplars.com.

Represent and Solve the Problem	Anticipate Misconceptions

Visualize	
Student Behavior **If a student…**	**They are ready for these targeted response lessons.**
…could not get started. …did not understand the context. …used the incorrect operation to solve.	I can act out the problem with math tools.
	I can remove the numbers or make them smaller to understand the context.
	I can retell the problem in my own words.

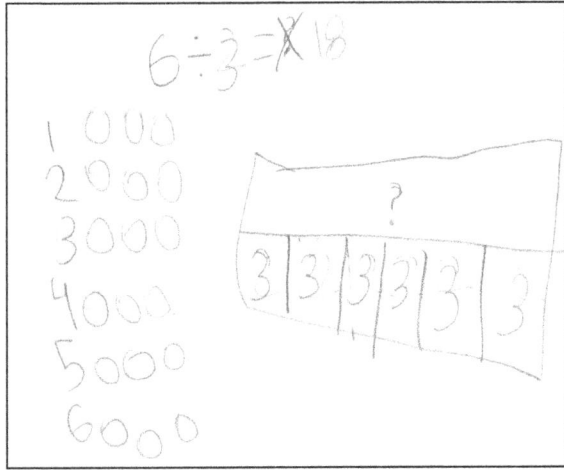

Strengths: The representations are organized. In the written equation, it appears the student knew that the answer of 3 didn't make sense. It is great that they are monitoring their understanding.

Areas for Growth: Some information in the problem was missed. The boats were left out of the student work. The equation has the division symbol, but the student did multiplication. The student needs to incorporate the context into what they put on paper.

Represent Visualization	
Student Behavior **If a student…**	**They are ready for these targeted response lessons.**
…represented the problem incorrectly. …couldn't see the relationship between the context and the math.	I can create a part-part-whole mat to match the problem.
	I can label the numbers with context.
	I can choose a representation to match my visualization.

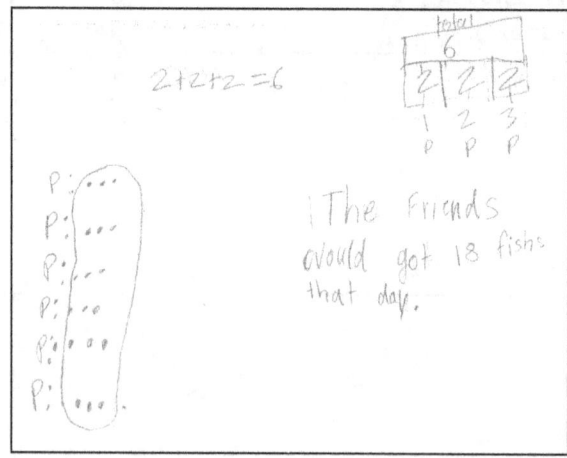

Strengths: The work was organized, and the student understood parts of the problem. There were labels for the context, and the answer statement was correct.

Areas for Growth: There was a misunderstanding about the boats and the people in the strip diagram. The student needs practice making sure the representation matches what they see in their mind.

How Do I Pinpoint the Needs of Each Student? ◆ 119

Identify the Question	
Student Behavior If a student…	**They are ready for these targeted response lessons.**
…did not answer the question from the problem.	I can write an answer statement to match the question.
…did not answer the problem thoroughly with context.	I can predict a reasonable answer to the problem.
	I can set up a workspace for each part of the problem.

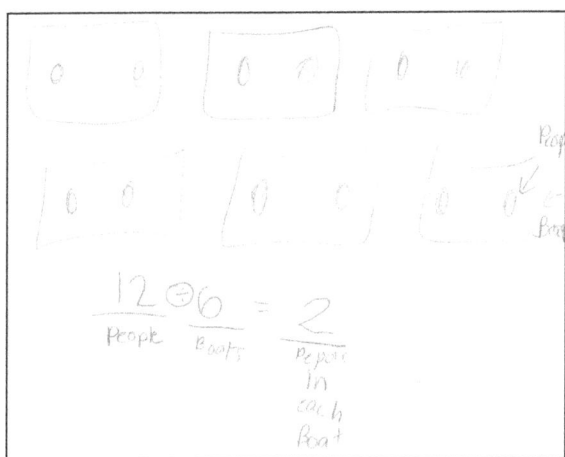

Strengths: Notice the organized representations labeled with the correct context from the problem. It is easy to see exactly what this student understood and worked out.

Areas for Growth: This student did not complete the second step of the problem – finding out how many fish the group caught. They need to develop the habit of paying attention to the question and returning to the problem to ensure they complete all the parts.

Organize and Solve	
Student Behavior If a student…	**They are ready for these targeted response lessons.**
…had unorganized work.	I can use a graphic organizer to organize my work.
…made simple mistakes.	I can monitor my comprehension as I solve the problem.
…had an unreasonable answer.	
	I can check to see if my answer is reasonable.

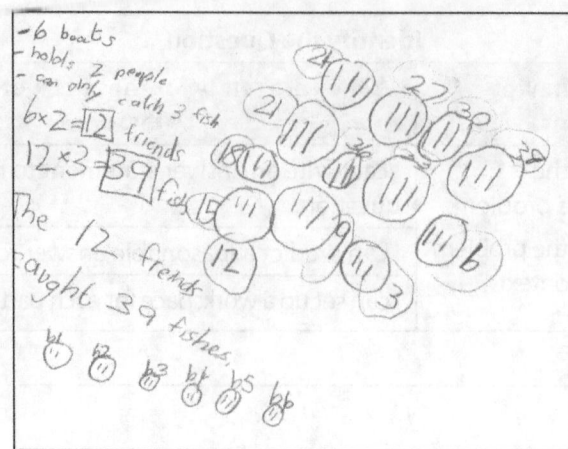

Strengths: Understanding of the problem is evident. The important information is listed, there are two equations to show the steps, and the pictures they drew to represent the problem were correct.

Areas for Growth: This student made a simple counting mistake because the work was not organized. They had the correct number of groups, but they accidentally counted one of them twice.

Justify Thinking	
Student Behavior If a student…	**They are ready for these targeted response lessons.**
…did not justify their answer. …did not justify their answer thoroughly.	I can prove my work another way.
	I can use sentence frames to justify my thinking.
	I can write a justification that includes my math and reading comprehension.

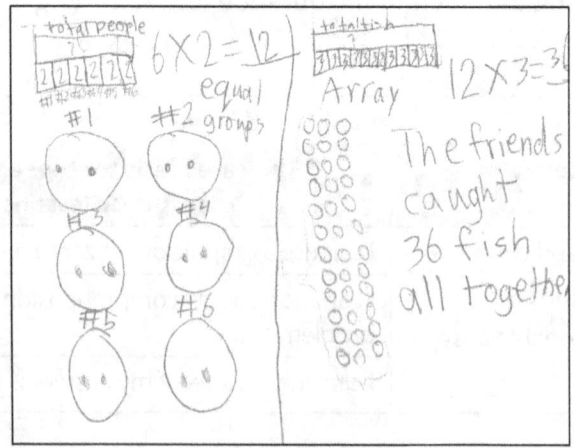

Strengths: Multiple ways to prove their thinking are shown, including strip diagrams, equations, and additional representations. The student labeled with context and had a complete answer statement with the correct answer.

Areas for Growth: To deepen this student's learning, they can be encouraged to improve their written communication about how they solved the problem.

Fourth Grade

Sharing Jelly Beans

There are five hundred eighty-eight jelly beans in a bowl. Hector, Michael, and Jolene decide to share the jelly beans equally. How many jelly beans do Hector, Michael, and Jolene each get? Their mother tells them that they cannot eat all the jelly beans at once. They can each eat an equal amount of jelly beans for four days. How many jelly beans do Hector, Michael, and Jolene eat each day for four days? Show all your mathematical thinking.

Copyright 2018, Exemplars, Inc. All rights reserved. Additional rubrics and task samples may be viewed at www.exemplars.com.

Represent and Solve the Problem	Anticipate Misconceptions

Visualize	
Student Behavior **If a student...**	**They are ready for these targeted response lessons.**
...could not get started. ...did not understand the context. ...used the incorrect operation to solve.	I can act out the problem with math tools.
	I can remove the numbers or make them smaller to understand the context.
	I can retell the problem in my own words.

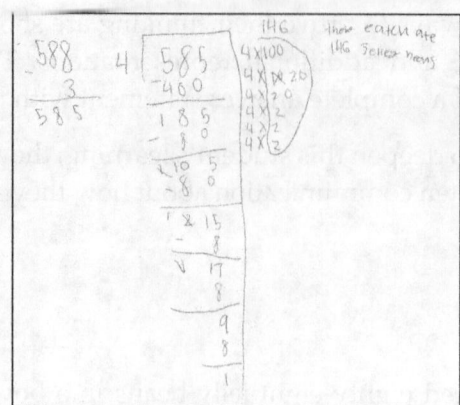

Strengths: The calculations for subtraction and division were correct. There is an answer statement in a complete sentence.

Areas for Growth: Notice how the student subtracted for the first step. They were unable to visualize each student getting jelly beans. The answer statement also did not match the problem because the problem asked how many jelly beans the kids would eat each day for four days.

Represent Visualization	
Student Behavior **If a student…**	**They are ready for these targeted response lessons.**
…represented the problem incorrectly. …couldn't see the relationship between …the context and the math.	I can create a part-part-whole mat to match the problem.
	I can label the numbers with context.
	I can choose a representation to match my visualization.

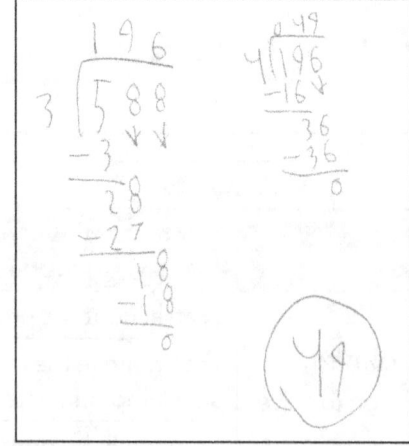

Strengths: The calculation for this problem was accurate, and the student is proficient in using the standard algorithm.

Areas for Growth: When students go straight to standard algorithms, they often struggle to represent their thinking in other ways. Because strip diagrams and other models are within the standards for students to master, the student must look beyond just getting the answer correct.

Identify the Question	
Student Behavior If a student…	**They are ready for these targeted response lessons.**
…did not answer the question from the problem.	I can write an answer statement to match the question.
…did not answer the problem thoroughly with context.	I can predict a reasonable answer to the problem.
	I can set up a workspace for each part of the problem.

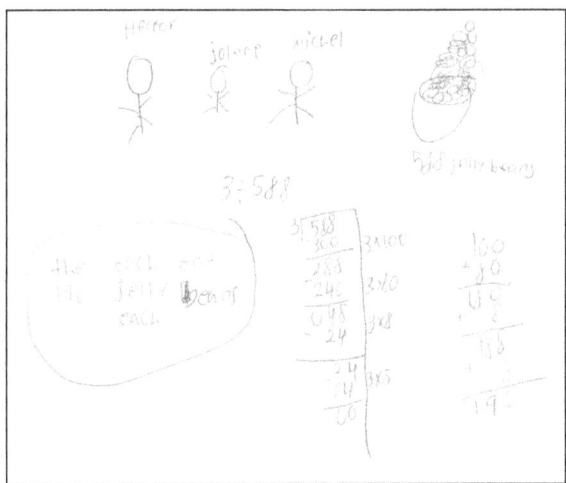

Strengths: The quick sketch matches the context, and the calculation for division is correct. An answer statement is present.

Areas for Growth: One misconception is within the equation. The student has the dividend and the divisor backward. The student only answered the first step, which was how many jelly beans each student will receive. The answer statement doesn't match the question in the problem.

Organize and Solve	
Student Behavior If a student...	**They are ready for these targeted response lessons.**
...had unorganized work.	I can use a graphic organizer to organize my work.
...made simple mistakes.	I can monitor my comprehension as I solve the problem.
...had an unreasonable answer.	I can check to see if my answer is reasonable.

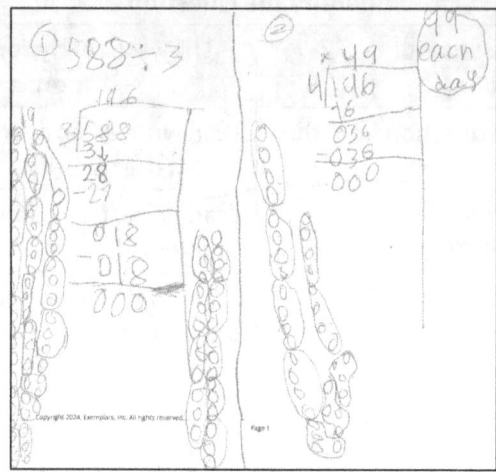

Strengths: The calculation for this problem was accurate. The student attempted to represent the problem and wrote an answer with context. The work is organized in two parts to keep the work in a designated space.

Areas for Growth: The representation for each step is unorganized and doesn't represent the context of the problem. The first step should have three groups, not three in each group, and the second step should have four groups instead of four in each group. Because the student solved with the standard algorithm, I would make a note that the student might not actually understand division conceptually and to investigate further.

Justify Thinking	
Student Behavior If a student...	**They are ready for these targeted response lessons.**
...did not justify their answer.	I can prove my work another way.
...did not justify their answer thoroughly.	I can use sentence frames to justify my thinking.
	I can write a justification that includes my math and reading comprehension.

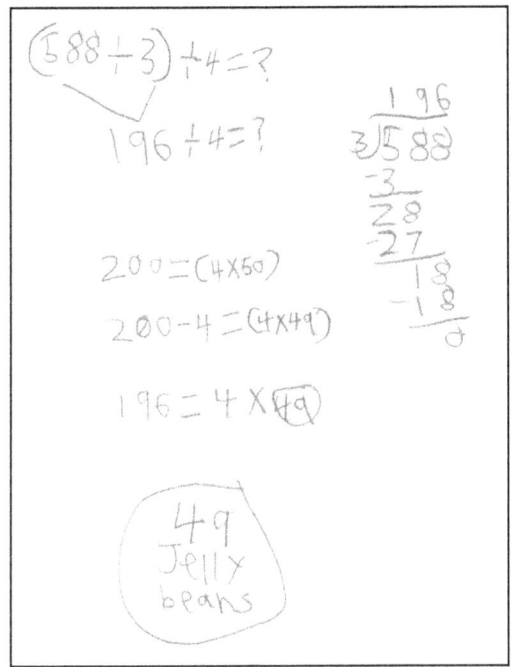

Strengths: In the middle, you see a unique strategy where the student shows strong number sense. The answer is paired with the context of the problem. The equation is multi-step, even using parentheses correctly.

Areas for Growth: This student is ready to show their understanding by writing about it and communicating using other models and strategies.

Fifth Grade

Collecting Insects

Jessica and Sarah collect insects. Jessica has two hundred thirty-four insects. Sarah has 2.5 times as many insects as Jessica. Jessica and Sarah's friend, Marie, wants to start an insect collection too. Marie buys ten insects. Marie also buys four times as many insects as Jessica has in her collection. Insects cost twenty-five cents each. Jessica, Sarah, and Marie each had three hundred dollars when they began collecting insects. How much money does each girl have now? Show all your mathematical thinking.

Copyright 2018, Exemplars, Inc. All rights reserved. Additional rubrics and task samples may be viewed at www.exemplars.com.

Represent and Solve the Problem	Anticipate Misconceptions

Visualize	
Student Behavior **If a student…**	**They are ready for these targeted response lessons.**
…could not get started.	I can act out the problem with math tools.
…did not understand the context.	I can remove the numbers or make them smaller to understand the context.
…used the incorrect operation to solve.	
	I can retell the problem in my own words.

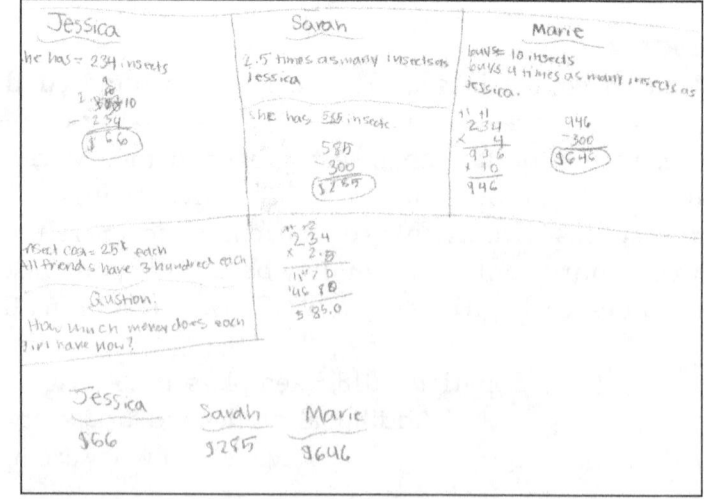

How Do I Pinpoint the Needs of Each Student? ◆ 127

Strengths: The first step of this problem is solved correctly. The workspaces are well-defined and organized. The student uses the standard algorithm for accurate subtraction and multiplication of whole numbers and decimals.

Areas for Growth: This student did not complete step two, and they completed step three incorrectly by subtracting the amount of money from the number of insects collected. They struggled to visualize what was happening in the problem.

Represent Visualization	
Student Behavior **If a student…**	**They are ready for these targeted response lessons.**
…represented the problem incorrectly. …couldn't see the relationship between the context and the math.	I can create a part-part-whole mat to match the problem.
	I can label the numbers with context.
	I can choose a representation to match my visualization.

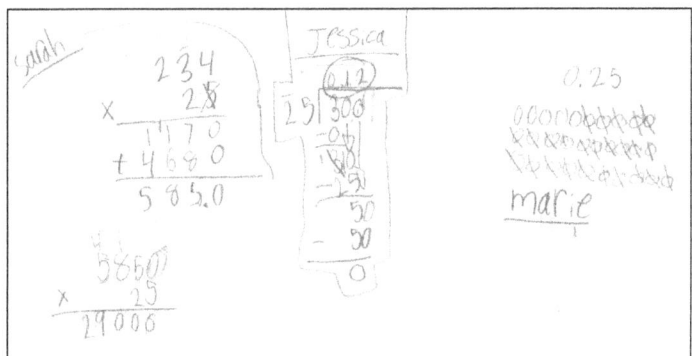

Strengths: The student was able to multiply and divide. They attempted several operations to try to make sense of buying the insects. This student showed great grit, trying multiple ways to attack the problem, such as drawing a picture, figuring out how much the bugs would cost, and figuring out how many insects could be bought with $300.

Areas for Growth: Here, they tried to figure out the operation by drawing circles to represent $0.25. Because they have a way to represent the numbers so they can see the relationship, they should be more easily able to choose the correct operation to solve. This student might also need help visualizing, so I would monitor this while pulling the small group.

Identify the Question	
Student Behavior If a student…	**They are ready for these targeted response lessons.**
…did not answer the question from the problem.	I can write an answer statement to match the question.
…did not answer the problem thoroughly with context.	I can predict a reasonable answer to the problem.
	I can set up a workspace for each part of the problem.

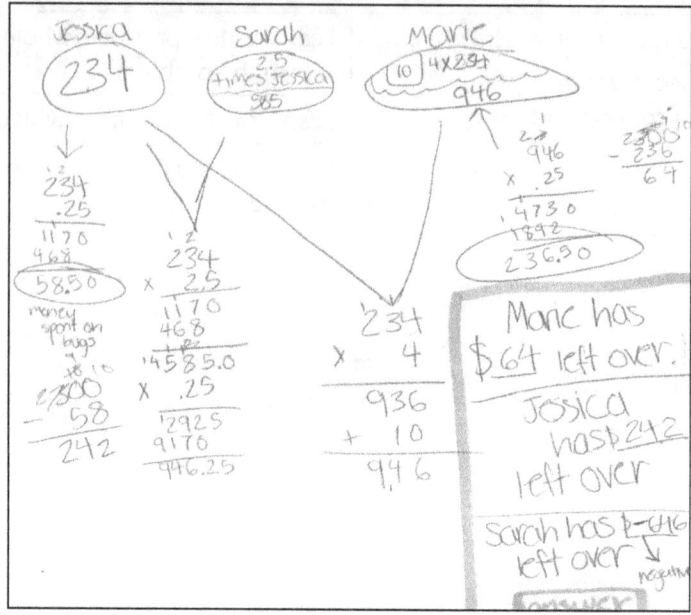

Strengths: The student knows which calculations will help her in each step of the problem. She has organized information for the first step, and her subtraction with regrouping across zeros is correct.

Areas for Growth: I see many things that lead me to believe a lack of understanding of place value exists. There is no zero on the second line of the standard algorithm for multiplication; there is a comma in 946, and when this student subtracts, they omit the decimal part of the subtracted value. Their answer for Sarah is in the negative numbers. This student needs to predict what would be a reasonable answer and that Sarah had the fewest insects, so she should have the most money left over.

How Do I Pinpoint the Needs of Each Student? ◆ 129

Organize and Solve	
Student Behavior If a student…	**They are ready for these targeted response lessons.**
…had unorganized work. …made simple mistakes. …had an unreasonable answer.	I can use a graphic organizer to organize my work.
	I can monitor my comprehension as I solve the problem.
	I can check to see if my answer is reasonable.

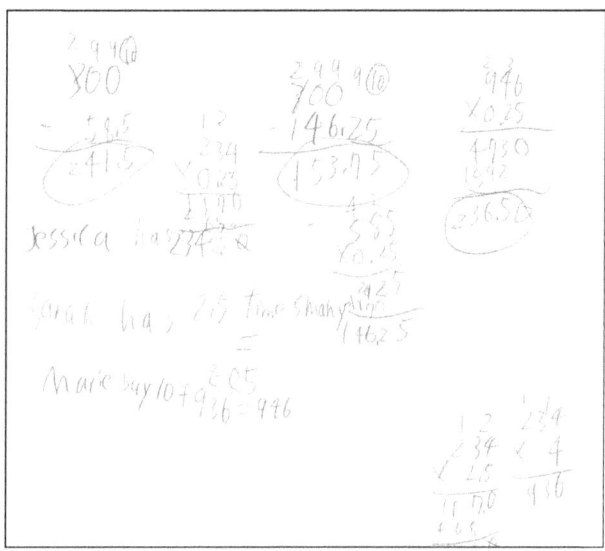

Strengths: The answers for each of the three girls in the problem are correct. The student shows strong computation skills for multiplication and subtraction of decimals.

Areas for Growth: Work for this problem is a little difficult to follow. This student could benefit from developing a habit of organizing their work. This will benefit them when communicating how they solved and how they know they are correct.

Justify Thinking	
Student Behavior If a student…	**They are ready for these targeted response lessons.**
…did not justify their answer. …did not justify their answer thoroughly.	I can prove my work another way.
	I can use sentence frames to justify my thinking.
	I can write a justification that includes my math and reading comprehension.

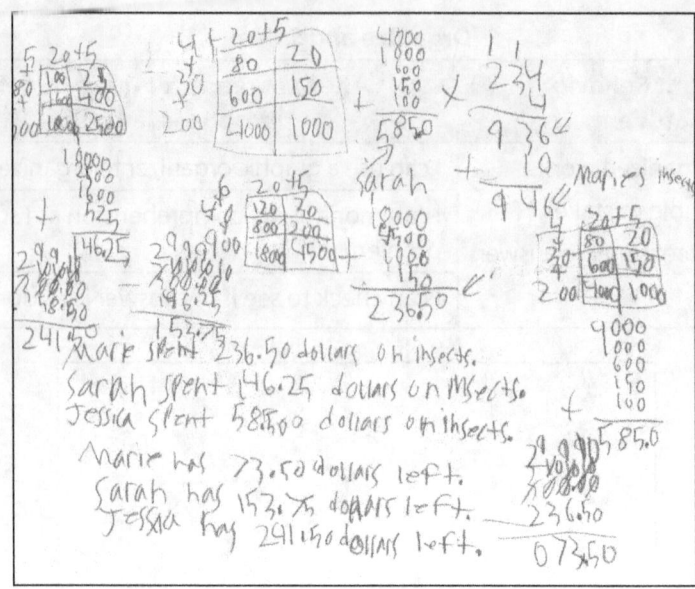

Strengths: You can see that this student has strong place-value understanding. Not only did this student tell us how much money the girls from the problem had left, but also how much they spent.

Areas for Growth: Based on the amount of work shown and the time it probably took to write all of it down, it might be time to move this student to the standard algorithm for multiplication to be less likely to make mistakes. This student is ready to elaborate on the problem by writing about their under-standing throughout the steps to solving.

When working with teachers, analyzing student work is where the most questions arise. This work takes practice and will be refined over time. There is no one-size-fits-all solution for student thinking. Still, when we can train ourselves to think in a way that helps students develop deeper, more inten-tional thinking, these skills can transcend all math concepts and even other disciplines.

Questions and Answers

How do I choose just one teach point for students who need a lot of help?

The significant part of this progression is that when students make many mistakes or don't know what to do, you can start them with visualizing lessons. In the next chapter, we will discuss how to track progress, but if students can't visualize or represent what they visualize, it will be tough to solve correctly.

I have some students who always get the correct answer. What do I do for them?

These students still need practice justifying and communicating their answers in multiple ways. This will help them become flexible thinkers and great communicators, which will benefit them throughout life. To push them even further, a more challenging version of the problem or an extension can be helpful. I love Exemplars, Inc. tasks because a more accessible and more challenging version of every task is already built into their platform.

Some students show more than one need, even in problem-solving skills. Where do I start them on the progression?

Sometimes, you just have to go with your gut and decide what will be best for the student right now that can be applied to future problems. It won't harm students to pull them into a group and have them practice a skill based on what you think they might need. Small-group instruction is not only about teaching students something, but also about gaining more information. You might see that they were ready for even more than you thought. When you know the student personally and have multiple experiences with their work, you will get a better view and can better assign the next steps.

What if students need to develop problem-solving skills AND computation skills?

A lot of students will fall into this category. You just put them in both groups. The next chapter will look at ways to track students for problem-solving skills and computation. When you separate the skills in small-group instruction, there is less confusion for the students about exactly what you want them to take away from a learning experience.

How often do students need to do a task like this?

Once you have responded to the needs of students from one task, or you feel like you need a fresh look, that's a great time. Students can also do tasks like this in a learning station with a partner to continue their growth and practice the deep thinking habits they are learning in their small groups with the teacher.

Is there an easier way to practice collecting feedback for students?

While developing an eye for analyzing student work through multiple lenses, you can use something like the following graphic organizer to support the development of this new habit. Writing down what you see can help pinpoint the most critical next step, but it is not required.

Student Name:		Task:	
	Strengths:	Areas for Growth:	Other Noticings:
Problem-Solving Skills			
Computation Skills			
Productive Struggle			

We will take a deeper look at the concept of productive struggle in Chapter 6.

Here are some questions you might consider for each component:

Problem Solving Skills

- Visualize
  - Did the student understand the context of the problem?
  - Did they use the correct operation to solve?
- Represent Visualization
  - Did the student try to represent the problem?
  - Did they represent the problem correctly?
  - Did they go straight to solving and choose the incorrect operation?
- Identify the Question(s)
  - Did the student answer the question from the problem?
  - Did they label their answer?
  - If there was more than one step, did they answer each step?
- Organize and Solve
  - Did the student have unorganized work? (Remember, organized work is different from neat work.)
  - Did they make simple mistakes?
  - Did the student have an unreasonable answer?
- Justify Thinking
  - Did the student have an answer statement?
  - Did they prove their answer in another way with another model, strategy, or the inverse operation?
  - Did they write about how they solved mathematically?
  - Did they write about how they used the context to determine what to do mathematically?
  - Did they include mathematical vocabulary in their justification?

Computation Skills

Did the student get the answer correct?
- Did they use any shortcuts or tricks that I want to address?
- Did they solve it efficiently?
- Did they solve it creatively?

Did the student get an incorrect answer?
- Did they perform any computation correctly (even if they used the wrong numbers or incorrect operation)?
- Did they make simple mistakes?
- Is the error in their computation related to place value or another foundational misunderstanding?

Productive Struggle

Did the student attempt to figure out the problem?
Did they have a positive attitude while solving?
When they got stuck, did they try to get unstuck?
- What did they try?
- What might have helped them that they didn't try?

How long did they attempt to solve the problem?
What behaviors did you notice that negatively or positively impacted the student's perseverance?

For the Other Noticings section, there might be behaviors or outside factors that don't necessarily fall right into one of the other categories, but you still want to note.

Chapter 3: Reflection

Analyzing student work can feel overwhelming. However, this work deepens students' and teachers' mathematical knowledge and develops a keen eye for attention to detail. Over time, this process becomes habitual, so pinpointing next steps for students will not always feel daunting or time-consuming.

The next chapter suggests several ways to quickly sort through student work and find one that makes sense in your classroom.

Because you have already anticipated the misconceptions and strategies for the tasks within your exploration of this chapter, here are some practice naming strengths, areas for growth, and where students fall on the progression. If you want to practice with your own students, administer the task from this chapter and try it out!

134 ◆ Math Problem Solving Through Small Group Instruction

Try It Out! – Kindergarten

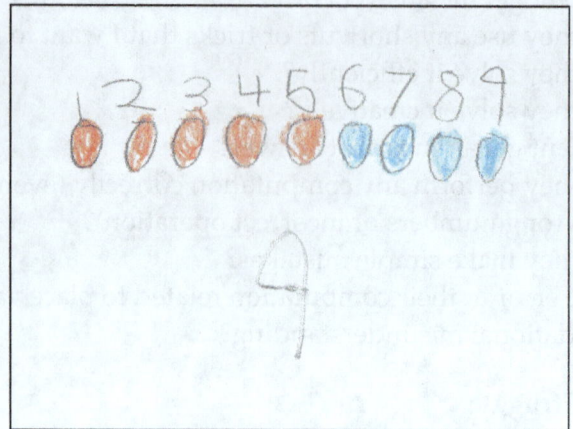

Figure 3.1 Sample K-1.

Strengths:
_____
_____

Areas for growth:
_____
_____

Phase of the progression to start with this student: _____

Figure 3.2 Sample K-2.

Strengths:
_____
_____

Areas for growth:
_____
_____

Phase of the progression to start with this student: _____

Try It Out! – First Grade

Figure 3.3 Sample 1-1.

Strengths:
_____
_____

Areas for growth:
_____
_____

Phase of the progression to start with this student: _____

136 ◆ Math Problem Solving Through Small Group Instruction

6 + 14 = 19

yes she has 19 bird

Figure 3.4 Sample 1-2.

Strengths:
_____
_____

Areas for growth:
_____
_____

Phase of the progression to start with this student: _____

Try It Out! – Second Grade

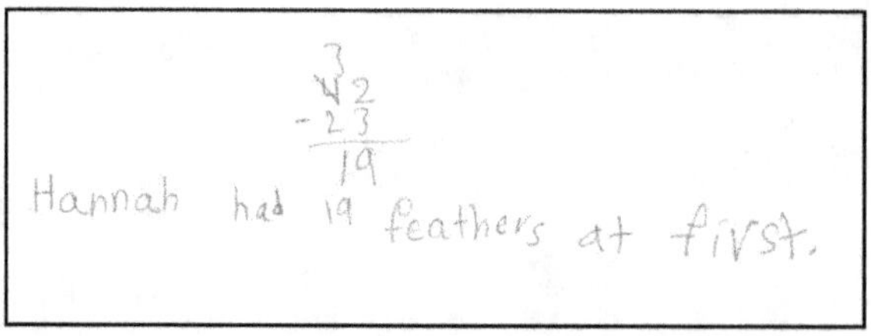

$$\begin{array}{r} \overset{3}{4}2 \\ -23 \\ \hline 19 \end{array}$$

Hannah had 19 feathers at first.

Figure 3.5 Sample 2-1.

Strengths:
_____
_____

Areas for growth:
_____
_____

Phase of the progression to start with this student: _____

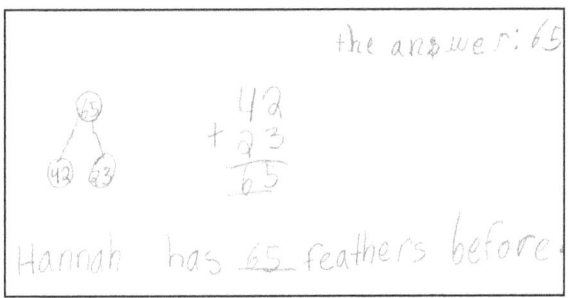

Figure 3.6 Sample 2-2.

Strengths:
_____
_____

Areas for growth:
_____
_____

Phase of the progression to start with this student: _____

Try It Out! – Third Grade

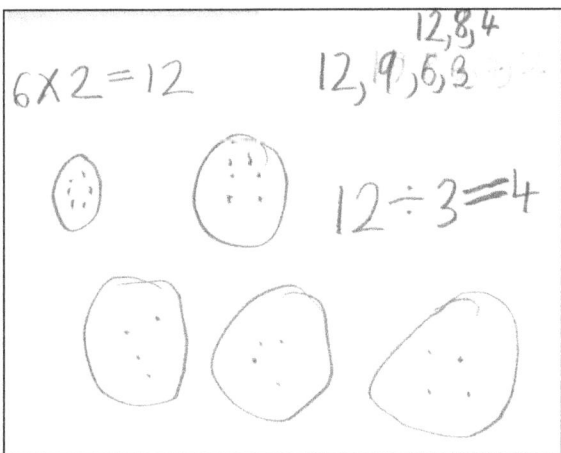

Figure 3.7 Sample 3-1.

Strengths:
_____
_____

Areas for growth:
_____
_____

Phase of the progression to start with this student: _____

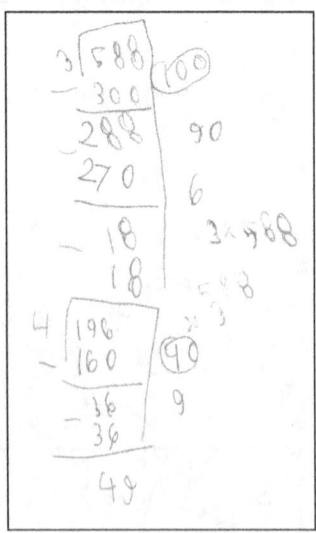

Figure 3.8 Sample 3-3.

Strengths:
_____
_____

Areas for growth:
_____
_____

Phase of the progression to start with this student: _____

Try It Out! – Fourth Grade

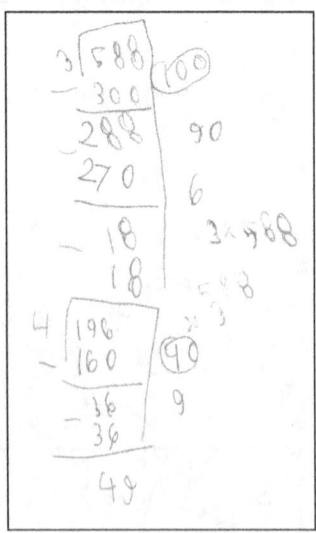

Figure 3.9 Sample 4-1.

Strengths:
_____
_____

Areas for growth:
_____
_____

Phase of the progression to start with this student: _____

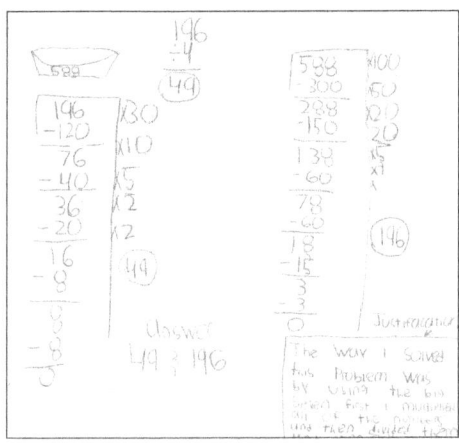

Figure 3.10 Sample 4-2.

Strengths:
_____
_____

Areas for growth:
_____
_____

Phase of the progression to start with this student: _____

Try It Out! – Fifth Grade

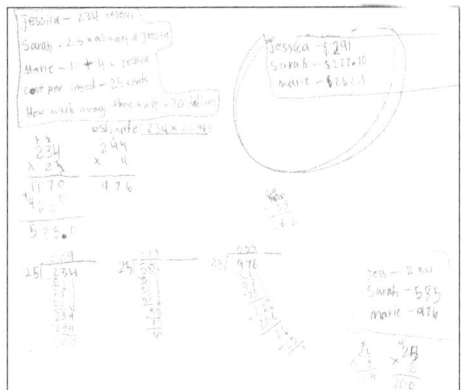

Figure 3.11 Sample 5-1.

Strengths:
_____
_____

Areas for growth:
_____
_____

Phase of the progression to start with this student: _____

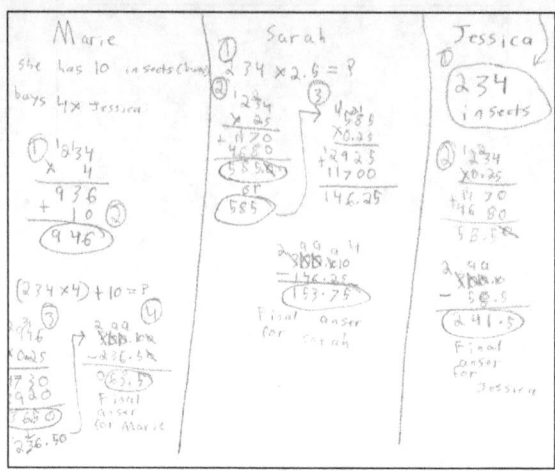

Figure 3.12 Sample 5-2.

Strengths:
_____
_____

Areas for growth:
_____
_____

Phase of the progression to start with this student: _____

References

Abu-Ghazalah, R. H., Dubins, D. N., & Poon, G. M. (2023). Dissecting knowledge, guessing, and blunder in multiple choice assessments. *Applied Measurement in Education, 36*(1), 80–98.

Hattie, J., & Timperley, H. (2007). The power of feedback. *Review of Educational Research, 77*(1), 81–112.

Smith, M. S., & Stein, M. K. (2018). *Five practices for orchestrating productive mathematics discussions.* Corwin.

4

How Can I Effectively Organize Groups for Differentiated Learning?

Now that we have figured out how to identify what students need, let's explore how to do that process quickly and efficiently to get started with small-group instruction. Small-group instruction supports the practice of differentiation. Differentiation is an instructional approach where all students get what they need. Carol Tomlinson's ideals about differentiation have changed the world of education and have given school districts and teachers everywhere a dream for education to aspire to. She wrote an article in 2015 called *Teaching for Excellence in Academically Diverse Classrooms*. Every classroom is academically diverse, and she writes about six key principles.

1. Human difference is needed and should be celebrated because it enriches learning. People need to learn from different kinds of people with unique perspectives and backgrounds.
2. Teachers must have a growth mindset and believe all students can learn at high levels. Teachers partner with students to help them grow on their unique learning journeys.
3. Teachers get to know their students by learning about them as people and through formative assessment. They use what they learn about students and their progress toward mastery to create the most effective learning environment.
4. Classrooms should have whole-group lessons that all students need and small-group lessons along with other learning experiences based on individual needs so that every student grows. Students will learn at different rates.

DOI: 10.4324/9781003510703-5

5 A rigorous and relevant curriculum should be used. Teachers must deeply understand the content they teach to help students reach that deep understanding themselves. What is most important for students to learn is clear, and students can apply their knowledge across disciplines.

6 Teachers must reflect on their teaching practices and frequently monitor where students are at a given time in relation to complex goals. They are always trying to analyze what is working or not working for each student. Teachers are flexible and evolve with the needs of their students. They believe they can get every student to learn at a high level.

Reading that article always gives me goosebumps as she describes what these classrooms embody and uphold with differentiation. However, creating this ideal classroom that we all would desire for even our own children is not easy, but it is so worth it. For differentiation to be doable, it is essential to have efficient ways to track data and progress toward mastery of skills. The following are tracking documents: one for problem solving skills and one for computation. The problem solving tracker is meant to be used as a living document where students can move from one phase to the next. The computation tracker will be used for isolated strategies, where students stay in those groups until they have mastered that specific strategy.

Problem Solving Small Groups				
Visualize	Represent Visualization	Identify the Question(s)	Organize and Solve	Justify Thinking

If a student starts in the Represent Visualization phase, they will likely need to progress through the other phases that follow. This can keep your small groups going for an extended period of time. The tasks and other formative assessment data you collect and what you observe in small groups will validate whether students need to stay within those phases or move on. Remember that groups are fluid. Don't think of students as a group, but individually. Some students may stay on the same learning target for multiple exposures, whereas other students may only need to see the new strategy once. Having documents like these in a digital format makes it easy to move students in and out of teach points as they learn.

Computation Small Groups				
(Learning Target)	(Learning Target)	(Learning Target)	(Learning Target)	(Learning Target)

Having no more than five to six students in a group is ideal. Each column has more than that many spaces because we are thinking about students by what they need. You may have ten students who need the same lesson. You can break those ten into two small groups. Because students will learn at different paces, you can condense the two groups into one group as students move on to other learning they need next. Students may not master a new concept on the first exposure. It typically takes at least three engagements with a concept for learning to occur. Every exposure must include students being engaged with the learning. Each time, it must be deliberate and explicit (Cooney Horvath, 2019).

Once you have developed an eye for identifying next steps for students, there are a few different ways you can sort students into meaningful groups, using a method called thin-slicing.

What Is Thin-Slicing?

I often hear teachers say that to assess students thoroughly, they need to give students 10–20 problems to get enough information to know what to do next. It is impossible to look deeply at that many problems for each student. By choosing one in-depth task or problem that shows a student's progress from multiple angles, a quicker approach can be taken to gain an accurate view of student thinking. Thin-slicing is the process of drawing conclusions from minimal information. Teachers have expertise and instincts in their field. When they practice and hone their skills at understanding learn-ing in a progression, they can make quick and accurate decisions about the next steps for students based on intuition and patterns (Gladwell, 2007). Students do need a lot of practice with skills, but teachers do not have to look deeply at every problem every student completes to understand what they need. Give yourself the permission to not look at everything students complete. Feedback is about quality, not quantity. This practice allows you to work smarter.

There are three ways to thin-slice:

- ◆ Choose one behavior to look for, and look through all student work with only that focus.
- ◆ Analyze one piece of work at a time to determine all of each student's needed teach points at that given time from that task.
- ◆ Look for behaviors in a live setting with eight to ten students.

Focus on One Teach Point at a Time

Suppose there is a specific teach point that you anticipate students need based on observation in class or within previous data. In that case, you can determine what you are looking for and acknowledge that you will ignore all other behaviors at this time. For example, if the assessment addresses the representation of problems with a part-part-whole mat, teachers could go through student work quickly to see exactly who needs that as a teach point, making a list of the students in that group. Then just repeat this process with as many teach points as necessary.

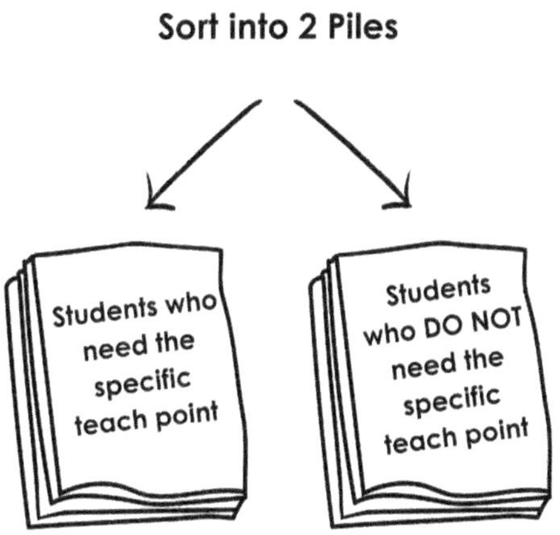

Sort into 2 Piles

Students who need the specific teach point | Students who DO NOT need the specific teach point

Figure 4.1 Thin-slicing one teach point at a time.

The students who end up in the pile who need that teach point would then be written down on a documentation tool so that you can track each student's learning progress.

Analyze Each Piece of Student Work for Multiple Teach Points

Another way teachers can thin-slice data is to examine each student's work sample in depth. For any teach points that are visibly needed, the student would be listed in a small group. For students who may need many teach points, the teacher could determine which problem solving group would be most beneficial and which computation group would be most helpful based on the order of importance. The teacher would think about the phases of the progression from chapter two and start with the earliest phase the student needs from left to right. This method of thin-slicing may be more timeconsuming, but the teacher has many groups to work with, making data collection less frequent.

For example, Student A is in first grade. They made a simple mistake because their work was not organized. The student will benefit from using a graphic organizer, so they were put into the Organize and Solve phase of the problem solving progression. Because they did not notice their answer was incorrect, they were also put into a computation group to learn the strategy of making 10 for addition.

Student B did not use the correct numbers for step one of this problem. They also pulled out the partial quotient of 10 multiple times. This is not an efficient strategy and could cause the student to make many computation errors. The student was put into a group for visualizing and also a group for dividing efficiently using partial quotients.

146 ◆ Math Problem Solving Through Small Group Instruction

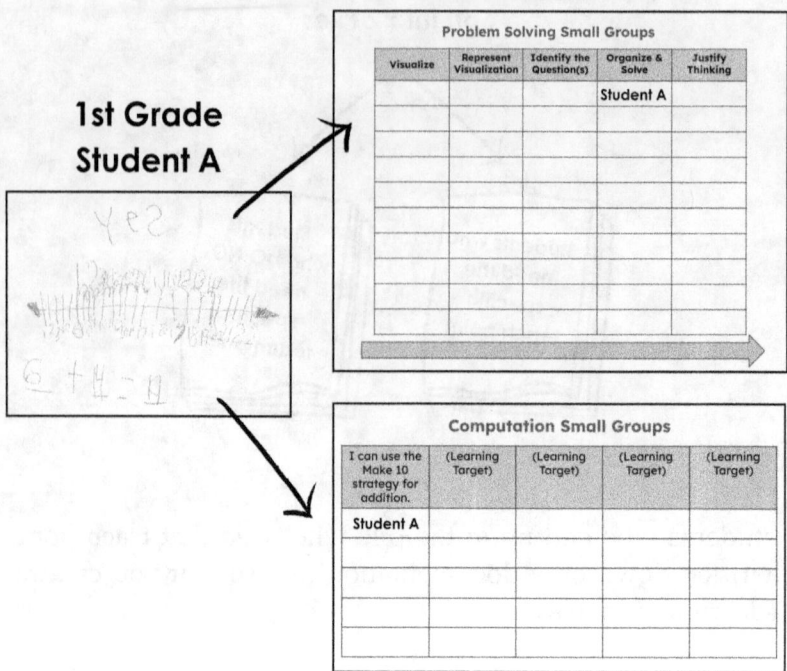

Figure 4.2 Thin-slicing one student at a time: Lower grade example.

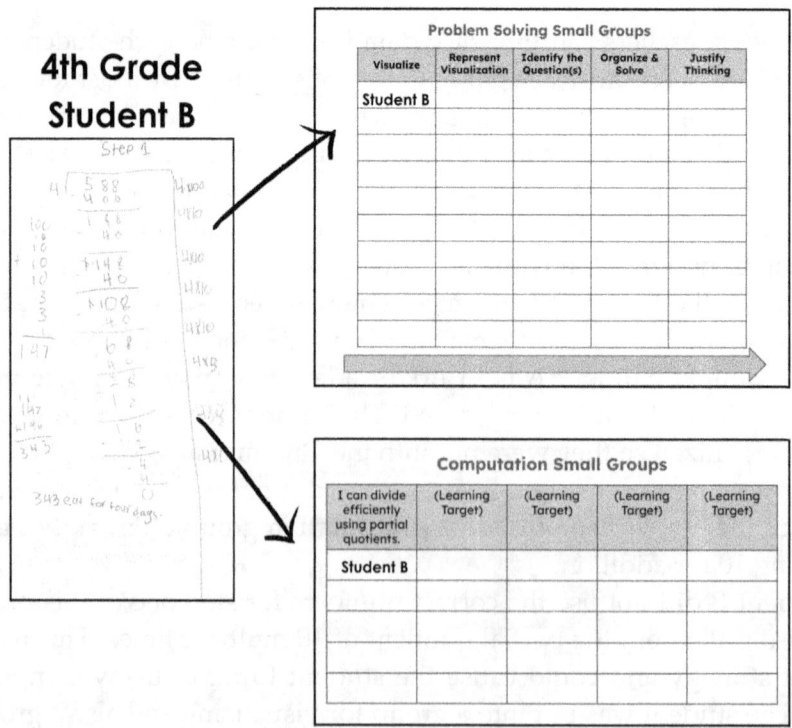

Figure 4.3 Thin-slicing one student at a time: Upper grade example.

This method of sorting students into groups would be used for each student. Some students may end up in only one group or not in a group at all. The students who mastered the given task can be given extension projects to work on during their learning station time to continue to grow in their application of the concept. The teacher could confer with those students between small groups to ensure they are on the right track.

Analyze a Large Group of Students in Real Time

Recently, I was working with a campus, and an instructional coach named Alyssa Durand came up with another way to partner with teachers regarding the progression and quickly name where every student in the class is within the phases of the progression.

- Preparation: Have chart paper ready to model the example. Ten slides are created, two for each part of the progression, to show the anchor chart and the problem being modeled. This is followed by another slide with the anchor chart again and a problem for the students to try.
- Step 1: Half of the class brings their journal to the carpet, and half of the class works on their learning station independently.
- Step 2: The teacher chooses one lesson from each progression phase to demonstrate and observe student behaviors.
- Step 3: The teacher demos each lesson and watches students work. As each student progresses through the phases, they are dismissed to return to their independent work once they show the need for that instruction phase. Each student is added to the problem solving data tracker for future small-group instruction.
- Step 4: If time allows, the teacher repeats this process with the other half of the class on the same day or the following day to get a current view of each student's progress.

The following second-grade example explains how a teacher might take students through this version of thin-slicing to get a quick view of students' thinking processes.

Second-Grade Example: Visualize Phase
Teacher Demo Problem
Sawyer went on a bike ride and traveled 73 miles in total. After riding for a while, he stopped to rest after 38 miles and again after 11 more miles. How many more miles does Sawyer have left to ride?

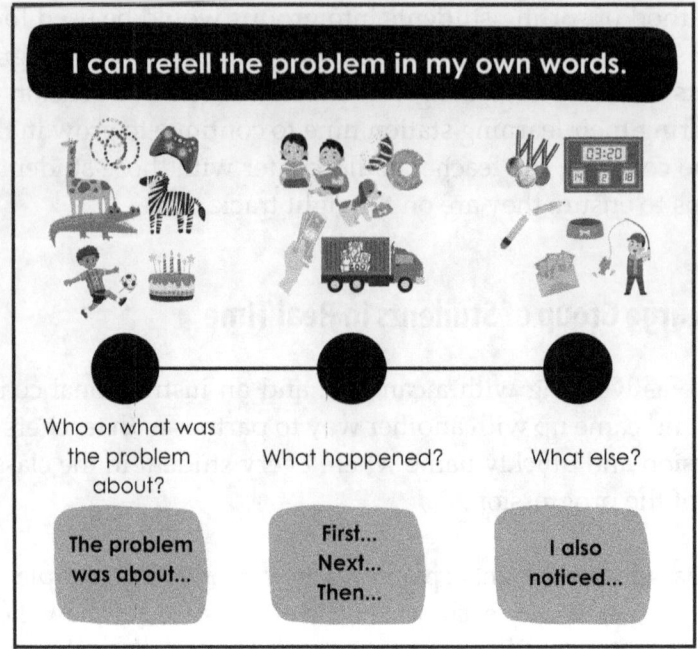

Figure 4.4 Anchor chart.

While the teacher shows the anchor chart and how to use it, they will think aloud as they trace the steps of retelling the problem. *Sawyer went on a bike ride. He got tired after part of it. Then he kept going. He stopped to rest again. He went a total of 73 miles.*

The students will then try retelling using a new problem and the anchor chart.

Student Try It Problem
Adrianna collected 64 pieces of candy in the first hour of Trick or Treating, then 78 pieces in the second hour. She ate 17 pieces on the way home. How many pieces of candy did she have left when she got home?

The teacher will observe students to see if they need additional instruction in the Visualize phase. If students can retell accurately in their own words, they stay at the carpet for the next "level."

If students exhibit the following behaviors, they should be placed in this phase on the data tracker for small-group instruction:

- They can only talk about how they would solve.
- They read the problem out loud or couldn't put it in their own words.
- They didn't know what to do even after coaching from the teacher.

Second-Grade Example: Represent Visualization Phase
Teacher Demo Problem
Sawyer went on a bike ride and traveled 73 miles in total. After riding for a while, he stopped to rest after 38 miles and again after 11 more miles. How many more miles does Sawyer have left to ride?

    The teacher walks through the creation of a part-part-part whole mat with the class as they think aloud. *I'm seeing the distance in my head as a total of 73 miles and broken up into three parts. We know one part is 38 miles. We know another part is 11 miles. Man, he must be tired after all of that riding! But we don't know how many more he needs to go before he is done with this long ride. When we draw out the problem as parts and wholes of the problem, it can help us to know what operation we need to use to solve. As mathematicians, we need to know what the numbers represent so we don't have to remember it and take up thinking space, so we label the numbers with context from the problem.*

73 total miles		
38	11	?
miles until he rested	miles he rode before resting again	miles he has left

The students will then try creating a part-part-whole mat with a new problem as the teacher watches them work.

Student Try It Problem
Adrianna collected 64 pieces of candy in the first hour of Trick or Treating, then 78 pieces in the second hour. She ate 17 pieces on the way home. How many pieces of candy did she have left when she got home?

    The teacher will observe students to see if they need additional instruction at the Represent Visualization phase. If students can create their own part-part-part-whole mat with labels accurately, they stay at the carpet for the next "level."

    If students exhibit the following behaviors, they should be placed in this phase on the data tracker for small-group instruction:

- ◆ They only tried to solve.
- ◆ They did not put the quantities in the correct spots.
- ◆ They could not label with context correctly or at all.

Second-Grade Example: Identify the Question(s) Phase
Teacher Demo Problem
Sawyer went on a bike ride and traveled 73 miles in total. After riding for a while, he stopped to rest after 38 miles and again after 11 more miles. How many more miles does Sawyer have left to ride?

With the remaining students, the teacher will show how to now focus on the question that is being asked in the problem. *As mathematicians, it is so important to pay attention to what the question is asking. If we don't pay close attention, we might accidentally just add all the numbers together, or if we make an error, we wouldn't be able to think about whether it makes sense. See on the anchor chart how the question is highlighted. That might help you focus your attention. I'm just going to point to the question in my problem. One way we can make sure we are answering the right question is to create an answer statement. To do that, we flip the question into a statement like this.*

Sawyer has _____ more miles left to ride.

Student Try It Problem
Adrianna collected 64 pieces of candy in the first hour of Trick or Treating, then 78 pieces in the second hour. She ate 17 pieces on the way home. How many pieces of candy did she have left when she got home?

The teacher will observe students to see if they need additional instruction in the Identify the Question(s) phase. If students can create their own answer statement accurately, they stay at the carpet for the next "level."

If students exhibit the following behaviors, they should be placed in this phase on the data tracker for small-group instruction:

- They only tried to solve.
- They could not create an answer statement.
- They could not create an answer statement in a complete sentence.

Second-Grade Example: Organize and Solve Phase
Teacher Demo Problem
Sawyer went on a bike ride and traveled 73 miles in total. After riding for a while, he stopped to rest after 38 miles and again after 11 more miles. How many more miles does Sawyer have left to ride?

In this phase, the teacher is going to focus on solving and checking to see if the answer is reasonable. *Now we are going to do what you have been excited to do this whole time, SOLVE! As you can see, there is a lot of thinking that has to happen before you get to this phase of problem solving. The thinking and strategies for staying on track help us ensure we are solving for the correct information and that our answer makes sense. As we look at this, our model for the problem we have been working on today, there are a few different ways we could* solve. We could subtract each of the parts from the whole distance of the bike ride, or we could add up the parts that we know Sawyer rode, then subtract them from the total bike ride. I'm going to follow the flow of the story and subtract each part. After I have my answer, I am going to plug it into my answer statement to make sure it makes sense. If my answer ends up being more than 73, that would not make sense because he only went that far. That would signal me to check my work to make sure I did the correct operation for each step and see if I made a computation mistake.

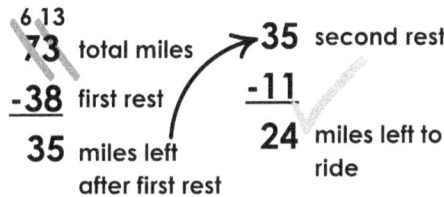

Student Try It Problem
Adrianna collected 64 pieces of candy in the first hour of Trick or Treating, then 78 pieces in the second hour. She ate 17 pieces on the way home. How many pieces of candy did she have left when she got home?

The teacher will observe students to see if they need additional instruction at the Organize & Solve phase. If students can accurately solve in an organized way, they stay at the carpet for the next "level."

If students exhibit the following behaviors, they should be placed in this phase on the data tracker for small-group instruction.

- Their work is unorganized.
- Their answer is unreasonable.
- They could not explain why their answer was reasonable.

If the student had a calculation error, they should be added to a computation group. If their answer was incorrect, but reasonable and organized, they would continue to stay at the carpet.

Second-Grade Example: Justify Thinking Phase
Teacher Demo Problem
Sawyer went on a bike ride and traveled 73 miles in total. After riding for a while, he stopped to rest after 38 miles and again after 11 more miles. How many more miles does Sawyer have left to ride?

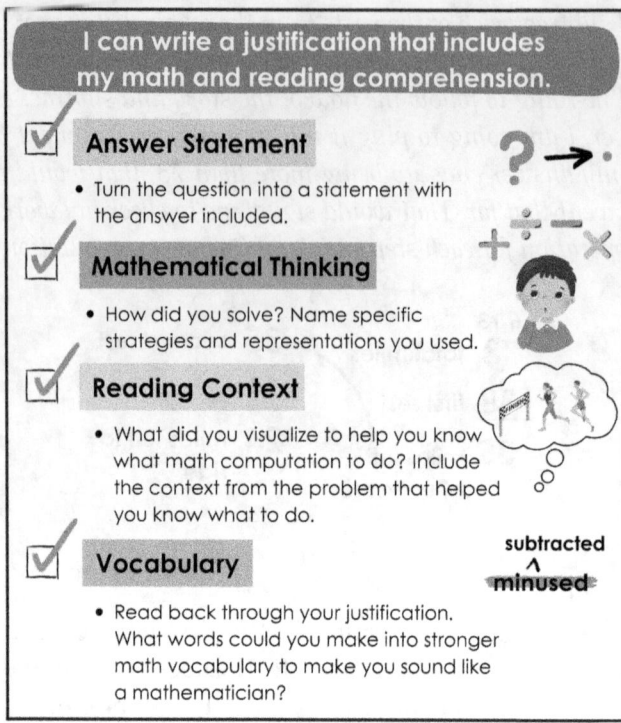

Figure 4.5 Anchor chart.

In this phase, the focus is communication about student thinking. Many students struggle to slow down their thinking and explain how they knew what to do. This is an essential skill for all people to be able to do in life and is part of process standards for all students. *Now that we've solved, we aren't done! We have to be able to defend that our answer is correct. There are four components that make a good justification. I can use this anchor chart to help me ensure that I have all four parts. I already did the first part in my answer statement.*

Write: *Sawyer has 24 miles left to ride.*

Then I need to ensure I am really explaining my math thinking with the reading context as to why I thought I needed to do that math based on what I was visualizing.

Add: *I know my answer is correct because I drew a part-part-part whole mat to show the total miles to ride and the parts of the bike ride where he rested in between. To find out how many miles he had left to ride, I subtracted the number of miles he rode before his first break from the total miles because I knew that would give me how many miles remained in the rest of her ride. Then I subtracted 11 miles from 35 miles to get 24 miles left. To check my work, I also added 38 + 11 + 24 to get 73 total miles. This proves the parts match the whole.*

Finally, I need to make sure I am using high-level math vocabulary. For example, I don't want to use the word "minused" for subtracting.

Student Try It Problem

Adrianna collected 64 pieces of candy in the first hour of Trick or Treating, then 78 pieces in the second hour. She ate 17 pieces on the way home. How many pieces of candy did she have left when she got home?

The teacher will observe students to see if they need additional instruction at the Justify Thinking phase. If students can write a justification with all the components, they could be assigned a project on the concept to complete during their learning station time to extend their learning.

If students exhibit the following behaviors, they should be placed in this phase on the data tracker for small-group instruction.

- They could not write using all the components.
- They struggled to write about their thinking.

Figuring out a system that works for you may take some time. You may try out several ways to document your data before you find the one that fits what you need. There might be different methods that work best at different times of the year, with different groups of kids, or when you are seeking different types of data. Don't be afraid to ask other teachers at your campus, your district, or even online forums to see what other ways are working for other teachers.

Questions and Answers

What if most of my students need the same teach point?

If 50 percent or more of your students need the same teach point, you can teach it to the whole group. That will save time and effort. Sometimes, if it is a difficult skill you want to monitor closely, teaching in small groups is still a better option because you can give targeted feedback and keep a close eye on students as they work.

This seems really time-consuming. When do I have time to do this?

Thin-slicing is a quick glance at data so you can go with your gut about what students need next. The more experience you have with this practice, the faster you will get. If you are expected to take grades, you are already doing this when you are grading papers. As you look over student work, choose one or two questions to analyze. You only need to analyze the amount of data that you have time to respond to. Write down your groups as you go, then you have both done at the same time.

Chapter 4: Reflection

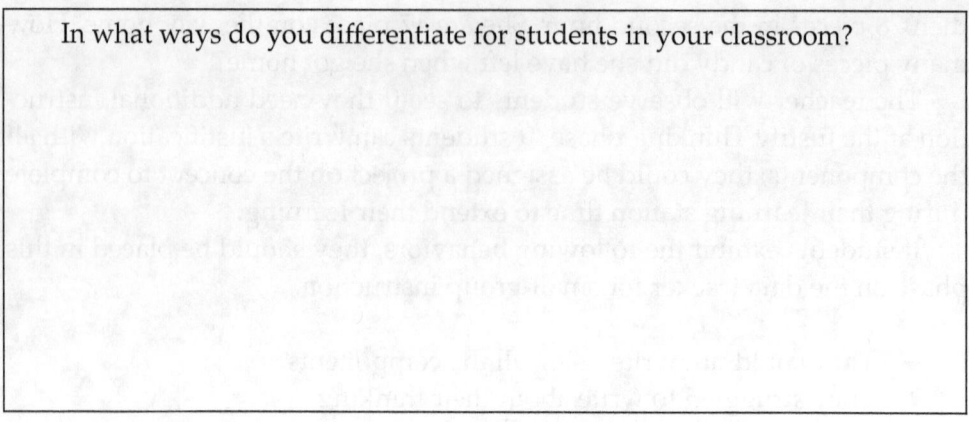

Try out one of the ways to thin-slice data for your students.
   I will try out:

   ◆ Focus on One Teach Point at a Time
   ◆ Analyze Each Piece of Student Work for Multiple Teach Points
   ◆ Analyze a Large Group of Students in Real Time

By _____ (date)

If it seems overwhelming, partner with a colleague or instructional coach. It helps to talk through the behaviors you notice.

References

Cooney Horvath, J. (2019). *Stop talking, start influencing*. Exile Publishing Pty, Ltd.

Gladwell, M. (2007). *Blink: The power of thinking without thinking*. Back Bay Books.

Tomlinson, C. A. (2015). *Teaching for excellence in academically diverse classrooms*. Society, 52(3), 203–209.

5

How Is Small-Group Instruction Implemented in the Classroom?

Every year, I aspire to be a better cook. Cooking meals at home is much better for my family than eating out. I also know that eating the same limited number of meals I have mastered is not what is best for my kids every night, or at least not in their eyes.

Sometimes, the stress of everything else I have going on keeps me from dedicating the time needed to improve. I want to be a great cook, but it will take practice and trial and error. Recently, I was inspired to make a great meal and bought everything needed to make pork chops, rice pilaf, and roasted broccoli. I prepared everything following what the experts told me from the recipe. Waiting anxiously, I thought, "I can do this. It's so easy!" Then, one by one, the components of my dinner were "done." The pork chops were super dry. The rice burned on the bottom of the pan and lacked flavor. The broccoli was just okay. My plan was a bust. I had spent all the money and time, and for what? I could have just stopped at my favorite chicken establishment on the way home for a similarly priced, way better-tasting bag of goodness.

It would be so nice to be able to throw in ingredients and know exactly when something is cooked right, but I am not there yet. With the proper research, practice, and feedback, I will eventually reach my goal.

I used to feel the same way about small-group instruction. I have worked with many educators who agree that small-group instruction is best practice. Knowing exactly what each student needs and providing them with opportunities to learn that are aligned with those needs is the "healthiest option."

DOI: 10.4324/9781003510703-6

I also know many teachers who have done all the preparation, had binders of lessons ready to go, the best intentions, and the initial confidence, but it just didn't click automatically. That is entirely normal and should, in fact, be expected. Wouldn't it be normal for me not to expect to be a gourmet chef early on in my cooking journey? Small-group instruction is the most challenging component of the math workshop to master and will require extensive practice and feedback to succeed.

> Small-group instruction is not merely watching students work on an activity or coaching them through redo work. These examples miss opportunities for meaningful learning to occur. Students need to be taught how to respond to their mistakes or misconceptions. Students should apply their new learning to their redo work independently, and they can do guided practice in collaboration with a peer. Small-group instruction is where new learning takes place in response to what students need that they can apply in future problems.

Creating specific, intentional, short, and meaningful learning experiences can seem overwhelming and require a lot of planning. Like any other complex teaching task, it requires a lot of practice. Mastery will not happen overnight, but if we take it a step at a time, with practice and perseverance, you will improve, and your students will benefit from your hard work!

Setting Up the Right Conditions

You can't just jump into small-group instruction and expect it to go perfectly. There are some conditions to set up to ensure success. Taking the time to go slow in setting up procedures and expectations for students when they are with you and working collaboratively with others will maximize learning time, reduce unwanted behaviors, and make this time manageable for you.

Phase 1: Set up and plan what your other students will be doing while you pull flexible small groups.

While the teacher teaches small-group instruction, the rest of the class must be highly engaged. One way to get much time daily in small groups is to incorporate a math workshop. A traditional math workshop involves daily number sense, a focus lesson, guided math (small-group instruction), learning stations, and share time (Lempp, 2022).

How Is Small-Group Instruction Implemented in the Classroom? ◆ 157

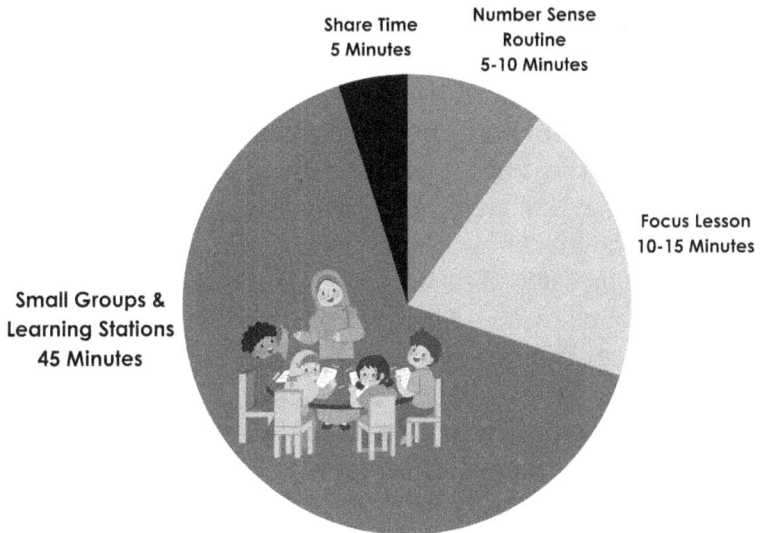

Figure 5.1 Math workshop model.

While some students are learning with you, other students should be engaged in meaningful math practice by accessing learning stations. Meaningful math practice includes hands-on games, independent and collaborative problem solving opportunities, fact-fluency practice using strategies, and working toward student-focused goals.

Students should move in and out of their independent level and instructional level so they can experience success along with challenging work. If students are still solidifying a skill at their instructional level, there should also be a feedback component, so students can tell if they are practicing correctly.

Your expectations must be clear for students, and solid routines will help you manage the classroom during this time. Here are some questions to consider and a few suggestions for each one.

- How will students be grouped? (pairs or triads are best)
- How will stations be organized? (crates, folders, bins)
- How often will students switch stations? (after a certain number of minutes, a new station each day)
- How often will you switch their partners? (as needed based on behavior, once per nine weeks)
- How will you incorporate voice and choice to increase engagement? (multiple stations in their tub to choose from, must-do/can-do chart, choice board, etc.)
- What will students do when they have questions? (ask three students before the teacher, assigned helpers, sticky note to teacher)

- How will students show their work during stations? (on a whiteboard, in their journal, recording sheet)
- How will you plan for a blend of resources? (current and past concepts, goal work, online/offline, hands-on, paper and pencil)
- When students are online, what are the rules? (which apps or websites, how long, how to record work)
- How will students know how to interact with each other? (voice level, coaching each other, interpersonal skills)
- How will hands-on stations be prepped to not become overwhelming? (send them home to volunteers; identify parents that help at school during the day to see if they can assist)
- What will students be expected to do if their partner gets pulled to work with the teacher in a small group? (continue by themselves, work on a different assignment, join a different group)
- Where will students get their supplies? (in a designated part of the room, within each station)

Students must know the expectations so they can make the most of their learning during the amount of time they are in this part of the math workshop. If students don't know what to do or are disengaged during this time, it is a lot of meaningful time lost. If you added up the time that students spend in stations over the course of a year, it would be well over 5,000 minutes if they spent even 30 minutes per day. It has to be strategically planned, but after it gets up and going, students love to collaborate and play games with their peers. It can quickly become their favorite part of the day.

Read more about learning stations or other workshop structures in Jennifer Lempp's book *Math Workshop: Five Steps to Implementing Guided Math, Learning Stations, Reflection, and More.*

> **Phase 2: Keep your whole-group lesson short (and don't teach that lesson again in small groups the same day to students who didn't master the learning).**

If the whole-group lesson goes too long, there is less time to differentiate instruction on essential learning each day. Those minutes add up and take away vital time for students to engage with the material they need in learning stations, math tasks, or with their teacher. Whole-group instruction is intended to meet the needs of most students as an episode of exposure to the content, to understand how to adjust the lesson for the following day, and to intervene for students who are not getting it.

The lesson's length, 10–15 minutes, is intentional because attention is vital to learning. Students must attend for an extended period, and sustained attention develops rapidly from about 5 to 12 years old (Wisniewski, 2024).

Students may not master learning a new concept on the first exposure. It typically takes at least three times of engagement with an idea for learning to occur. Each exposure must include students being engaged with the learning. Each time, it must be deliberate and explicit (Cooney Horvath, 2019).

A separate engagement with learning occurs when students sleep between learning episodes to process and store the information in their long-term memory (Cipeda et al., 2006; Diekelmann & Born, 2010). Using small-group instruction to reteach the same lesson from that day is an ineffective use of instructional time. Distributed practice over several days is more beneficial for processing. If you want to help students who did not understand the whole-group lesson, consider backing up to a prior grade-level standard and teaching a prerequisite skill in small groups.

> *Phase 3: When you start pulling small groups, use lessons already created to give you a starting place.*

Even though lessons may be prepared already, be sure to examine them and the problems you present to students. Work out the problems yourself to anticipate what students might struggle with. Think of ways you can help them avoid those mistakes themselves.

> *Phase 4: Create your own lessons.*

The lessons included in this book are just a starting point to get you moving in the right direction. Considering the diverse needs in your classroom, you can tweak them or use something additional. The key to making small-group instruction easy and less overwhelming is to internalize the structure. Four components make a lesson flow and help with pacing: the introduction, the teach portion, the try it portion, and the send-off. Knowing these components can equip you to quickly pull together a lesson about any skill naturally.

To make learning the most effective, focus the lesson on one specific skill or strategy. When multiple skills are addressed within the same lesson, students will jump between the topics, losing the depth of learning on one topic (Cooney Horvath, 2019). Attention plays a significant role in math problem solving. Being able to focus on one thing will greatly impact the amount of intentional learning that takes place within your small group (Cuder et al., 2023).

When teachers write their own lessons or need to teach in the moment, they can use these moves to guide them.

	Small-Group Lesson Components		
Intro	Link the new lesson to prior learning.	Start with a compliment about a common strength you noticed in their work, and tell them they are ready for the next challenge.	Tell a story that is relevant to their lives to grab their attention.
Teach	Model the skill for students when the learning is new for them.	Use a piece of another student's work to show what the new skill looks like.	Have students analyze a piece of work with an error. Have them find it, then show them a skill to avoid it.
Try It	Give the student work on which they made errors to try out the new strategy.	Give students a new problem to try it out.	Give students a hands-on matching game or sorting activity to practice the new skill.
Send Off	Give students a mini anchor chart to use as a reminder.	Remind them of the skill and how it will help them as mathematicians.	Give students a specific compliment on something you saw them do well with the new skill.

Intro (1–2 minutes)

The first component is an opener to the lesson. I've seen it called many things, but it's key to setting up students' brains to hear what teachers are about to present for students to learn. This is not a time to ask students questions for them to respond. That can make this part last much too long and get the lesson off to a distracted start. Feel free to give them a prompt to visualize or think about something. This is just not a time for them to share. There are a few different moves that can be made here.

Link to Prior Learning

When you can ground new content in something students already know about, you make it attainable and less scary. This strategy activates schema (information students already know) so students see the learning as relevant to them. You get the brain to start retrieving what the students know about the topic so they can expand their thinking attached to what they already know. This makes the learning more likely to stick. When students feel learning is relevant, they are more likely to activate selective attention or focus on the current task while tuning out distractions (Wisniewski, 2024).

Common Compliment

Another intentional move is to compliment students on a common strength. When students have a lot of growth that needs to occur, this builds their confidence and helps them continue the behaviors that they are doing well so they don't lose them. Oftentimes, they aren't aware of the moves they are making, so it helps to name them and call them out as things that good mathematicians do. I started this work when working on math conferring with teachers, and I noticed that whenever a student received a compliment, their body language changed. They sat up straighter, and they started to smile. Then, their motivation would visibly improve. So I needed to know why. A part of the brain called the striatum is responsible for reward-related processing and is linked to dopamine functioning. Rewards shape human behavior and enhance learning and motivation to replicate the behavior. When compliments are given to a student by a teacher, this social interaction sends signals to the striatum, which evaluates it and assigns a high value to the interaction (Bhanji & Delgado, 2014; Grill et al., 2021; Sugawara et al., 2012).

Not all compliments are equal. There is an art to giving compliments. They must be authentically specific and emphasize process rather than ability. This language is not natural to use. The more you practice it, the easier it becomes.

Example Language to Use

- I noticed something in your work that only amazing mathematicians do. (Explain in detail what you noticed.)
- You guys are the kind of mathematicians who …
- I noticed something in your work that shows you're thinking like a real mathematician. (Explain in detail what you noticed.) I want you to continue doing that.
- You're the kind of mathematician who doesn't give up when things get tricky. That's amazing!
- Wow, you're solving problems like mathematicians! Let me show you what I mean.
- I can tell you've been working hard on (specific skill), just like expert problem-solvers do!
- You're showing the kind of creativity and perseverance mathematicians need to tackle big challenges. When you (Describe your specific noticing of their creativity and perseverance and how it will help them to solve other complex problems.)

- Mathematicians like you are always finding new ways to think about problems. That's exactly what you did here!
- Your work reminds me of the way mathematicians …

At the end of a compliment, it is helpful to tell students what that behavior you noticed will do for them. A great structure for this is a Value-Value Potential statement. Telling students to continue what they are doing well is crucial for repetition (Kee et al., 2010).

Value: Acknowledge something positive about the individual or their work that good mathematicians do.

Value Potential: Highlight the impact it will have on their learning if they continue doing the named behavior.

For example, if I have a group of students who have only solved the first step of a problem, they all solved that part correctly but did not go back into the problem to see there was more to do.

Value: "I can tell you've been working hard on representing the problem with a model, just like expert problem-solvers do! You each had a representation of what you saw in your mind for this problem." (Have students point to where they did that skill in their work, so I know they understand what I want them to continue doing.)

Value Potential: "When you represent the problem, it helps you understand what is going on and makes the relationship within the problem visible. If you continue doing this, you will be able to understand problems more and more as they get more difficult."

Then, I would show them how to write an answer statement or set up a workspace to help them use the skill of representing for both steps, reiterating that this skill will help them even further as they grow to use it even better.

Learn more about compliments in the math classroom in an article I wrote on Edutopia: https://www.edutopia.org/article/benefits-praising-students-math-class

Tell a Story

Something is to be said about telling a story that grabs people's attention and keeps them engaged. Oftentimes, students need to feel something is relevant to them personally or to their learning to be able to pay attention (Wisniewski, 2024). This reminds me of a time I wrote a lesson about being organized, where I showed students a picture of a messy closet. I told students that my closet looked like that when I was getting ready, and I ended up being late for work. I asked them if their closet had ever looked like that. They were immediately involved with connection. I asked them how it made them feel. Their responses were so insightful: "anxious," "frustrated," and "I wouldn't be able to find anything I need!" I told them that organizing their work is like organizing your closet. "You can find everything you need, and it keeps you from getting frustrated and anxious when you are organized." From then on, we giggled about their "math closet." They made an authentic connection to something in their life and how taking the time to be organized can make them more successful mathematicians.

Teach (4–6 minutes)

The key to keeping this component short and sweet is having one very targeted teach point. Say the teach point multiple times throughout the teach component and use academic vocabulary. This will help students be very clear about where their focus should be. Many lessons do not require students to solve. This will probably be new for them. Remind them of the importance of the process and the habits they create by not focusing solely on getting the answer.

Example Language to Use

- You are ready for…
- I have a challenge for you… Are you ready?
- You've got the skills to tackle this!
- I can't wait to see how you approach this!
- I know you can handle this next step!
- Let's try something new together!
- You're going to grow so much from this challenge!
- This is going to push you, but I know you're up for it!
- You're ready to take this to the next level!
- You've already built a strong foundation—now let's build on it!

Explicit Demonstration

When students are learning something very new to them, it is important for them to understand how to use it, when to use it, and why to use it. We have to be very careful in demonstrating that we are not just having students mimic our behavior or follow a set of steps without thinking about why. Students still need to apply what they have learned when they try it out in new situations.

Always have something students can refer back to as they are learning. That way, students don't have to hold that information in their working memory when they try to use the strategy on a new problem. One consideration is whether the students need access to the whole visual for that specific lesson. You should hide parts of anchor charts that students won't need because it can distract from the intended learning (Ashman et al., 2020).

Worked Example

A worked example is another visual that could be used to teach a skill. This impact is noted in the worked example effect from cognitive load theory. The worked example effect is when students are shown a worked-out example of what is expected. This is a highly effective strategy because it reduces the number of elements to be processed compared to having to solve the problem from the beginning. This method reduces the cognitive load (amount of information to process) so students can understand more easily and not have to remember all the contents of the problem as they try out the new strategy (Ashman et al., 2020; Sweller, 2011). Not only does it reduce the load on the working memory, it also makes the lesson go much quicker.

An effective way to use this type of teach component is to collect exemplar pieces of work from students throughout the school year to use as your worked examples. It is a good idea to ask the student who completed the worked example if you can use their work to teach others. Usually, students see this as a compliment and are happy for teachers to share their work.

Error Analysis

This method allows for an inquiry approach. Students search for a misconception or mistake in a piece of work. Then they draw conclusions about it in discussion with the teacher and other students in the group. It is helpful to have prompts for students to see while they quietly find the error, so everyone can use the amount of time they need. Show the students these steps.

ERROR ANALYSIS

1. Find an error in this piece of work.

2. Once you find it, think about why the student might have made this mistake.

3. Then think about what the student could do differently next time to avoid this mistake.

4. If you think it was a misunderstanding, what do you think this student needs to learn about to be able to fix up their understanding?

Unlike the worked examples, error analysis should not be performed on other students' work. This would hurt your math community to show a student's mistakes to others. These can be created by the teacher to emphasize a specific misconception or mistake commonly seen in the work of the students in the group. Looking at the work of others is less intimidating than finding their own mistakes, but once they do it and talk openly about it with the group, it is impactful to then go into a piece of their own work to identify and correct the mistake noticed in the error analysis.

Other Considerations

During small-group instruction, students can view it as a competition with the other few students to get the answer first. Every student needs to be given the opportunity to think and process. Adding in some simple accountability moves can help students understand that they all need time to think and that shouting out an answer can steal the opportunity to learn and process from others.

One example is for students to give a simple thumbs up when they have an idea or answer. Another is to ask students to look up at you when they are ready to move on. A third strategy involves giving students a green and a red card. They can show the green card when they are ready and the red card if they are not ready. Make sure to verbally celebrate students who give thorough responses or for perseverance. This creates a culture of responsibility for their own learning and the learning of others.

Try It Out (4–6 minutes)

This component may be the most difficult for the teacher. Teachers need to take on the role of a curious cheerleader, asking questions to put thinking back on students and cheering them on as mathematicians. This section of the lesson aims for students to try something new in a safe place while thinking for themselves. One of the ways teachers can get students to think for themselves is through implementing wait time. Wait time, also known as "think time," allows students time to process and create a thorough response to a question or task the teacher poses. Students need 3–5 seconds of wait time after being asked a question to formulate a response, and even more than that to try out something new. Sitting and being quiet while watching students work is so uncomfortable, but it is the key. This is when students can practice monitoring their thinking while trying out a new skill. They learn to rely on themselves instead of the teacher to remind them of all the tools and strategies they have acquired. You will learn more about wait time in Chapter 6.

The teacher needs to create space for students to think and struggle, so they truly know what each student needs next. Do they need to move on to the next phase of the progression? Do they need to experience a lesson with this teach point again? Do they need something else altogether? If you help them complete it or ask leading questions, students will not be able to apply it on their own when they are not with you.

Example Language to Use

- Try rereading to see if you can figure it out.
- Look at our example and the anchor chart to remind yourself what we did.
- What could you try first?
- What's something you can try before asking for help?
- What makes sense to you so far?
- Can you explain your thinking to me?

New Strategy on Student's Own Work

This one is my favorite to use with students in all grade levels. Using a problem on which the student made errors is such a powerful move. It helps to get buy-in from students for the strategy you taught them. They can immediately see the value, it builds confidence that they will know what to do next time to avoid the mistake, and they can see how relevant the learning is to them specifically. Similar to using a worked example, using a problem students have already experienced makes the lesson progress faster because they already have background knowledge of the problem and can focus on the isolated skill you are teaching (Ashman et al., 2020; Sweller, 2011).

New Problem

Have a new problem for students to try out the new skill. The problem should have a different structure to ensure that students think and apply the skill. They should be able to justify their thinking process. If you need to use a new problem, it might take longer for them to complete. During this time, getting up to go confer with other students as they work could be a good use of the extra time.

Sort or Other Interactive Option

Using a sort where students can see problems and match a correct option with them can provide a scaffold as a first attempt at the lesson. Sometimes students are not quite confident enough to try out the new skill on their own yet. Let's say a lesson is about choosing a representation to match what they are visualizing. There could be a few problems with several different completed representations with the numbers from the problem and they could then think about which one makes the most sense to them instead of having to create their own representation before they are ready. They could then copy that representation as practice. The next time they do the lesson, they would be more confident to attempt it on their own.

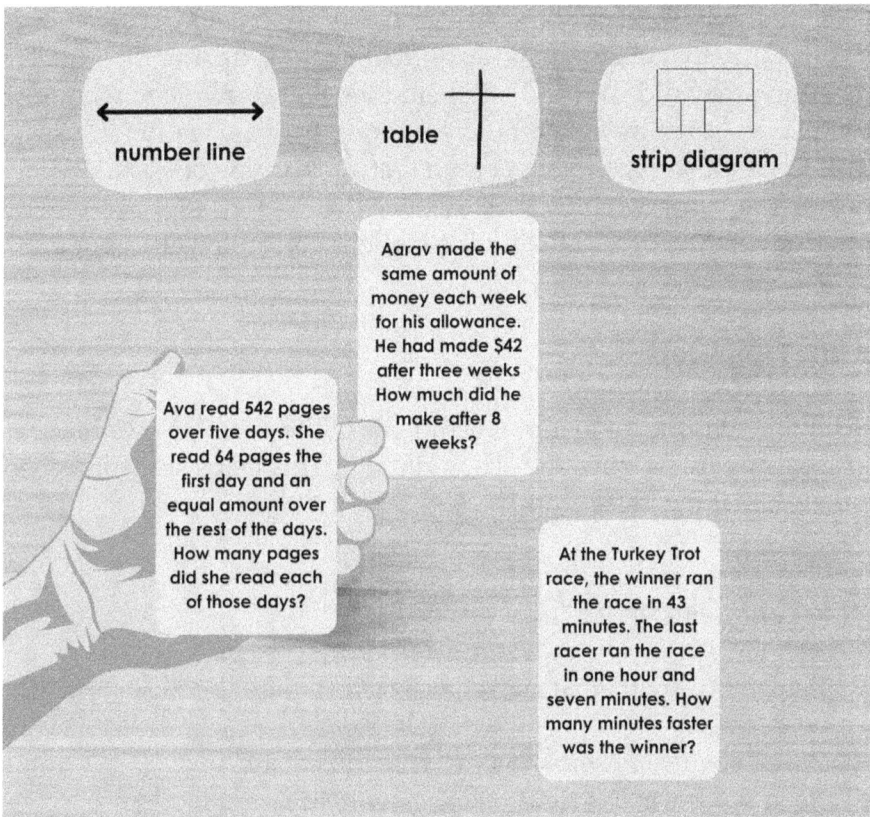

Figure 5.2 Example sort for Try it component of a lesson.

Another interactive option during the Try it component is to use it as an opportunity to introduce or practice a station using the new strategy. This practice can help ensure that students know how to practice the station correctly when you are not beside them. They could practice using sentence stems, collaboration, and game rules while recognizing pitfalls.

It is helpful to see if students know when to use a strategy and also when it would not be beneficial. This allows the student to have multiple opportunities in a short time to think about using the new strategy learned.

Other Considerations

If students start to make mistakes that are unrelated to the teach point, it will take everything inside you to do it, but *do not* address the mistake unless it directly impacts what they are trying to practice. For example, if the lesson is about using a graphic organizer to have organized work, and they do not regroup correctly while subtracting, tell them what a great job they did while using the graphic organizer and send them on their way. Their calculation misconception had nothing to do with their organized work. What you *can* do is make a note about it and put them in a group for subtraction with regrouping.

If you realize that the lesson is too difficult for a student, compliment them on something they did well and tell them they will continue to work toward this with you. Assign them to a different group they are ready for. Assigning students to the wrong group happens. It is still a learning opportunity for you and them. You can get more clarity about what they need when they work right in front of you, especially if it is a student you are unsure about.

Send Off (1 minute)

This component is meant to remind students of the skill they learned and the importance of why or when they should use it. This helps students reflect on what they are taking away from the lesson.

Example Language to Use

- Remember, mathematicians (insert teach point) because (how it helps them).
- When you use (insert strategy) you will be able to …
- As you solve problems, you can (insert strategy) to …

Mini Anchor Chart
Print your anchor charts four to a page and give each student one as they leave the lesson. There may even be specific students who need this more than others. I have seen teachers put a sheet protector with cardstock, in students' math folders, so students can tape anchor charts to it for easy access. Students could also have a dedicated section of their math journal for gluing these charts as references.

If the anchor chart is related to a student's current goal, they could attach it to their desk to remind them as they work to master it.

Verbal Reminder or Note
A verbal reminder or a simple note can be an effective way to close out the lesson. Sticky notes in fun shapes can be a fun token for students to save and use as a future reminder of what they learned.

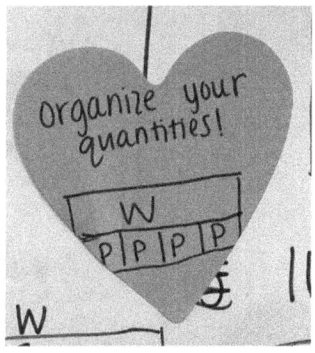 

Figure 5.3 Example note to use for Send-off component of a lesson.

Another option could be a label that the student or teacher could put on the student's next assessment, so they use the strategy soon. This allows the teacher to check back in on the student's independent understanding of the skill. See more about this in Chapter 7.

Specific Compliment
Use the guidance from earlier in this chapter to give meaningful compliments. When compliments are given as the send-off, they must be linked to what the student did during the Try it portion. Tell students what they did well during that time that will support them in using the new skill as a mathematician.

Other Considerations
When students leave the group, don't forget to take some notes about what learning they might need next. Here is an example of a data tracker that could be used to record student behaviors and progress.

Anecdotal Notes Page to be Used During Small-Group Instruction

Date and Learning Target	Student Names	Anecdotal Notes

Date and Learning Target	Student Names	Anecdotal Notes

Dismiss students as they complete the Try it component. They should not wait for all students to finish. This allows students who are still working to remain focused without the pressure of other students watching them, and the ones who have completed their work to go back to meaningful work in learning stations.

Small-Group Instruction Recap
Powerful reminders that make a difference: • Anticipate misconceptions before the lesson. • Build in some accountability moves to ensure all students participate. • Keep the lesson in context. Avoid straight computation. • Have students build on each other's thinking. It doesn't only have to be you. • Keep the lesson targeted and to the point. • Refrain from correcting mistakes unrelated to the teach point. Just make notes on what students need next. • Dismiss students as they finish. Send them off with a reminder of the skill they learned. • Refer students to the anchor chart or worked problem for support instead of relying on you. • Give students as much wait time as they need. Get up and walk around as students work or sip water to keep you from helping them too early. There is more about wait time in Chapter 6. • The lesson should be at the instructional level. The lesson should not be too easy or too difficult. If it seems too difficult, dismiss the student with a compliment and make notes to adjust to another teach point.

> - Walk around to confer with other students while small-group students work independently to maximize small-group time and implement more wait time.
> - Using a problem that students are familiar with in the Try it component can keep the focus on the teach point because they already have prior knowledge. It can also get buy-in from students on using the strategy.
> - Small-group instruction is two-way communication. You are teaching them something and gaining information on where to go next.

Use this table tent as a reminder from this chapter.

Small Group Instruction Components					
Intro	Link the new lesson to prior learning.	Start with a common compliment you noticed in their work, and tell them they are ready for the next challenge.	Tell a story that is relevant to their lives to grab their attention.	1-2 min	Keep the lesson targeted and short.
Teach	Model the skill for students when the learning is new for them.	Use a piece of another student's work to show what the new skill looks like.	Have students analyze a piece of work with an error. Have them find it, then show them a skill to avoid it.	4-6 min	
Try It	Give students their work back that they messed up on to try out the new strategy.	Give students a new problem to try it out.	Give students a hands-on matching game or sorting activity to practice the new skill.	4-6 min	
Send Off	Give students a mini anchor chart to use as a reminder.	Remind them of the skill and how it will help them as mathematicians.	Give students a specific compliment on something you saw them do well with the new skill.	1 min	

- -

- Try rereading to see if you can figure it out.
- Can you draw a picture of what you are visualizing?
- Who are the characters? What are they doing? What happened throughout the story?
- Can you find all of the steps and set up a workspace for each one?
- What kind of representation could you use that matches what you are visualizing to help you solve?
- What do these numbers represent? Be sure to label them so it matches the problem.
- How do you know your answer is correct? Does it answer the question/s?
- Can you defend or prove your answer with another strategy?
- Does your justification include the context of the problem and connect it to the math?
- Did you write about how you used the context to know what to do?
- Is your explanation clear and organized? Could someone read it and know exactly what you are trying to say?
- Can you write what you just said?

- -

Figure 5.4 Table tent for tips on small-group instruction.

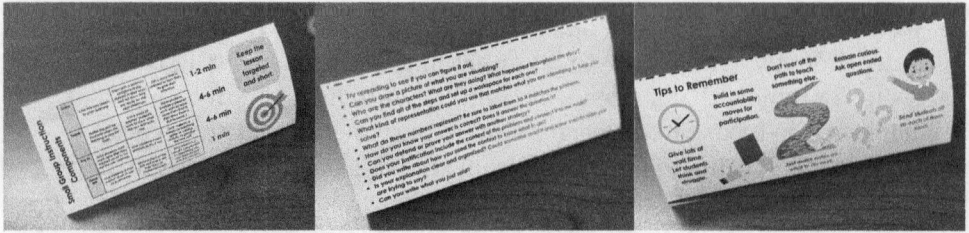

Figure 5.5 Photo of table tent in use.

There was a lot packed into this chapter about small-group instruction. Remember, you will not be a master at this overnight, just like I still practice my cooking skills. Take small steps.

- At first, you could just use the lessons provided in this book.
- Once you are ready to create your own lessons, use the Small Group Instruction Components printable as a guide. Choose one option to try for each of the components: Intro, Teach, Try it, and Send off. Master delivery of those before moving on to the other options.
- Try out the lessons with just a couple of students at first to get your feet wet.
- Do not spend hours prepping lessons. Keep it simple. You need a problem for the teach portion and one for them to try it out (Remember, this can be one that they have already done.) You can even use the same problems for different teach points with different students.
- Give yourself grace. Small-group instruction will never look perfect and go exactly as you planned. Learning is messy and beautiful.

Questions and Answers

If my students don't master the content of the whole-group lesson, won't this cause them to grow further and further behind?

Sometimes, students need more time to practice a concept before it clicks. Because a concept is taught over many days, students might get it after another exposure to it the next day. You might notice that students have gaps that prevent them from mastering the current concept. That is even more of a reason to have more time for small-group instruction. Some students may need to learn prerequisite skills to access the current level of a concept. Giving a formative assessment in the middle of the current concept can help you target specific needs for student understanding so that small groups can be held on current learning before a summative assessment occurs. Students who can access the learning in the whole-group lesson should not have to sit and wait longer for other students. Learning stations allow everyone to maintain a high level of engagement and needed practice with prior and current concepts.

Can I have a small group as a rotation in my stations so I can meet with each student for the same amount of time each week?

Meeting with students for the same amount of time provides your students with equality. Students deserve equity. Equity happens when each student is receiving what they need. That might mean you don't meet with specific students in small groups some weeks. Providing an activity that will still challenge and grow that student is okay. Each student will likely need at least one of the teaching points within the progression. Groups should be created with data and an action that will grow every student. There is an exception. When primary school students are just learning how to be students in school, flexible groups might be too much. Once procedures are solidly in place, teachers should transition to flexible groups promptly.

If I keep the lessons short, I will need even more lessons. What are some ways to prepare that easily?

As you grow in experience with the content and the learning targets, the lessons will take less and less brain power for you to create. Pinpointing what students need becomes easier if you know the standards deeply. Because teachers should only talk for a short part of the lesson and then refer students back to the problem and anchor charts to think, there is not much to plan for each lesson, so don't let it intimidate you. This part of the math workshop is the most important for student growth. If lessons are provided for whole-group instruction, planning time can be used for small-group instruction. Consider sharing the preparation with your team. If anyone creates a lesson, you can keep it in a shared drive for easy access for everyone. Generating problems can be made simpler by using an artificial intelligence program. You can just type in the problem structure you want with the exact parameters and how many you need. For example, "Generate 10 to 20 one-step comparing problems." Then, sift through them to find the ones you like.

Can I use the Gradual Release model or "I do, We do, You do" during small-group instruction?

In math, we must be mindful when using this model that students are not just mimicking the teacher without knowing the why and how to apply it across multiple situations. When students mimic, they can typically replicate the strategy on problems just like the one presented, but not in new situations. Students should not all solve the same way and think the same way. We are trying to develop their problem solving skills and how to think for themselves. One way to examine this practice is to present your students with a problem to solve. When you look through their student work, does it all look the same? You should see various models and strategies to know if students are thinking for themselves and if they have various tools to apply and justify their thinking.

We don't do math workshop in my district. What other ways can I implement small-group instruction?

First, is it a firm requirement that you do not do a workshop model? If you can't, are there other times throughout your instructional day that differentiation occurs? Some districts or schools have a set time in the school day called WIN time (What I Need) or I&E time (intervention and enrichment). Small-group instruction is perfect during this time as well. If these are not options, partner with your instructional coach or campus administration to brainstorm what might work. It might help to take data with you to show the need for differentiation and a plan for what you think would work best for your campus or classroom.

How do I know if students are doing meaningful work during stations? How can I monitor them?

This is where it's essential to let go of some control. Students need to feel empowered to own their learning. You can make many strategic moves to ensure this time is meaningful.

1. Feedback: You can ensure stations have feedback to see if their answers are correct or incorrect to ensure they practice correctly. This could be a QR code with the answers they can check, access to a calculator, partners checking each other's work, or an answer key available in the station. You could even have a way for students to watch a video on the strategy from the station or a structure to let you know if they are struggling with a concept so they don't keep practicing incorrectly.

2. Accountability: Students could have work to turn in or be checked by each other to create accountability for their learning. This could be a reflection sheet or journal work.
3. Technology: You can use apps to monitor what students are doing on their computers from your small group. Technology options also give the students feedback on whether they are doing well or adjusting to their needs. Most programs have a way for teachers to monitor their progress.
4. Have explicit expectations and actively monitoring during this time is key. Once you dismiss students to stations and call your first group, take a lap around the room to ensure students are getting started right away and compliment the behaviors you want to see. During your small groups while students are trying out the new skill, make another quick pass through the room to ensure students are still on task. If there are students who are being disruptive, you can have a paper and pencil assignment for them to complete at their desk as an alternative to working collaboratively with other students. They can try again the following day to follow the expectations for learning stations.

Why isn't there daily problem solving listed in the workshop model?

Daily problem solving that is led by the teacher is not included in the math workshop. Students should be doing problem solving within stations collaboratively or independently. This allows the teacher to respond to more students in small-group instruction. One way to incorporate daily problem solving is to give students a problem to complete as they leave the focus lesson to go to stations. This gives them daily practice, allows them to use the time they need, and allows them to check in with others to justify their answer. These problems should visit concepts already taught as a form of spaced retrieval. Learn more about retrieval practice in Chapter 7.

Can I create small groups from my exit tickets?

Exit tickets are a great tool to inform what to do for the whole-group lesson the following day. Students need to sleep in between learning episodes so that their brains can consolidate the learning before a new exposure (Cipeda et al., 2006; Diekelmann & Born, 2010). Small-group instruction should prioritize responding to what students need from their independent assessments on the most important skills they need to master before the end of the year.

Chapter 5: Reflection

Time your whole-group lesson to see how close it is to 10–15 minutes. You might video it so you can see which parts take the longest. Come back to write your time here and reflect on how you will adjust to make it shorter to allow for maximum time pulling flexible small groups.

Whole-group lesson time: _____

If your lesson went beyond 15 minutes, what part took the longest? Why?

How could you adjust your next lesson to keep it to the allotted time?

Sometimes, the scariest part is jumping in and trying it out. Choose a small-group lesson and deliver it to students. Come back here and reflect.

What went well in your lesson?

What do you want to do differently next time?

What did you learn about students that you didn't know before?

Do it again tomorrow. You've got this!

References

Ashman, G., Kalyuga, S., & Sweller, J. (2020). Problem-solving or explicit instruction: Which should go first when element interactivity is high? *Educational Psychology Review, 32*, 229–247. https://doi.org/10.1007/s10648-019-09500-5

Bhanji, J. P., & Delgado, M. R. (2014). The social brain and reward: social information processing in the human striatum. *WIREs Cognitive Science, 5*, 61–73.

Cepeda, N. J., Pashler, H., Vul, E., Wixted, J. T., & Rohrer, D. (2006). Distributed practice in verbal recall tasks: A review and quantitative synthesis. *Psychological Bulletin, 132*(3), 354–380. https://doi.org/10.1037/0033-2909.132.3.354

Cooney Horvath, J. (2019). *Stop talking, start influencing*. Exile Publishing Pty, Ltd.

Cuder, A., Zivkovic, M., Doz, E., Pellizzoni, S., & Passolunghi, M. C. (2023). The relationship between math anxiety and math performance: The moderating role of visuospatial working memory. *Journal of Experimental Child Psychology, 233*. https://doi.org/10.1016/j.jecp.2023.105688

Diekelmann, S., & Born, J. (2010). The memory function of sleep. *Nature Reviews Neuroscience, 11*, 114–126. https://doi.org/10.1038/nrn2762

Grill, F., Nyberg, L., & Reickmann, A. (2021). Neural correlates of reward processing: Functional dissociation of two components within the ventral striatum. *Brain and Behavior, 11*, 1–12. https://doi.org/10.1002/brb3.1987

Kee, K. M., Anderson, K. A., Dearing, V. S., Harris, E., & Shuster, F. A. (2010), *Results coaching: The new essential for school leaders*. Corwin.

Lempp, J. (2022). *Math workshop: Five steps to implementing guided math, learning stations, reflection, and more*. Heinemann.

Sugawara, D., Tanaka, M., Okazaki, R., Watanabe, K., & Sadato, N. (2012). Neural correlates of social praise: The striatum as a key structure of social reward processing. *PLOS ONE, 7*(6), e41207. https://doi.org/10.1371/journal.pone.0041207

Sweller, J. (2011). Cognitive load theory. *Psychology of Learning and Motivation, 55*, 37–76.

Wisniewski, R. (2024). *Promoting student attention: How to understand, assess, and create conditions for attention*. ASCD.

6

What Strategies Can I Use to Foster Productive Struggle in My Students?

Imagine you are on your way to a new restaurant. You plug the address into your phone. Every time you have to make a turn, your speakers tell you what move you are about to make and even which lane to be in. You also have a watch that buzzes as you approach to remind you to take the turn. A wreck occurs on the route, but you don't even know that because your phone has redirected you around it to get you to your destination. You are thinking about your grocery list, what conversations happened that day, and what you will wear next week for picture day. You didn't have to think about the task at hand actively, and you effortlessly arrived at the new restaurant.

Now imagine students at the small-group table or meeting with their teacher on the carpet. They start a new problem, and every time they get to a challenging part, the teacher alerts the student that there is a tricky part coming. Then, the student gets to another challenge and looks to the teacher for guidance. The teacher says, "What does it say about how many are in each bag?" The student gets back to work and makes a computation error. The teacher says, "Remember, when we have a smaller number on top in the ones place, we have to regroup." The student then gets to the end, and the teacher believes the student can do it now because they got the answer correct.

The teacher did a lot of the thinking for the student. Just like the driver would not remember how to get back to the new restaurant without the support of the navigation app, the student would not be able to get through a complex problem without support.

Instead of creating a safe space for students to make mistakes and giving thinking prompts, the students remained at low-level thinking, not having to monitor their comprehension or learn ways to get themselves out of misunderstanding.

What Is Productive Struggle?

Productive struggle is essential within mathematics and throughout life. Its presence is necessary for self-efficacy to exist. So, let's define it. The book *Productive Math Struggle* defines it as "purposefully reacting to an unclear challenge so that progress is made or learning advanced" (Sangiovanni et al., 2020). When learning gets really difficult, students choose to stay with the task and try to solve it.

When students learn to get past challenges through thinking and persevering, learning can then be applied to new situations, eliminating the need for directions to be given at every turn.

The National Council of Teachers of Mathematics (NCTM) book *Principles to Actions* (2014) names eight research-based, highly effective instructional strategies.

1. Establish Mathematics Goals to Focus Learning
2. Implement Tasks That Promote Reasoning and Problem Solving
3. Use and Connect Mathematical Representations
4. Facilitate Meaningful Mathematical Discourse
5. Pose Purposeful Questions
6. Build Procedural Fluency from Conceptual Understanding
7. Support Productive Struggle in Learning Mathematics
8. Elicit and Use Evidence of Student Thinking

Although the NCTM acknowledges productive struggle as one of the most impactful teaching practices, it is not explicitly stated and explained within process standards that states have listed for teachers to follow. It is presented as shown in the following examples:

- **Common Core**
  Mathematical Practice 1 – Make sense of problems and persevere in solving them.
    Mathematically proficient students start by explaining to themselves the meaning of a problem and looking for entry points to its solution. They

analyze givens, constraints, relationships, and goals. They make conjectures about the form and meaning of the solution and plan a solution pathway rather than simply jumping into a solution attempt. They consider analogous problems, and try special cases and simpler forms of the original problem in order to gain insight into its solution. They monitor and evaluate their progress and change course if necessary. Older students might, depending on the context of the problem, transform algebraic expressions or change the viewing window on their graphing calculator to get the information they need. Mathematically proficient students can explain correspondences between equations, verbal descriptions, tables, and graphs or draw diagrams of important features and relationships, graph data, and search for regularity or trends. Younger students might rely on using concrete objects or pictures to help conceptualize and solve a problem. Mathematically proficient students check their answers to problems using a different method, and they continually ask themselves, "Does this make sense?" They can understand the approaches of others to solving complex problems and identify correspondences between different approaches (Common Core State Standards Initiative, 2010).

- **Texas Essential Knowledge and Skills Process Standard B**

    The student uses mathematical processes to acquire and demonstrate mathematical understanding. The student is expected to use a problem solving model that incorporates analyzing given information, formulating a plan or strategy, determining a solution, justifying the solution, and evaluating the problem solving process and the reasonableness of the solution (Texas Education Agency, 2012).

- **Mathematics Standards of Learning for Virginia Public Schools K–12 Mathematical Problem Solving**

    Students will apply mathematical concepts and skills and the relationships among them to solve problem situations of varying complexities. Students also will recognize and create problems from real-world data and situations within and outside mathematics and then apply appropriate strategies to determine acceptable solutions. To accomplish this goal, students will need to develop a repertoire of skills and strategies for solving a variety of problem types. A major goal of the mathematics program is to help students apply mathematics concepts and skills to become mathematical problem solvers (Virginia Department of Education, 2016).

These three examples mention persevering, being problem solvers, or using a problem solving model, but do not explicitly mention productive struggle.

It is so important to understand what productive struggle does for students so we do not "rescue" them when problems present a challenge. So let's take a look at how this practice can be embedded within the math classroom through the actions of teachers and students.

The Power of Mistakes

Telling students it's okay to make mistakes so they will try again is great, but understanding what is happening in their brain when they do can get their buy-in (and yours, too). First, the brain is aware when we make mistakes, even if we aren't. When a mistake is made, there are two different types of reactions the brain can have. There can be an error-related negativity, or ERN, response, which is increased electrical activity when there is a discrepancy between what was solved and the correct answer. The other response is called error positivity, or Pe, which is where there is conscious awareness that there is a mistake and more attention is focused on it. Why is this so important? It means the brain is learning from our mistakes, even if we are not conscious we are making them. The brain is sparking and aware. It is more active when there are mistakes than when there are correct answers. In times of struggle and challenge, the brain grows the most (Boaler, 2016).

Creating Opportunities for Students to Experience Productive Struggle

Classrooms are often set up for students to only experience success. Students may always get work that the teacher knows they have a high chance of getting correct. This may be so that students are happy at school, or even to avoid uncomfortable questions from parents about grades. (Learn more about meaningful grades in Chapter 7.) Having low expectations of students creates a lack of growth.

In addition to *productive* struggle, students can experience *unproductive* struggle. When problems are consistently out of a student's reach, they start to believe they cannot solve problems, which reduces their self-efficacy or their belief they can do math. Many experiences like this can lead students to develop an aversion to math, which can be difficult to recover from.

To avoid unproductive struggle, students need to practice problem solving often with differentiated opportunities. Learning stations are the perfect places for this to occur, but we must be ready to differentiate for students so that problem solving is not too hard or too easy.

Ways to differentiate problems to scaffold include the following:

- Having the same multi-step problem as others, but having smaller numbers
- Giving students one step of a problem at a time, gradually increasing the number of steps you give at one time
- Providing a checklist to remind students of resources they can access
- Including a partially worked example
- Providing a graphic organizer
- Adding an extension question to the problem
- Requiring students to show multiple ways to solve the problem
- Having students write and solve an additional question that goes with the context of the problem
- Partnering students to tackle difficult problems together

Avoid giving students a scaffold until they are at the point of unproductive struggle. We can anticipate what they might need, but wait until they actually need it. This will grow them more and more each time to not need the scaffolds.

Another way this can be described is in the language of independent, instructional, and frustrational levels. Emmett Betts wrote about levels of differentiated guidance for reading instruction in his book *Foundations of Reading Instruction*. These levels very similarly align with math support. He described three levels. The independent level was ideal for recreational or self-directed reading. The instructional level is most effective for learning because it balances challenge with support. The last level he described was the frustrational level, which was described as too difficult and can lead to disengagement or frustration (Betts, 1946).

This is supported by John Sweller's cognitive load theory; when there is too much cognitive demand overwhelming the working memory, it impedes learning (2011). In the same way it was described by Betts for reading, problem solving lessons and other problem solving opportunities need to be at the instructional level where students can practice while experiencing productive struggle, getting themselves unstuck, and learning from mistakes. There has to be a balance present between challenge and support, so students can get comfortable in the uncomfortable and gain self-efficacy as they solve hard problems.

I have recently been reflecting on feedback I have given teachers when observing small-group instruction. I get so excited when lessons go well, and students show they can master new skills they are learning. I'm rethinking my reaction. Think about this. If students can quickly and easily do what we teach in small-group instruction, it's probably not the right teach point for them. Small-group instruction should be at the student's instructional level, not their independent level. The instructional level will include students taking time to think and struggle through it. This is when their brain will grow, and we will actively know what to do with them next because we can see where they may stumble.

Students should have to think deeply and reason about whether they have used new skills correctly and whether their work makes sense. It should not be easy. It should be just out of reach, so they are growing, and it has been proven that they need our support and facilitation. Teachers should not get discouraged if students don't get what they are teaching them right away! It means they are learning something new. Instruction is two-way communication. That's why it is okay to dismiss students who don't get it the first time. Information is gained on where they need to go next. It might be that they need that lesson more than once, or it might be that they need something different altogether. If teachers do find themselves in a position where students struggle to show what they know on an assessment after they thought students would do well, the teacher may have provided too much support throughout the new learning.

There must be ample opportunities for students to experience productive struggle in the math classroom. Providing many ways they can engage with complex problem solving is a way for them to gain the confidence and self-efficacy to be applied in school and in life.

- Math tasks in collaborative groups in a whole-group setting, also known as a task and share structure
- Collaborative problem solving with partners during learning stations
- Providing meaningful open-ended problems on independent work with interleaved concepts. (You will learn more about this in Chapter 7.)

The Secret Ingredient

Over the years, I have often heard some version of this: "They can do it when they are with me! Then, when it comes to an assessment, they can't!" This is so often true, but what causes it? Teachers are some of the most caring and supportive people who exist. That is, ironically, one of the issues. As teachers, we have this innate pull to care for students. We want them to love school and be happy and successful. Sometimes, we don't want to watch students struggle, so we jump in to save them before they can experience negative feelings. This action harms learning. John Hattie is an educational researcher who identifies the level of impact that factors have on student learning and achievement. Throughout his work, he has noted that teaching strategies with an effect size above 0.4 are considered above average and worth implementing because they are likely to lead to meaningful gains in student achievement. Teacher–student dependency harms learning at an effect size of –0.24 (Visible Learning MetaX, n.d.). When students are overly dependent on their teacher, it no longer benefits their learning and has a negative impact. We have to instill confidence in students to know they can learn and persevere through mistakes and obstacles when they are learning.

An additional component must be present for productive struggle to occur in the classroom. Without it, the hard work teachers put in every day is exponentially less successful. What is this component?

The answer is wait time.

Research shows that teachers and students experience many learning benefits when proper wait time is provided (IRIS Center, 2018; Takayoshi & Van Ittersum, 2018). Some of those benefits include the following:

- It reduces the number of responses of "I don't know."
- It creates accountability for all students to formulate a response.
- More extended responses can be attained instead of one-word answers.
- An increase in scores on assessments has been found.
- Increased participation from striving learners was noticed.
- Students develop confidence and have less reliance on the teacher.

Here are some tips for implementing wait time because it can feel uncomfortable.

- Create a habit of counting in your head to allow for 3–5 seconds or reading of students' body language. If they are still thinking and working, let them continue in silence.
- If students start to look to you for answers, try to encourage them that they can do it themselves. Use the anchor charts from the lessons in this book to give them ways to find answers that foster student independence.
- If you are tempted to intervene when students make mistakes, take a sip of water. If the student needs more time to try something, confer with another student at a learning station and come back.

- Remain curious and ask open-ended questions or give prompts that put the thinking on the student. When students arrive at the conclusion themselves, it is more beneficial for their learning. Some helpful questions or prompts include the following:
    - Can you go back and reread it?
    - Tell me about what you were doing here.
    - Are there any tools that would help you?
    - Look back at our example and see if you can figure it out.
    - What is something you could try?
    - Hmmm.

Usually, the amount of wait time is the biggest takeaway for teachers during learning sessions. One time, I was working with a fourth-grade group, and one student got stuck. He looked up and asked me a question about the problem. I literally just said, "Hmmm," with curiosity. He went right back to work. When we can create an environment where it's okay to be wrong and to try novel ways to solve problems, students raise their own belief in themselves.

As you start to try this out, it is helpful to know your current reality. The following is a protocol for analyzing the interactions within your small groups.

1. Video yourself (just with your cell phone is fine) doing a small-group lesson.
2. Scribe in the document exactly what you and each student said. Use different colors to represent each person in the group. You will also document the time each interaction happens within the video.
3. For each interaction, decide who did the thinking required for the learning.
4. If the teacher did the thinking for the student, look through the list of questions provided and find a better question that would elicit thinking from the student instead of what you asked.
5. Then, decide if more wait time would have been beneficial.

Wait Time Protocol

Part 1: Once the students start to work independently or with a partner, script the conversation and document the time in the video.

Part 2: Reflect on who did the thinking and fill in the checkbox.

Part 3: If the teacher did the thinking for the student, look at the questions/prompts and determine what could be used in that situation instead or whether wait time would help.

Time	Teacher Said/ Student Said…	What Happened in Response?	Who Did the Thinking?		What Question, If Any, Could Be Used to Get the Student to Think More Deeply?	Would More Wait Time Help in This Situation?
			Teacher	Student		
Ex: 1:03	What does it mean when the problem says "each"?	To multiply or divide	X		Can you draw a picture of what you are visualizing?	Yes
Ex: 3:07	I'm confused.	Try rereading the problem to see if it becomes clearer.		X		

Questions/Prompts to Encourage Student Thinking

Problem Solving	Try rereading to see if you can figure it out. Can you draw a picture of what you are visualizing? Retell to yourself or a friend what is happening in the problem. Who are the characters? What are they doing? What happened throughout the story? Can you find all the steps and set up a workspace for each one? Why did you solve it that way? Is there an additional way to solve it?

Representation	What kind of representation could you use that matches what you are visualizing to help you solve?
	What manipulatives could you use to help you see the relationship in the math?
	What do these numbers represent? Be sure to label them so they match the problem.
Justification	How do you know your answer is correct? Does it answer the question/s?
	Can you defend or prove your answer with another strategy?
	Does your justification include the context of the problem and connect it to the math?
	Why does this work? Does it work every time?
	What did you mean when you said…?
	How did you know you were finished?
Communication	Did you write about how you used the context to know what to do?
	Is your explanation clear and organized? Could someone read it and know exactly what you are trying to say?
	Can you write what you just said?
	Can you draw a picture or representation to help you better communicate what you are thinking?

This process can be done as a checkpoint throughout the school year to mark improvements in this practice and to see what impact you notice on the thinking and learning of your students.

Helping Students Understand Productive Struggle

Normalizing productive struggle in classrooms is an imperative part of a student's work ethic. One way to help students understand is by growing their knowledge about how their brain works and the importance of a growth mindset.

Remember how I said in Chapter 1 that a classroom is filled with students who are either learners or nonlearners? It can also just as easily be said that a school is also filled with teachers who are learners and nonlearners. The National Council of Teachers of Mathematics names productive and unproductive beliefs about professionalism in mathematics education. One of the productive beliefs is that "[d]eveloping expertise as a mathematics teacher is a career-long process. The knowledge base of effective mathematics teaching and learning is continually expanding" (National Council of Teachers of Mathematics, 2014, pp. 101–102). I work with kindergarten through fifth-grade teachers every day and I learn something new every time. We can always be growing in our craft of teaching mathematics effectively as we get new students and new teammates to learn from.

New research shows that there will be little gain even when a student has a growth mindset if the teacher does not. However, if the teacher also believes that all students can grow and learn and that mistakes create learning, students did have more gains than in other classrooms where a growth mindset was absent. Students are impacted by their environment and pick up on cues that influence their behaviors (Yeager et al., 2022). Teacher beliefs impact student outcomes.

Do you have a growth mindset or a fixed mindset?	
Fixed Mindset	**Growth Mindset**
• Believe only certain students will ever be capable of getting an A • Talent will measure success • Some people are just not "math people." • Have low expectations for certain students • Group students by ability	• Believe mistakes are learning opportunities • Celebrate growth on assessments • Give the amount of time needed for students to process • Have high expectations for everyone • Group students by common skills needed

If you are unsure, think about your students and how they feel about struggle and learning.

Students might exhibit these behaviors…	
Fixed Mindset Classroom	**Growth Mindset Classroom**
• Afraid to try new things • Afraid to ask questions • Do not solve creatively • Avoid risk-taking • Think something is wrong with them if they don't learn quickly like other students • Avoid challenging tasks or turn them in without trying to stick with them • Pass judgment on students who answer incorrectly • Do not value feedback • Threatened by the success of others	• Seek challenges • Not afraid to ask questions • Solve creatively • Encourage each other to keep trying • Work hard and see effort as a way to learn • Persist through difficult tasks • Ask questions • Coach each other • Want feedback to get better • Celebrate the success of others

Remember earlier when we talked about mistakes? Research has found that when students have a growth mindset, the brain lights up more when mistakes are made than in students who have a fixed mindset. This leads to students being able to actively correct mistakes more often when they have a growth mindset because the brain is more likely to spark again to bring conscious attention to the mistake (Boaler, 2016). The greater picture of this is that when students have a growth mindset and high self-efficacy, their brain is more active and helps them to learn more.

Lessons in the math classroom don't always have to be about math content. When students need to learn what to do when they are struggling, you can respond to what they need through explicit instruction. Noticing behaviors that signal avoidance, frustration, lack of grit, or low confidence can help the teacher pinpoint how to build skills that help students become more independent when solving.

Productive Struggle Lessons	
Student Behavior **If a student…**	**They are ready for these targeted response lessons.**
…thinks they cannot learn. …does not try. …shows little effort.	I can use a growth mindset to tackle problems.
…is afraid to make mistakes. …gets upset when they make a mistake.	I can explain the importance of mistakes in my learning.
…is a perfectionist. …erases their work even when it is correct. …second guesses themselves.	I can acknowledge the hard work I've done.
…lacks confidence but has the skills to solve. …needs a lot of teacher reassurance through the solving process.	I can use positive self-talk to help myself persevere.
…tries to solve in their head and gets frustrated. …doesn't understand why they need to show their work.	I can offload information in my head to my paper to help my brain process.
…gets overwhelmed when they can't figure out what to do. …might cry or get emotional when they can't solve.	I can take a break and come back so I can think more clearly.
…gives up when they get stuck. …only try the same strategy when they get stuck each time.	I can use my resources to get unstuck.

Here are some lessons that will support students in understanding ways to persevere in solving complex problems.

Productive Struggle
Kindergarten to Fifth-Grade Lessons

Lesson 1: I can use a growth mindset to tackle hard problems.

Intro: *Do any of you play sports, dance, play an instrument, or anything like that?* Students don't need to share, just get an example in their mind. *Think back to when you first started. You probably weren't very good at it. When you practiced, you got better. The more you practice and persevere through making mistakes, the more you will learn, and your brain will grow smarter in that area.*

Teach: *The brain is like a muscle that grows stronger and smarter when you encounter challenges. It is important to have a growth mindset when you are learning to remind yourself that when things get hard, it's going to be worth it.* Show students the anchor chart with the different mantras students might have with a fixed or growth mindset. *Your success in anything you do is highly dependent on your mindset and whether you believe you can do it or not. You have the power to decide. You can determine how much you learn by how much effort you put in, how willing you are to try something in a different way, and how you value mistakes as part of learning.*

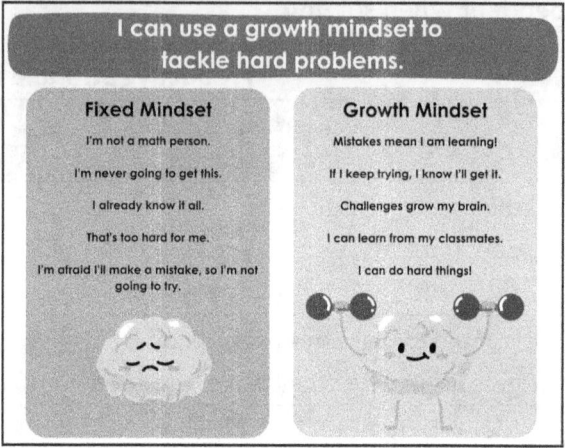

Figure 6.1 Anchor chart for using a growth mindset to tackle hard problems in kindergarten-fifth grades. To view this anchor chart in color, access the online Support Material: https://resourcecentre.routledge.com/books/9781032839875

Try it: Give students some manipulatives and have them build the tallest tower they can. Watch them as they approach it in different ways, learn from each other, and persevere. Point out every time you see them show a growth mindset. Example: "I saw you try again in a different way. That's what people with a growth mindset do." "I saw you work so hard and then it fell, but you tried again. I see your growth mindset!"

Send off: *When you get stuck on tricky problems, or you make mistakes, it is important to take control of your mindset. You can impact how much you learn and grow by how you think about things.*

Lesson 2: I can explain the importance of mistakes in my learning.

Intro: *How many of you have gotten frustrated when you made a mistake? I want you to imagine you are a scientist experimenting in a lab. Do you think they get the perfect mixture the first time? No way! They learn through making mistakes, finding what works, and finding what doesn't. Think about all the inventions that we would not have if we didn't value mistakes.*

Teach: *Mistakes are not just okay. They are a vital part of the learning process. Today I want to talk to you about what happens in your brain when you make a mistake. When you make a mistake, your brain lights up. Even if you don't notice your mistake, your brain does. Sometimes your brain will signal again to get you to focus more attention on it so you can fix it. When you have a growth mindset and believe mistakes are how we learn, your brain brings more attention to mistakes so you can learn from them. So it is so important to believe mistakes are good for your learning. This is true not only in math but in life. I am going to give you an example. The other day, I put way too much salt into the soup I was making. I learned and made notes on the recipe to do half as much next time. Do you remember the mistake I made in the lesson the other day? I learned ….* Give an example of a mistake you recently made in class.

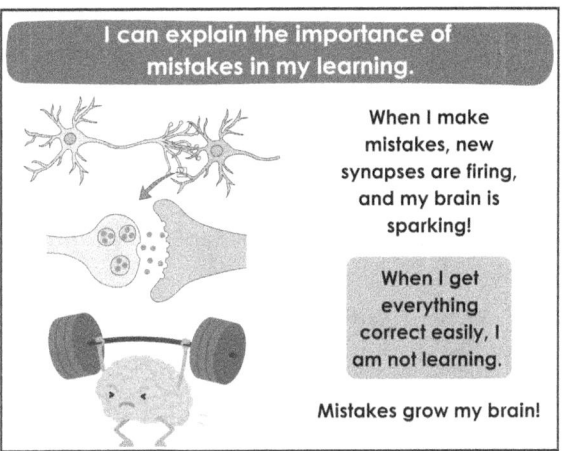

Figure 6.2 Anchor chart for explaining the importance of mistakes in my learning in kindergarten-fifth grades. To view this anchor chart in color, access the online Support Material: https://resourcecentre.routledge.com/books/9781032839875

Try it: *Think of a time when you recently made a mistake. Give me a thumbs up when you have it. Now I want you to think about what you learned from your mistake.* Students can share out and you can reiterate the importance of valuing those mistakes and what they learned from them.

Send off: *When you get frustrated about mistakes, just remember they are a vital part of learning. Without them, we would not learn as much or as quickly. Mistakes are a sign your learning is growing.*

Lesson 3: I can acknowledge the hard work I've done.

Intro: Note: This lesson is probably better suited for a one-on-one conference because it is very personal for students who struggle with perfectionism and fixed mindsets. *Think of a time when you worked really hard at something. Maybe it was learning to dance or playing soccer. Remember, at one point, you were a beginner and did not have any skills. You had to work hard to grow and learn. Math is the same way. You won't just automatically be good at all the concepts you are learning. It will take effort and hard work. There was a time when you didn't even know how to count! Think of all you know now!*

Teach: *Today we are going to practice finding all the things you are doing really well in your work, and then reminding yourself how this contributes to growing as a mathematician.* Show the student an example piece of math work that did not get the correct answer. Model noticing and naming what is going well for that mathematician. Then let them try it out on something else they notice. Use the sentence stems on the anchor chart.

Figure 6.3 Anchor chart for acknowledging the hard work I've done in kindergarten-fifth grades. To view this anchor chart in color, access the online Support Material: https://resourcecentre.routledge.com/books/9781032839875

Try it: Now the student will try it out themselves on a piece of their own work. Remind them that when problems are hard, their brain is growing and learning. Eventually, with hard work, they will be able to do the part of their work that is incorrect right now.

Send off: *When you feel overwhelmed or have a voice in your head that is telling you that you can't do hard math problems, it is important to take a step back and look at all the things you are doing well and give yourself a compliment. This will help you keep going to succeed!*

Lesson 4: I can use positive self-talk to help myself persevere.

Intro: *Did you know your brain is like a muscle? When you challenge it and push yourself, it can become stronger and learn more. One of the ways you can do this is by believing in yourself when problems are tough!*

Teach: *Instead of getting frustrated when we get stuck, we can give ourselves a pep talk to keep us calm and remind ourselves that we CAN do it. Some of the phrases we can use are on our anchor chart.* Have one printed for each student so they can take it with them and put it in their journal or math folder to refer to later.

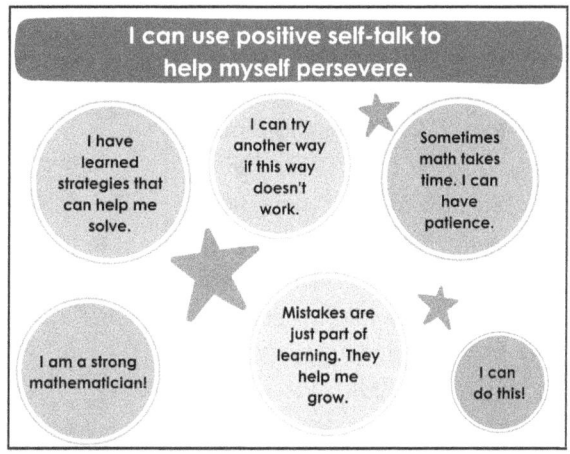

Figure 6.4 Anchor chart for using positive self-talk to help myself persevere in kindergarten-fifth grades. To view this anchor chart in color, access the online Support Material: https://resourcecentre.routledge.com/books/9781032839875

Try it: Have students read through the anchor chart and see if they can think of anything else that can be added. Have them think of a place they can put it so they can refer to it when needed. Talk about some times in math or in life where they have used this strategy or where they think it might be useful. Examples are shooting free throws in a basketball game, trying to get a new belt in taekwondo, trying to brainstorm a story in writing, etc.

Send off: *Put this anchor chart in a place where it can remind you that you CAN do it! View challenges not as something frustrating but as an opportunity to learn and exercise your brain. Sometimes, all you need to do is give yourself a pep talk!*

Lesson 5: I can offload information in my head to my paper to help my brain process.

Intro: *Give me a thumbs up if you have ever been trying to solve something in your head and then your brain just can't go any further. Or have you ever repeated something to yourself over and over so you don't forget?*

Teach: *Writing things down is about more than just "showing your work." It helps your brain process more clearly. Today, I want to talk to you about how to do something called "offloading" information. When you are solving complex math problems, your brain needs you to do it in pieces in an organized way so it can process the information more clearly. This can look like creating a representation of the problem of what you visualized, or even jotting down important things to remember. Then your memory has more space to look at the information and make sense of it.*

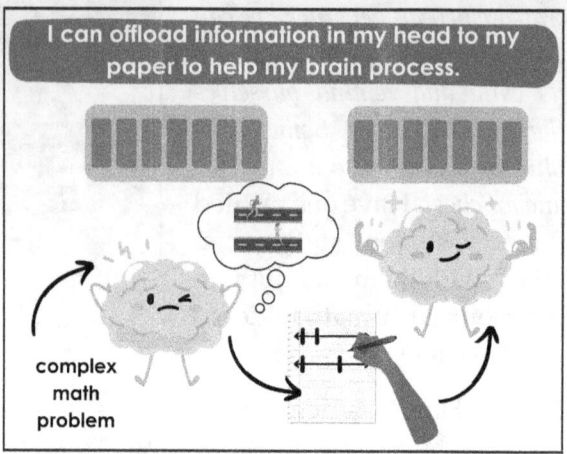

Figure 6.5 Anchor chart for offloading information in kindergarten-fifth grades. To view this anchor chart in color, access the online Support Material: https://resourcecentre.routledge.com/books/9781032839875

Try it: Show students a really complex problem. Have them represent it like they do in the Represent Visualization phase of the progression. *I want you to really pay attention to the relief you feel once you get the problem represented on paper. Pay attention to how it feels when you read the problem again. Describe how it feels.* Students will not solve. They are just noticing how much more clearly they can think.

Send off: *As you are solving tricky problems, it helps to "offload" information or show your work so that your brain can have more room to process the information.*

Lesson 6: I can take a break and come back so I can think more clearly.

Intro: *The other day I was writing some lessons, and I did it for so long that I started to not be able to think very clearly. I sat there staring at my computer for a long time, trying to come up with ideas, but they just weren't coming. I finally put my head down for a minute and took some deep breaths. Then I drank some water, and I was ready to go! I finished in no time after that.*

Teach: Show the anchor chart. *When you get overwhelmed by problems or you feel like you're stuck, there are a few things you can try so that your brain can think more clearly. When you close your eyes and take some deep breaths, it can reset your focus and make you feel calmer. When you drink water, your brain can work better because it needs hydration to think* clearly. *When you take a walk, your heart pumps more blood (which carries oxygen), to your brain so you can think better. Now, remember, these strategies are not to be overused. They are reserved for times when you really feel like you are stuck and need something to try to get you back to work.* Give parameters that work for your classroom.

Figure 6.6 Anchor chart for taking a break and coming back so I can think more clearly in kindergarten-fifth grades. To view this anchor chart in color, access the online Support Material: https://resourcecentre.routledge.com/books/9781032839875

Try it: You could allow them to take a walk, just so they know what your parameters are. This might be a time when they could talk through times when they felt overwhelmed or stuck at the level you are referring to, so they understand when to use these strategies.

Send off: *Remember, when you get stuck and frustrated, there are things you can do that will help your brain to get reset. You can take deep breaths, drink water, or even take a quick walk.* Print this on a mini anchor chart for them to refer to, or have some printed out that you can hand to students when they reach a high level of frustration to remind them.

Lesson 7: I can use my resources to get unstuck.

Intro: *I know there have been times when you have gotten stuck on a really tricky problem. Maybe you thought to yourself, "I am never going to get this!" That's actually a good sign because it means your brain is working hard, and you are about to learn something new! When you get stuck, it can kind of feel like you're a detective. You're looking for clues for what you might be able to try next.*

Teach: *When you get stuck, you can think of resources that can help you get back on track. You could go look at our anchor charts in the classroom. You could look in your journal to find a strategy that might work. You could even go get manipulatives or think about the representations we know that might help us get started.* Model this with a problem where you show getting stuck, then show how to find one of these resources to spark an idea for getting started again.

Try it: Have students look at a new problem and imagine they got stuck. Have them identify the anchor chart that could help them, something from their journal, which manipulatives, and which representation. This way they can name exactly where these things are in the classroom and how to use them as tools.

Send off: *As you are solving really challenging problems in math, it is normal to get stuck. Just remember that you can also get yourself unstuck. You have so many tools to use that can get you started again.*

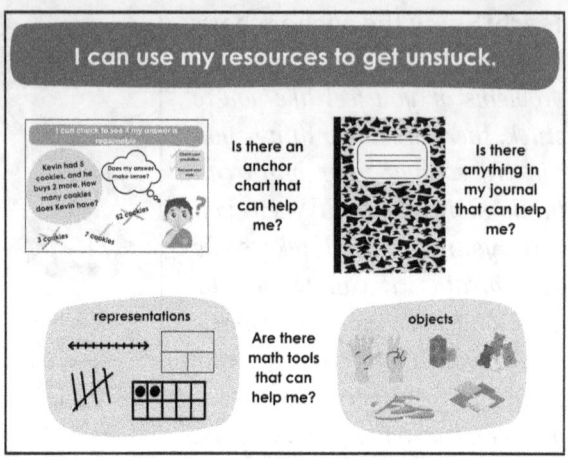

Figure 6.7 Anchor chart for using my resources to get unstuck in kindergarten and first grade. To view this anchor chart in color, access the online Support Material: https://resourcecentre.routledge.com/books/9781032839875

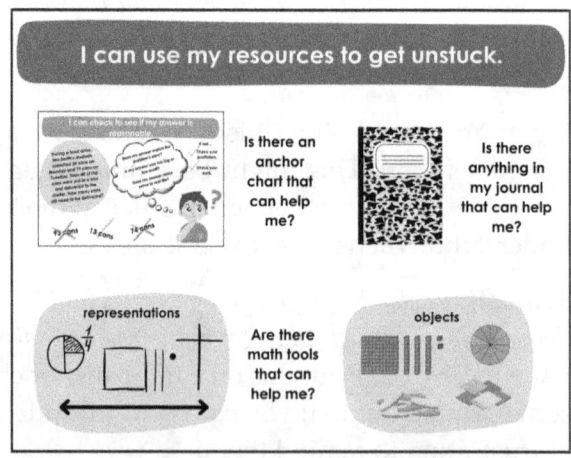

Figure 6.8 Anchor chart for using my resources to get unstuck in second–fifth grades. To view this anchor chart in color, access the online Support Material: https://resourcecentre.routledge.com/books/9781032839875

Questions and Answers

Should I wait to give students challenging work until they can handle it?

When students struggle to do something, this is not the signal to do it less. For students to get better, they need to do more of it. It will be uncomfortable at first, but that's why you can balance tasks by helping them have success and then also have opportunities to struggle so they gain confidence. A perfect way to do this is to have them collaborate with a peer so they are not alone. The lessons provided are great, even for conferring with students. You can build their ability to work independently by letting them get to a point of challenge, then do one of those lessons to remind them what they can do to get themselves back on track.

How do I handle situations where some students finish quickly while others are still struggling?

This is a vital part of differentiation. We must not forget that students are new at solving complex math problems. They need time to process. Allowing students this time, as long as they are on task, is what will help them realize they can solve challenging problems on their own. They will get faster the more they practice. You might give some students a timer if they have a habit of taking way too long. They still need the opportunity to practice getting faster instead of avoiding finishing problems.

What should I do if students don't arrive at the correct solution after struggling?

That's ok! You have gained insight into what they can do correctly and more specifically where they are still struggling. This is the perfect piece of data to drive what you do next for them in differentiated small-group instruction. To build grit and perseverance with students, sometimes we must ignore incor-rect answers and praise the behavior that got them to try. Building grit and perseverance is more important than the correct answer in the long run.

How do I ensure that students with learning differences or lower confidence can benefit from productive struggle?

Every student has to learn how to struggle and get unstuck. This means that you might have to differentiate the tasks given to students so they don't automatically get to the frustration level and unproductive struggle. One way to keep the rigor high but also accessible to all students is to make the numbers of a problem smaller, utilize students' accommodations of oral administration or graphic organizers, and so on. The tasks provided in this book from Exemplars, Inc. already have an accelerated version and more accessible version of each task ready for teachers to use. This could be a great option for differentiation.

How do I explain the value of productive struggle to parents who might see it as unnecessary frustration?

Providing parents with the process standards that apply to your state or district can help, or showing parents the most sought-after skills in the job market right now from the introduction of this book can help. We are preparing students for the future jobs they will have and for life. Productive struggle is not solely about math instruction.

Chapter 6: Reflection

What are your beliefs regarding intelligence? To learn more about mindsets, read the book *Mindset* by Carol Dweck. Think about the students who struggle in your classroom. Do they have a growth mindset? If not, how could you foster that?

Video yourself teaching a small group. Fill out the wait time protocol. Reflect here on what you learned and what you are trying next.

References

Betts, E. A. (1946). *Foundations of reading instruction*. American Book.

Boaler, J. (2016). *Mathematical mindsets: Unleashing students' potential through creative math, inspiring messages, and innovative teaching*. Jossey-Bass.

Common Core State Standards Initiative. (2010). *Standards for mathematical practice*. Retrieved January 9, 2025, from https://www.thecorestandards.org/Math/Practice/

Dweck, C. S. (2006). *Mindset*. Ballentine Books.

IRIS Center. (2018). *Wait time*. Vanderbilt University. https://iris.peabody.vanderbilt.edu/wp-content/uploads/misc_media/fss/pdfs/2018/IRIS_fundamental_skill_sheet_wait-time.pdf

National Council of Teachers of Mathematics. (2014). *Principles to actions: Ensuring mathematical success for all*. National Council of Teachers of Mathematics.

Sangiovanni, J. J., Katt, S., & Dykema, K. J. (2020). *Productive math struggle: A 6-point action plan for fostering perseverance*. Corwin.

Sweller, J. (2011). Cognitive load theory. *Psychology of Learning and Motivation, 55*.

Takayoshi, P. & Van Ittersum, D. (2018). *Wait time: Making space for authentic learning*. Kent State University Center for Teaching and Learning.

Texas Education Agency. (2012). *Texas essential knowledge and skills for mathematics: Elementary*. Retrieved January 9, 2025, from https://tea.texas.gov/about-tea/laws-and-rules/sboe-rules-tac/sboe-tac-currently-in-effect/ch111a.pdf

Virginia Department of Education. (2016). *Mathematics standards of learning for Virginia public schools*. Retrieved January 9, 2025, from https://www.doe.virginia.gov/home/showpublisheddocument/3038/637982465171900000

Visible Learning MetaX. (n.d.). *Teacher-student dependency*. Retrieved January 25, 2025, from https://www.visiblelearningmetax.com/influences/view/teacher-student_dependency

Yeager, D. S., Carroll, J. M., Bluontempo, J., Cimpian, A., Woody, S., Crosnoe, R., Muller, C., Murray, J., Mhatre, P., Kersting, N., Hulleman, C., Kudym, M., Murphy, M., Duckworth, A. L., Walton, G. M., & Dweck, C. S. (2022). Teacher mindsets help explain where a growth-mindset intervention does and doesn't work. *Psychological Science, 33*(1), 18–32.

7

What Other Small Adjustments Can I Make in My Classroom to Help My Students Develop Problem Solving Skills?

A teacher can have the most amazing lessons and learning experiences, but still miss out on some huge learning accelerators that take little more effort than each teacher already uses daily. A few little changes based on how the brain learns and processes can make a world of difference in the amount of learning that is retained by students.

Understanding Memory

Memory is a three-step process. Encoding occurs when information enters the brain, storage occurs when information stays in the brain, and retrieval occurs when information emerges from the brain. Sometimes, encoding and storing information are mistakenly considered the most important, but retrieval is the key that is often overlooked. When we retrieve, memories become deeper and more accessible (Cooney Horvath, 2019).

Spaced Practice

Instead of having an extended event of massed learning with the learning all together, it is beneficial to come back to the topic several times with time in between. Spaced practice increases long-term retention (Latimer et al., 2021).

An example of massed practice would be getting four professional development sessions in a row in one day. Compare that to spaced practice, which

DOI: 10.4324/9781003510703-8

involves getting the same four sessions but just one per week for four weeks. The brain needs time for consolidation to occur between learning sessions. Consolidation is when the brain reorganizes and "files away" learning into long-term memory. Sleep helps with the consolidation process. The brain deeply processes new learning and connects it to prior learning over a period of time (Brown et al., 2014).

Retrieval

When discussing retention of learning, we have to mention the forgetting curve. Humans lose about 70 percent of what they have just heard or read. The last 30 percent falls off more slowly. Reread that. So, even if you teach it, only about 30% of it will be remembered by students. What?! This does not bode well for retaining student learning if teachers do not cycle back to essential concepts through assessment, instruction, and practice throughout the school year. That is why we must disrupt the forgetting curve by presenting opportunities to retrieve that information. Retrieval interrupts forgetting and keeps our knowledge accessible (Brown et al., 2014; Latimer et al., 2021).

One of the most impactful ways to increase learning is to combine both of these topics of spaced practice and retrieval to create spaced retrieval. When teachers space practice of a concept throughout the year, it creates opportunities for retrieving previous learning and practicing it in new situations. Every time you recall what you have learned, the brain reconsolidates the memory, strengthening the connections to what you already know and making it easier to remember in the future (Brown et al., 2014; Kang, 2016). Spaced retrieval is most impactful over a more extended period, instead of having retrieval instances closer together (Carpenter et al., 2022; Lyle et al., 2020).

An example of this is a beginning-of-year assessment. New teachers want to see what students know about the most critical content from the previous year. The teacher can provide an assessment opportunity with a couple of problems from each essential piece of learning. This can help them see what their new students were able to retain and remember from the previous year. It also starts the retrieval process of information that students will need to build upon in this year's learning, allowing the teacher to go ahead and start targeted small-group instruction and retrieval practice in learning stations.

One form of retrieval is reflection. When we reflect on our mistakes, the brain retrieves earlier knowledge and learning and then connects it to recent experiences and plans for what to do next time. This strengthens the learning, making it easier to recall. Unless you keep recalling what to do with certain concepts, it will not be automatic when needed later. Repeated recall helps the brain establish lasting connections because the brain labels it as important. When foundational knowledge is present, creativity in complex problems is achievable. An example is when students move to the standard algorithm too quickly; they cannot use their number sense to solve any other way, and might try to rely on keywords or a similar cue to trigger using the procedure.

Being exposed to the same information multiple times is not considered retrieval practice. Exposure includes rereading, restudying, or copying information (Butler, 2010). Some examples of retrieval for the math classroom would be playing games on a concept, taking assessments, problem solving a concept from a past cluster of learning, etc. Students must actively recall the information instead of being taught the information again or longer. Instruction should be saved for response to assessment work and be specifically targeted to the student's needs (Latimer et al., 2021).

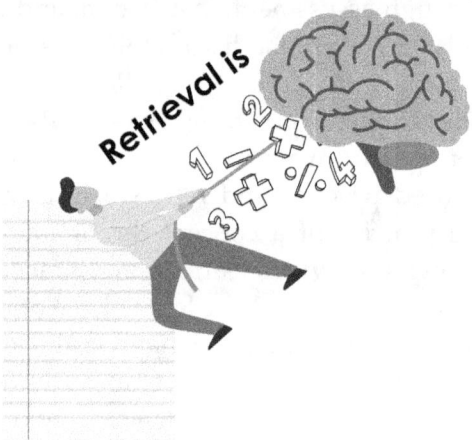

Figure 7.1 Retrieval is pulling out information from long-term memory.

Figure 7.2 Retrieval is *not* putting more information in.

One of the biggest misconceptions that can happen with retrieval is to stop practicing a concept once students master it. Students still need to retrieve the content they are good at for the brain to still deem it important. I used to think that when students mastered certain math facts, they could set those aside and work on the ones that did not come as easily. The opposite of that is true. Students need to continue using the skills that they are good at to keep performing the skill well.

Interleaved Practice

Over the years, this one sticks out to me as an easy tiny tweak that can create rich student learning. Cue interleaved practice. Interleaved practice is when problems on an assignment are all from different topics, so students have to switch between skills they have already learned (Cooney-Horvath, 2019). This creates the need for the students to choose a strategy to solve based on each problem in front of them (Rohrer et al., 2015). Assessments and practice need different skills embedded throughout them to be true problem solving. If a title on the top of an assessment says, "Addition with Regrouping," students immediately enter the assignment with a low level of thinking. Many students may not even read the problems and just skim enough to know which numbers to pull out and add together.

To maximize interleaving in primary grades, include different types of problems with various unknowns. An example of this might be to have a joining problem with the start unknown along with a problem with the comparing structure with a result unknown.

In upper grades, there are so many concepts to resurface for practice throughout the year. This is the perfect opportunity for purposeful learning by retrieval of many concepts. Getting fresh data often about all the major concepts for the grade level allows mastery to happen much more effectively in preparation for the next grade.

Assessments That Tie It All Together

To tie these three ideas together, a different type of assessment can be created and planned throughout the course of the school year.

If your grade level assigns graded work, be sure that the graded work matches what you value. Graded work is a communication of values to students and parents. If students only gain points for correct answers but not any of the correct processes, the process of solving will not be valued. If teachers grade assessments with 10–20 questions and make questions worth 5 or 10 points for the correct answer, this sends the message that students need to finish quickly and skip the representation phase.

Instead, teachers can do fewer problems and have students go deeper. Providing a checklist for students can give them a better idea of what you value and also actually assess the process standards intentionally. For example, a fifth-grade assessment could look like this.

Name _____

1. Carter's dad was making a workbench in his garage. He needed to cut four pieces of wood that were 4 ½ inches and eight pieces of wood that were 3 ¼ inches to make some shelves. How long were all of those pieces together?	Student Teacher
	☐ ☐ Model
	☐ ☐ Labels
	☐ ☐ Answer statement
	☐ ☐ Equation
	☐ ☐ Correct answer
2. At Jefferson Supermarket they were having a sale on peaches. Peaches last week were $2.67 per pound. This week, they were only $2.09 per pound. If someone bought 5 pounds of peaches every week, how much money will they save this week?	Student Teacher
	☐ ☐ Model
	☐ ☐ Labels
	☐ ☐ Answer statement
	☐ ☐ Equation
	☐ ☐ Correct answer

Figure 7.3 Example of an asset-based assessment.

At first, students may need to see the checklist in more of a question format as they get used to it. Then, students could have less support and eventually not even need a checklist. There are two checkboxes for each item: a place for students to assess themselves and a place for teachers to check if students have done that skill correctly. A checklist ensures the student is practicing both the process and computation standards.

The checkbox behaviors are created based on the problems on an assessment like this. Going deeper with problems takes more time, so doing fewer problems makes sense. Students can then get points for what they did well,

	Student	Teacher	
	☐	☐	Do I have a model to match the problem?
	☐	☐	Is it labeled with context from the problem?
	☐	☐	Did I write an answer statement that matches the question?
	☐	☐	Do I have an equation?
	☐	☐	Is my answer correct?

	Student	Teacher	
	☐	☐	Model
	☐	☐	Labels
	☐	☐	Answer statement
	☐	☐	Equation
	☐	☐	Correct answer

Figure 7.4 Checklist scaffold.

instead of losing all points on a question if they did not get the answer correct. It helps the teacher, student, and parent to pinpoint where misconceptions lie and what the expectations of learning are on the pathway to proficiency. Although this should not be the case all the time, when the teacher wants to check in on a specific strategy or model, they can name it on the checklist to gain a narrower view of student mastery. For example, if teachers notice students have not been using an open number line, they can add that to the checklist for a problem where that strategy would be efficient. This can push students out of their comfort zone and help the teacher create very targeted small groups.

This type of assignment would be graded based on how many check boxes there are. For example, if there were four problems with five checkboxes each, each checkbox would be worth five points. This approach places equal value on the answer and other behaviors exhibited on the assessment.

In primary grades, this may be in the form of a graphic organizer, where students have to include many aspects of the problem solving process. You can have multiple representations on it and let students choose which one to use, or even challenge them to represent it multiple ways.

When this type of assessment is first given, students require a lot of support in understanding what high-quality work looks like and what the vocabulary means. It is helpful to have anchor charts that show them what exemplar work looks like and how to identify when it is time to check the box that they have completed a task.

When this work is returned to students, it can increase learning by giving them time to reflect. When students get feedback that is specific and are given time to reflect, they typically perform even better on later assessments because they spend time analyzing and retrieving again to try to fix what they did or on making a plan to do better next time based on prior learning and this experience (Carpenter et al., 2022).

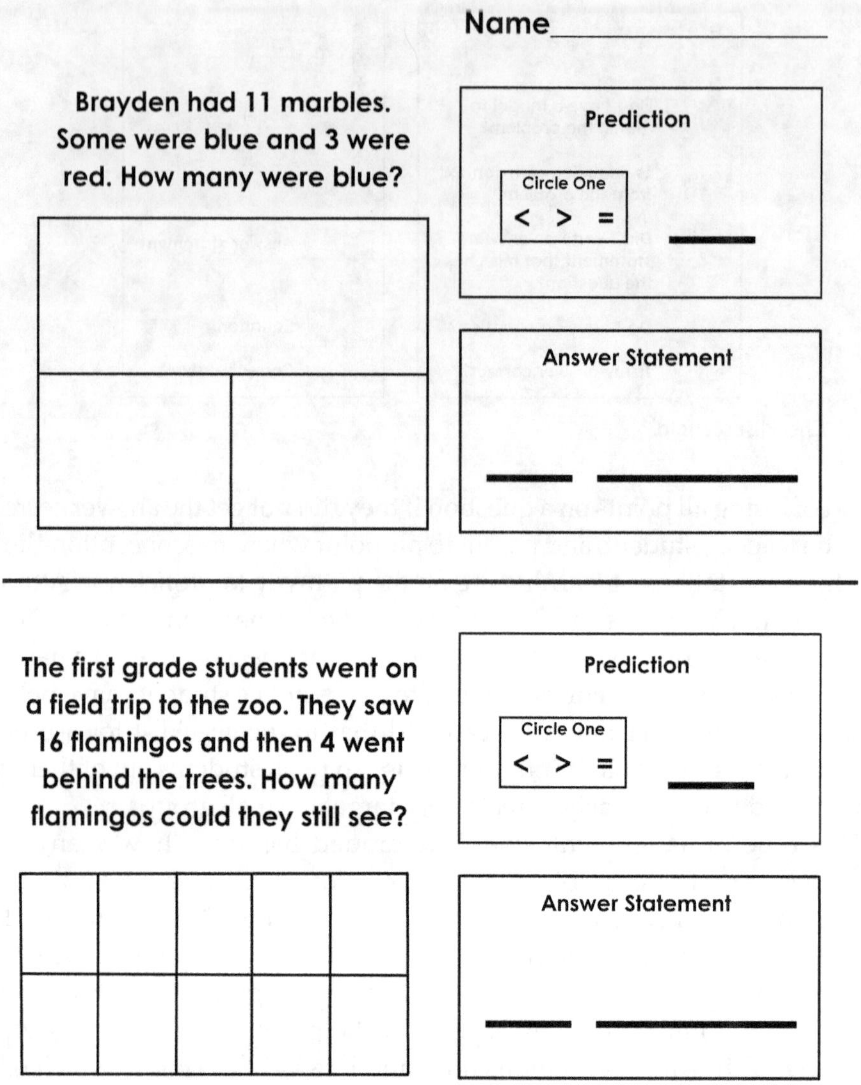

Name_____

Brayden had 11 marbles. Some were blue and 3 were red. How many were blue?

Prediction

Circle One

< > =

_____

Answer Statement

_____ _____

The first grade students went on a field trip to the zoo. They saw 16 flamingos and then 4 went behind the trees. How many flamingos could they still see?

Prediction

Circle One

< > =

_____

Answer Statement

_____ _____

Figure 7.5 Lower grade example to support deeper thinking.

Creating an Assessment Plan for Spaced Retrieval and Interleaving

First: Identify what content standards are most important for students to learn. Your state probably defines some that are more important than others. Remember, process standards are embedded within every content standard, so we will address those later. In Texas, these standards are called "Readiness Standards."

Second: Unpack those standards. One at a time, in the order that they show up in the scope and sequence, get to know these standards deeply. Investigate the ways they are assessed, what vocabulary is used, the different models, and so on. Make a list of learning targets that fall under each standard. Oftentimes, when we assess students based on a standard, we do not cover all its parts. We see if students master a few aspects of it instead of in its entirety. When you plan for it this way, you can ensure that all parts will be assessed at some point in the year, allowing time for a response.

Here is an example of what this might look like. As stated by the Texas Education Agency (2012), the multiplication readiness standard for third grade is: *3.4K The student is expected to solve one-step and two-step problems involving multiplication and division within 100 using strategies based on objects; pictorial models, including arrays, area models, and equal groups; properties of operations; or recall of facts* (section "Grade 3, Adopted 2012").

1. I can explain what multiplication means using groups of objects or arrays.
2. I can represent multiplication problems using pictures, models, and number sentences.
3. I can use strategies like skip counting, repeated addition, or patterns to solve multiplication problems.
4. I can find the product of two numbers within 100.
5. I can explain what division means by sharing objects into equal groups.
6. I can represent division problems using pictures, models, and number sentences.
7. I can relate division to multiplication and use fact families to check my work.
8. I can find the quotient when dividing within 100.
9. I can solve one- and two-step word problems involving multiplication and division.
10. I can explain my thinking and show how I solved a multiplication or division problem.

Third: Decide how often students will be assessed. Every week or every other week would ensure students get ample retrieval practice.

Fourth: Map out when you will assess each standard over the course of the year. Assessments should occur at least a week after the content was learned, so the teacher has a chance to reteach if necessary. Choose four standards to assess for each assessment.

Fifth: Make sure the behaviors you listed as you unpacked are represented throughout the year, so students get to practice all the skills tied to each of those standards.

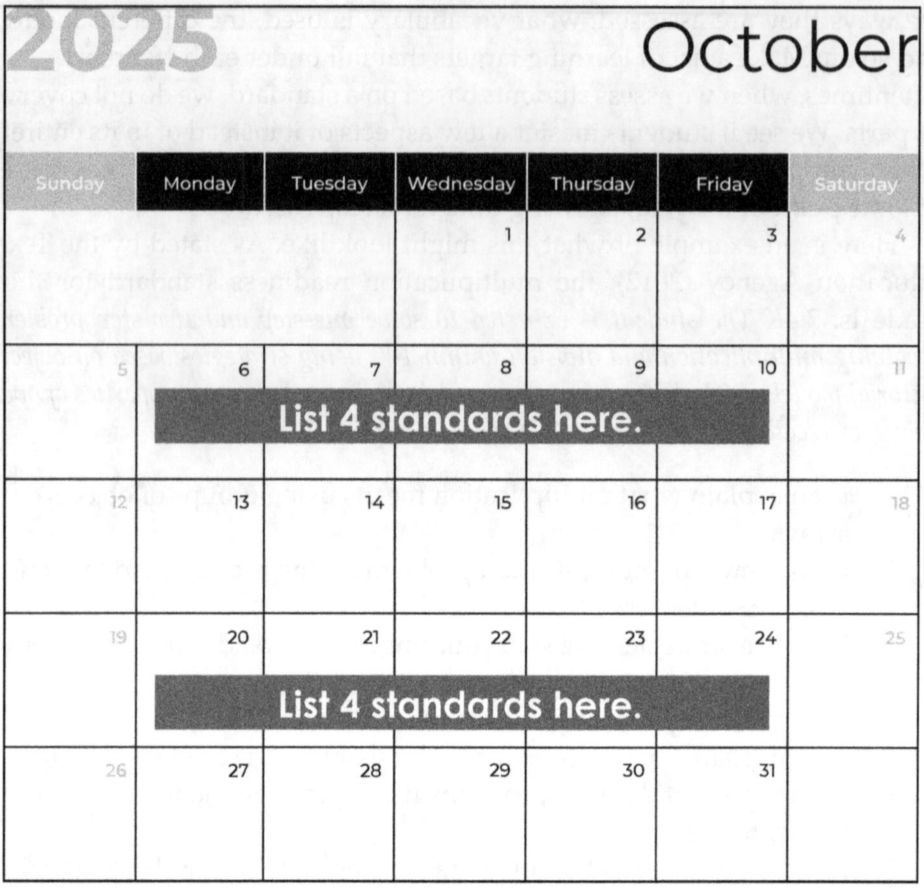

2025						October
Sunday	Monday	Tuesday	Wednesday	Thursday	Friday	Saturday
			1	2	3	4
5	6	7	8	9	10	11
		List 4 standards here.				
12	13	14	15	16	17	18
19	20	21	22	23	24	25
		List 4 standards here.				
26	27	28	29	30	31	

Figure 7.6 Example calendar to show pacing of assessments.

Last: Create the assessments. Choose one question for each standard on the assessment. This is where the interleaving is represented. Students will have to retrieve each of the concepts, creating a valid problem solving opportunity with deep thinking. Anticipate the misconceptions by solving each one. Create checklist behaviors you want students to complete based on what you want them to retrieve and practice.

Bringing Students Into Their Learning With Goal Setting

When teachers assess students in a way that is relevant to them and their learning goals, it creates ownership and motivation to learn. Assessments that allow students to reflect and do deep thinking create ownership and curiosity about what to learn to do better next time. This informs students, teachers, and parents of what students know and don't know, allowing focus to improve in areas where they are weak.

One of the assessment questions could be tailored to a problem solving goal the student is working on. The teacher could have a stack of labels when students are in their small-group instruction. As students finish the lesson, as part of the send-off, the teacher could write the learning target on a label. That can be stuck onto the student's assignment the following week to have spaced retrieval and application of their new learning.

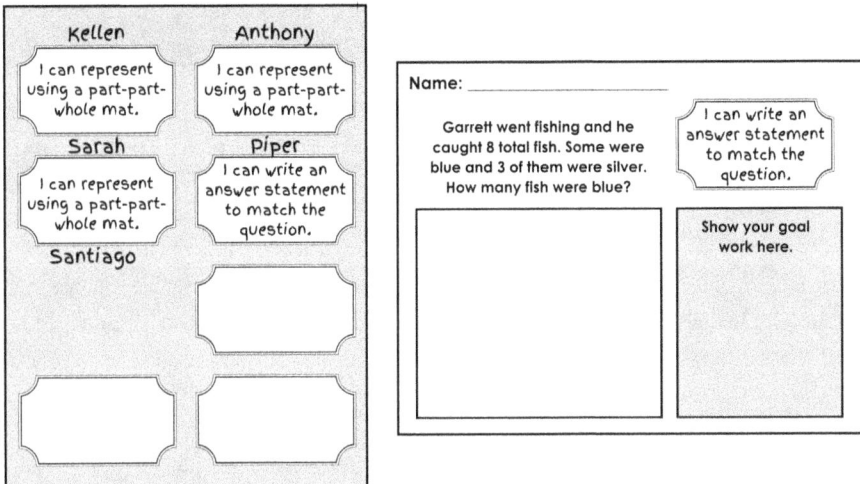

Figure 7.7 Transfer teach point to practice.

To keep track of what they are working on to practice while in learning stations or doing independent work, students could use a goal-setting foldable. Using a sticky note or paperclip, they could mark where they are working on the progression at a given time. Once folded, they can just open up to that phase of the progression and see each skill they can try, along with a graphic to remind them of what they might have done in a small group with the teacher. The graphics match the kindergarten to first-grade progression or the second-grade to fifth-grade progression.

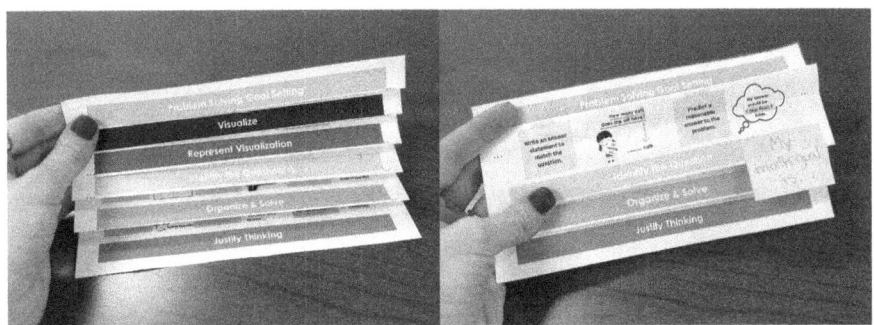

Figure 7.8 Goal-setting foldable.

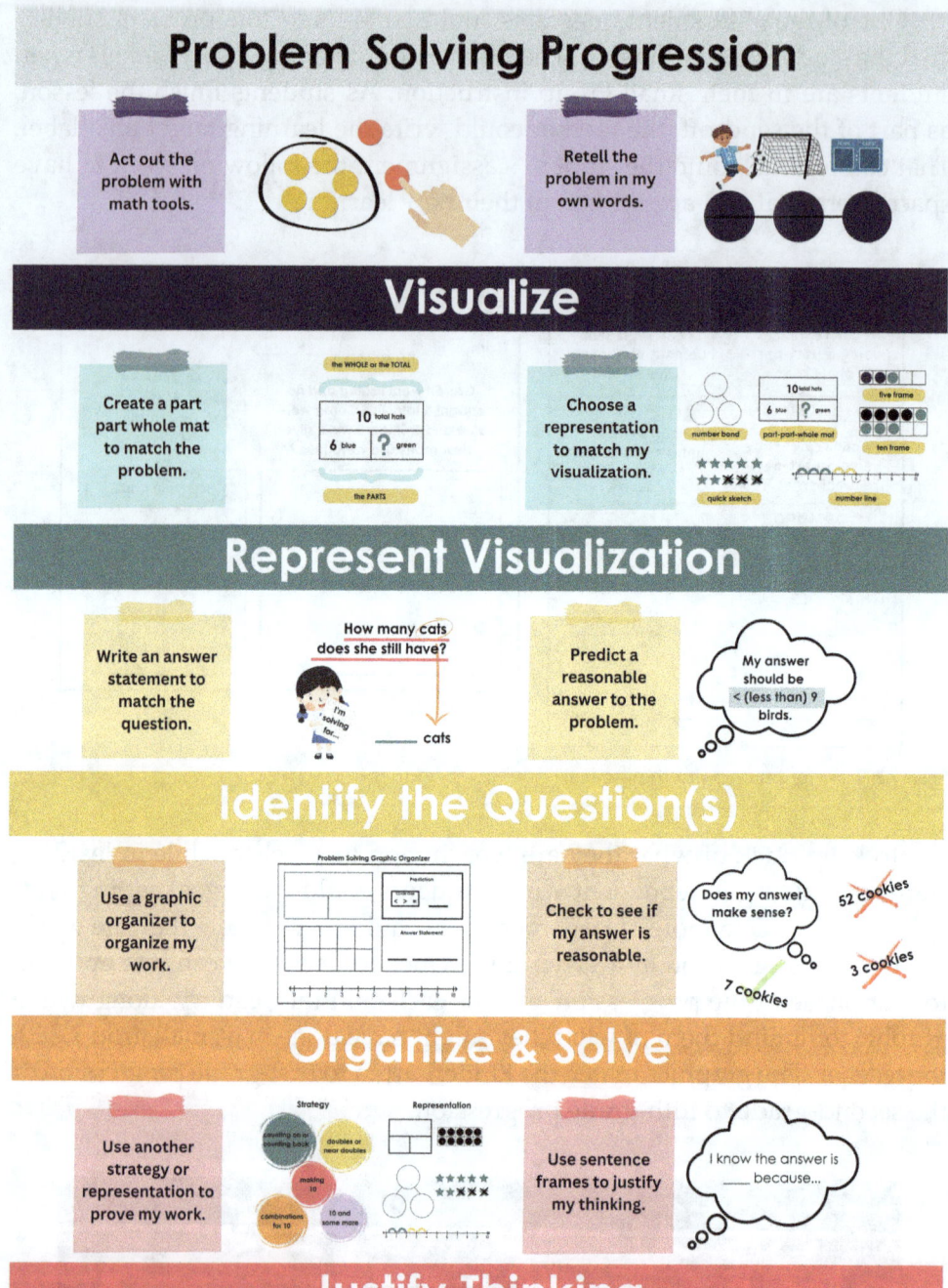

Figure 7.9 Kindergarten and first-grade goal-setting foldable.

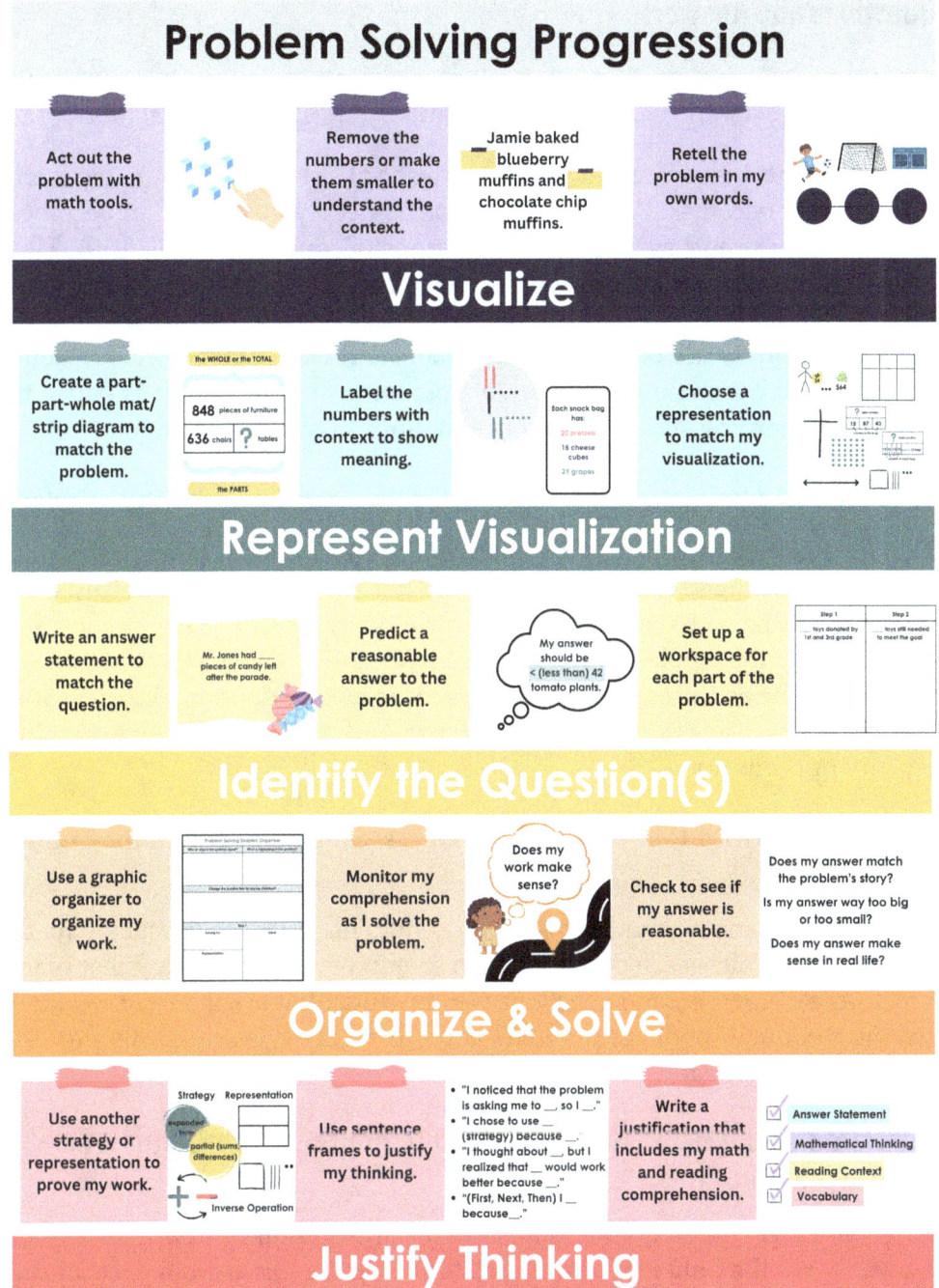

Figure 7.10 Second- through fifth-grade goal-setting foldable.

Questions and Answers

In addition to problem solving, shouldn't students also practice straight computation?

When students have repeated practice of a specific skill in isolation, the more automated it becomes. When a skill becomes deeply automated, it becomes harder to access and apply in new situations (Cooney Horvath, 2019). This essentially separates that learning in their mind from contextual situations. We need students to practice within context and choose the models and strategies they want to use based on the numbers and the context of the problem. Students will never do operations in isolation in real life, so it is better to ensure this learning stays attached to situations they may encounter.

How should I administer an assessment like the one proposed in this chapter?

This type of assessment can take students longer to work through because they are exhibiting several mathematical behaviors and thinking deeply. One option could be to have students complete one problem a day as they are released from the whole-group lesson to go to stations. Then, the assignment would be done by the end of the week. It could also be done as a learning station. Retrieval is an essential part of learning, and this would be a meaningful practice opportunity.

If students only do four problems on an assignment, how will they build stamina?

If you follow a math workshop structure, students could be practicing math for up to 45 minutes each day. They gain stamina every day during that practice. Going deeper into the questions is more difficult work than just working out the computation of the problem, and has students practice vital process standards intentionally.

If my student got the answer correct but didn't show all the other components, do they get all the credit?

When you read the standards that students are learning, getting the correct answer is not the only part. Assessments should comprise more parts of the standards to be more valuable learning and information for where to go next. We are teaching students to value the process of solving complex problems and communicate their thinking in ways that might be uncomfortable for them. This is a good indication that they are learning something new and being prepared for the future.

Chapter 7: Reflection

Write your own definitions for these words.

Retrieval:

Spaced Practice:

Interleaving:

Create an assessment that includes interleaving and checklists. Administer it to students and come back to reflect on how their work is different than it was on previous assessments.

References

Brown, P. C., Roediger, H. L., & McDaniel, M. A. (2014). *Make it stick*. The Belknap Press of Harvard University Press.

Butler, A. C. (2010). Repeated testing produces superior transfer of learning relative to repeated studying. *Journal of Experimental Psychology: Learning, Memory, and Cognition, 36*(5), 1118–1133.

Carpenter, S. K., Pan, S. C., & Butler, A. C. (2022). The science of effective learning with spacing and retrieval practice. *Nature Reviews Psychology, 1*, 496–511.

Cooney Horvath, J. (2019). *Stop talking, start influencing*. Exile Publishing Pty, Ltd.

Kang, S. H. (2016). Spaced repetition promotes efficient and effective learning: Policy implications for instruction. *Policy Insights from the Behavioral and Brain Sciences, 3*(1), 12–19.

Latimer, A., Peyre, H., & Ramus, F. (2021). A Meta-Analytic Review of the Benefit of Spacing out Retrieval Practice Episodes on Retention. *Educational Psychology Review, 33*, 959–987.

Lyle, K. B., Campbell, R. B., Hopkins, R. F., Hieb, J. L., & Ralston, P. A. (2020). How the amount and spacing of retrieval practice affect the short- and long-term retention of mathematics knowledge. *Educational Psychology Review, 32*, 277–295. https://doi.org/10.1007/s10648-019-09489-x

Rohrer, D., Dedrick, R. F., & Stershic, S. (2015). Interleaved Practice Improves Mathematics Learning. *Journal of Educational Psychology, 107*(3), 900–908.

Texas Education Agency. (2012). *Texas essential knowledge and skills for mathematics, §111.5. Grade 3, adopted 2012.* https://tea.texas.gov/academics/curriculum-standards/teks-review/texas-essential-knowledge-and-skills

Conclusion

To conclude the book, I wanted to pull out the big ideas from each chapter to discuss how they are all connected.

Introduction

- Learning how to problem solve is not solely about math. Students need problem solving as a life skill. Students build this skill throughout their school experience to use it in life.
- The data show a large need to focus on math problem solving starting early. By the time students get to "testing grades," it's too late.

Chapter 1

- When teachers and students understand a bit about their working memory, they can create more space for thinking deeply.
- Reading comprehension, math computation, and self-efficacy are all important aspects that impact the function of working memory and being able to solve complex problems.

Chapter 2

- Process standards and content standards are intertwined. It is difficult to talk about one without the presence of the other when the topic is complex problem solving.
- Creating habits for students is teaching the brain to do these strategies in the progression with minimal effort because of practice.

Chapter 3

- Look for strengths for students to continue and areas for growth. Choose the most important next thing for students to work on that will make the most impact.
- Go with your gut. Think about what students need next, but if you get into the instruction with them, and it isn't right, just write down what to do with them next. It was still a meaningful time for you to get to know the students' needs.

Chapter 4

- Sorting through data should be a quick decision.
- There are multiple ways to thin-slice student work. Teachers need to find a way that works for them.
- Teachers can't possibly review every single piece of work that students produce. Give yourself permission to focus on the assignments you plan to provide feedback on or have the time to address through instruction. Only review additional work if you need more information about specific students' understanding.

Chapter 5

- Small group instruction is meant to be a time to cycle through the most essential standards to help students have the opportunity to master them. If we focus on everything, nothing becomes important.
- The right conditions must be set up for small group instruction to have the biggest impact.

Chapter 6

- In times of struggle and challenge, the brain grows the most.
- Students have to do the thinking for themselves. Teachers have to allow the space for it to occur.

Chapter 7

- There are strategic changes that teachers can make to the practices they already have in place to maximize learning for students based on how the brain functions.
- Assessments and grades should measure strengths in addition to areas for growth. When the answer is not the only way to get credit, more accurate communication is provided to the teacher, parents, and the students themselves.

Small group instruction has the power to transform learning and provide students with the focused support to master essential skills they need throughout their lives. The key is to start – without the pressure of perfection. By making small, intentional shifts, you can create an environment where students engage more deeply, think more critically, and build confidence in their problem solving abilities. The most impactful teaching happens when we meet each student where they are and guide them forward in meaningful ways. So don't wait! Trust your instincts, embrace the process, and take the first step toward meaningful differentiation in math problem solving. Your students will thrive because of it.

For Product Safety Concerns and Information please contact our EU
representative GPSR@taylorandfrancis.com
Taylor & Francis Verlag GmbH, Kaufingerstraße 24, 80331 München, Germany

www.ingramcontent.com/pod-product-compliance
Lightning Source LLC
Chambersburg PA
CBHW080936300426
44115CB00017B/2845